WOMEN
IN THE 1920s
PAMELA HORN

No. 69   *The*   May 1928

Needlewoman

A Magazine of Exclusive Fashions in Dress and in the Home.   Monthly 4d.

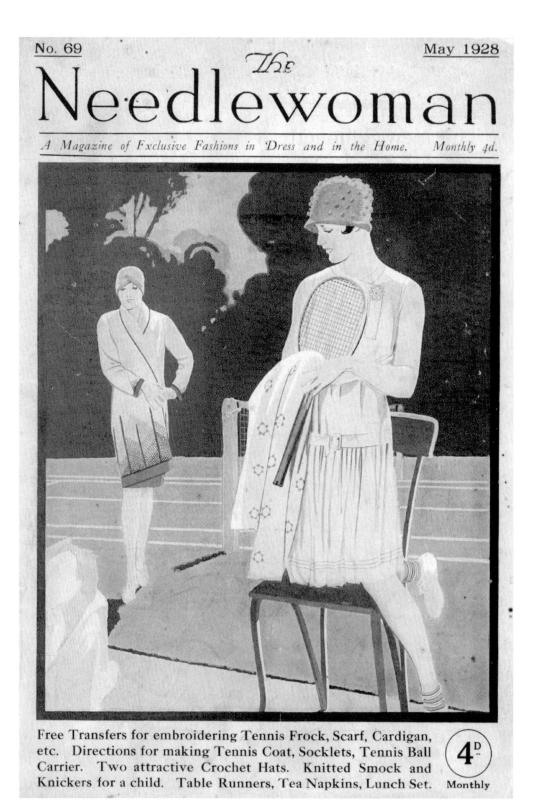

Free Transfers for embroidering Tennis Frock, Scarf, Cardigan, etc. Directions for making Tennis Coat, Socklets, Tennis Ball Carrier. Two attractive Crochet Hats. Knitted Smock and Knickers for a child. Table Runners, Tea Napkins, Lunch Set.

4^D

Monthly

Cover illustration for The Needlewoman, *showing the tennis fashions of the day*

WOMEN
IN THE 1920s

PAMELA HORN

ALAN SUTTON PUBLISHING LIMITED

First published in the United Kingdom in 1995
Alan Sutton Publishing Ltd
Phoenix Mill · Far Thrupp · Stroud · Gloucestershire

British Library Cataloguing in Publication Data

Horn, Pamela
  Women in the 1920s
  I. Title
  305.420941

ISBN 0-7509-0526-3

Jacket illustration: In the Library *by Delphin Enjolras (Fine Art Photographic Library Ltd).*

Typeset in 11/12 Ehrhardt.
Typesetting and origination by
Alan Sutton Publishing Limited.
Printed in Great Britain by
Butler & Tanner Ltd, Frome, Somerset.

Contents

There are no yard measures, neatly divided into the fractions of an inch, that one can lay against the qualities of a good mother or the devotion of a daughter, or the fidelity of a sister, or the capacity of a housekeeper. Few women even now have been graded at the universities; the great trials of the professions, army and navy, trade, politics and diplomacy have hardly tested them. They remain even at this moment almost unclassified.

from Virginia Woolf, *A Room of One's Own* (1929)

Acknowledgements

I should like to thank all those who have assisted me in the preparation of this book by providing information and illustrations or who have helped in other ways. In particular, my thanks are due to the National Westminster Bank plc and their archivist, Mrs F. Maccoll, for permission to quote from Group Archives; to Cadbury Ltd, Bournville, and their librarian, Mrs H.M. Davies, for making available company records; to the Chairman of the Conservative Party for allowing me to quote from archives at the Bodleian Library, Oxford; to Loughborough University of Technology and their archivist, Mrs J.G. Clark; to the National Museum of Labour History, Manchester; the Rural History Centre at the University of Reading; the University of Reading Library and, in particular, the archivist, Mr Michael Bott; the Fawcett Library, Guildhall University; the Bradford Heritage Recording Unit; the Welsh Folk Museum, National Museum of Wales, and, in particular, Mr Lloyd-Hughes, the archivist, and Mrs Minwel Tibbott; the staff at the National Council for One Parent Families; and the Wellcome Centre for Medical History, London.

I have also received much efficient and friendly assistance from staff at the various Libraries and Record Offices where I have worked or who have provided information. These include the Bodleian Library, Oxford; the British Library; the British Library Newspaper Library, Colindale; the Public Record Office; the Library and Photographic Library of the Imperial War Museum; the Tameside Local Studies Library, Stalybridge; the Greater London Library and Record Office; Cardiff Central Library; Derby Central Library; Great Yarmouth Central Library and the Local Studies Library, Oxford. I should like to express my appreciation, too, of help given by staff at the Glamorgan Archives and at Suffolk Record Office, at both Ipswich and Bury St Edmunds.

Finally, I must express my appreciation of the help given to me by members of my family – my brother and sister-in-law, Mr and Mrs Ian Horn, and my aunt, Mrs Phyllis Knight. But most of all my thanks are due to my husband for his constant help, support and advice. Without him this book could not have been written.

Pamela Horn
November, 1994

CONVERSION TABLE

Shillings and pence and some illustrative decimal coinage equivalents.

1d.	½p	1s.	5p
2d.	1p	2s.	10p
3d.		3s.	15p
4d.	1½p	3s. 6d.	17½p
5d.	2p	10s. 0d.	50p
6d.	2½p	12s. 6d.	62½p
7d.	3p	25s. 0d.	£1.25p
8d.	3½p	30s. 0d.	£1.50p

CHAPTER 1

From War to Peace: 1914–20

During the war women's powers and capacities were called into full play and no one denies that there was a response beyond all expectation. To-day there is little call to a strenuous and sustained effort, entailing full use of powers and faculties. Instead, interesting work is taken out of their hands, and they are being forced back into the routine of their hitherto normal occupations.

Annual Report of the Chief Inspector of Factories and Workshops for 1919,
Parliamentary Papers 1920, vol. XVI, p. 9.

When war broke out in August 1914 countless women found their lives thrown into turmoil as accustomed routines were destroyed by the departure of their menfolk for the dangers and uncertainties of the battlefield. A contributor to the feminist journal, *Common Cause*, commented on the sense of helplessness experienced by many as they saw 'all that they most reverence and treasure, the home, the family, the race, subjected to irreparable injury, which they are powerless to avert'.[1]

Those dependent on men in the regular army and the reservists were entitled to separation allowances but often they were unable to read and write well enough to complete the requisite claim forms. At Ancoats, Manchester, Stella Davies, a local telephonist, remembered attending at the University Settlement to advise some of those faced, possibly for the first time, with the need for literacy:

Not only forms but letters from . . . husbands and fathers had to be read and answered. . . . The orders on the post office for the separation allowances were slow in coming through and many women found themselves penniless. Moreover, a suprising number were not married although they had several children as the result of an association which had lasted for, in some instances, many years. At first these women could claim no allowance but later a children's allowance was granted if the father admitted paternity. All this meant a great deal of 'paper work'.[2]

In country districts women who had never travelled beyond the nearest market town soon had sons or husbands serving in far-off Flanders or France. The *Mark Lane Express* in September 1914 described one mother waiting patiently at her cottage door for the arrival of the carrier with his slow-moving cart, coming from town. 'He had been amongst the newspapers and the special editions, and must know something . . . [she] has got two sons at the war and is naturally anxious.'[3]

In Bury many of the men were territorials in the 5th Battalion Lancashire Fusiliers, and they were initially sent to camp in the nearby village of Turton, on the edge of the moors. Each weekend large numbers of parents, wives and sweethearts made their way by tram, train and waggonette to visit them. Among them was Sarah Scowcroft, whose husband James had been employed by the Corporation prior to joining up. He and his wife were also caretakers of their local Methodist chapel and Sunday school. James had never been farther than the Isle of Man, but within weeks he was posted to Egypt. From there he was sent to Gallipoli, where he was killed in June 1915. Sarah, like many other war widows, was left to bring up their two children on an inadequate income. She boosted her meagre military pension with part-time work as a cleaner. She also took in washing and occasionally had lodgers, but it was a constant struggle to make ends meet. For Sarah, her husband's death meant not only an aching sadness but the end of the modest comfort and security she and her family had hitherto enjoyed. Later, when her daughter Alice was offered a place at Bury High School, the opportunity had to be missed. Mrs Scowcroft could not afford the special uniform and other items this would have entailed. Instead Alice left school as soon as she was able to work in a toffee factory.[4]

Among the well-to-do also the outbreak of war led to widespread changes. There was an upsurge of patriotic fervour which encouraged many women to take up a variety of charitable activities. Typical was the widowed Lady Airlie, a Lady of the Bedchamber to Queen Mary. Before the end of 1914 all three of her sons and a son-in-law had departed for the front and, like others in her situation, she learnt to dread the arrival of a telegram which might bring bad news. But she was also involved in philanthropic work, including meetings of the Army Nursing Board and recruitment of Voluntary Aid Detachment (VAD) nurses for the Red Cross, as well as long sessions on duty in the out-patients' department of St Mary's Hospital, Paddington. She handed over most of Cortachy Castle, her Scottish home, to the Red Cross for use as a hospital although she continued to manage the estate. 'My entire horizon was bounded by potatoes,' she wrote on one occasion. 'Every vine house was stuffed full of them; even the little hut at the back of the gardens was stacked with potato boxes from the floor to the roof.'[5] When the war ended she had lost one of her sons and a son-in-law, both killed in action, while her daughter Mabell had died shortly before the Armistice as the result of a fall while exercising Army remount horses.

Some members of the aristocracy, such as the Duchess of Sutherland, set up hospitals, either in Britain or in France, while others, such as Lady Londonderry, promoted organizations designed to utilize female labour for the war effort. One of Lady Londonderry's pet projects was the Women's Legion. This consisted of a band of uniformed volunteers whose duties ranged from military cooking and

WAACs recruiting sergeants in Trafalgar Square, London, 1918. (Trustees of the Imperial War Museum, London)

running canteens for munition and transport workers to acting as ambulance drivers and driving for the Army Service Corps and the Royal Flying Corps. Some worked on the land. The largest group of volunteers served as cooks and waitresses at military establishments and by 1917 they numbered about thirty thousand. In that year they formed the nucleus of the Women's Auxiliary Army Corps.[6] Soon after came the Women's Royal Naval Service and the Women's Royal Air Force Service, as well as special groups of women employed in the Army Pay Office, the Remount Department, the Forage Corps and the Army Service Corps, among others. In all, around one hundred and fifty thousand women were enrolled in these various uniformed services. They were under the control of their own officers and although not enlisted in a legal sense they regarded themselves as members of the armed forces.[7] Most were from a working-class or lower middle-class background; only their leaders were upper-class. However, among the general public there was sometimes hostility towards females in uniform. Even the redoubtable Lady Londonderry complained of the behaviour of male porters, who squeezed her out of lifts when she was in uniform. On one occasion she was turned away from the front door of a large house by an indignant maid, who directed her to the trademan's entrance instead. The maid later explained that she had 'thought you was one of them 'orrible Army women'.[8]

WAACs marching in Rouen, 24 July 1917. (Trustees of the Imperial War Museum, London)

Those well-to-do females who had more modest ambitions, or perhaps smaller means, than Lady Londonderry organized sewing guilds, raised funds to send parcels to the soldiers or prisoners-of-war, arranged entertainments for the wounded, and promoted endless flag days for war objects. They administered welfare schemes to cater for munitions workers and took a leading part in the War Savings Campaign. When all else failed they knitted socks and mufflers for the men at the front, or as Caroline Playne put it: 'The great era of knitting set in; men should fight but women should knit.'[9]

Many younger people, such as Lady Diana Manners, opted to become VAD nurses. Lady Diana worked first at Guy's Hospital in London and then in the hospital opened by her mother, the Duchess of Rutland, at their Arlington Street home. There, with her sister Letty and a close friend, Phyllis Boyd, both fellow members of staff, she was able to combine nursing with an active social life. But there was a darker side to Diana's apparent light-heartedness. From time to time she resorted to heavy drinking – usually vodka and absinthe in the early hours of the morning – and sometimes even drug-taking (particularly chloroform and morphia), when the sorrows and tensions of war became too great. 'Strange that grief should be so infinitely the biggest emotion,' she wrote on one occasion. 'In

VAD nurses with convalescing patients during the First World War. (The author)

no ecstasy that we know of can there not be found a thousand touches of chance that will reverse our state; . . . Whereas in sorrow nothing can lighten one's darkness.'[10]

Leah Manning, a Cambridge teacher, worked as a part-time VAD when she left school each day. She had strong socialist and pacifist beliefs but argued that if she could not prevent men from being 'torn to pieces, perhaps [she] could do something to comfort and assuage'. She began by meeting the trains bringing wounded men back from the battlefield. They arrived lousy, their uniforms caked in mud and blood, and, later in the year, with toes and fingers dropping off from frostbite. 'Some men were too tired to raise to their lips the mugs of tea we brought them.' Leah, like other VADs, was treated with contempt and hostility by the regular trained nurses.[11] They seem to have feared that after the war these 'amateurs' would seek to undercut and supplant them by entering the profession on a permanent basis. 'The presence of Red Cross nurses drove some of them almost frantic with jealousy and suspicion, which grew in intensity as the VADs increased in competence', was the judgement of another of the despised 'amateurs'.[12]

But while the well-to-do engaged in voluntary work and charitable activities, for many of those lower down the social scale the immediate impact of the war was the loss of a job. A high proportion of those industries most adversely affected by the hostilities were, in peacetime, major users of female labour. The cotton industry, for example, was already in recession before the war but it was further hit by disruptions in the supply of raw materials and by a decline in exports. In response to the new mood of austerity, demand for luxuries such as silk, lace, jewellery, millinery, china and glass suffered a sharp decline. Wealthy households even reduced the size of their domestic staff, although this was sometimes involuntary, the maids leaving to seek more remunerative work elsewhere. By

September 1914 over 40 per cent of female industrial workers were unemployed or on short time; indeed, in dressmaking alone about 34 per cent of the women were out of a job, and in the jam and confectionery trade 39 per cent.[13] Not until the beginning of 1915 did the situation improve, as the needs of the armed services for clothing, food, and leather goods increased the demand for labour. But it was April of that year before employment levels again reached their pre-war position. By then women were replacing men in offices, shops, the transport system, and even in the metal-working industries, including munitions factories, as well as in traditional 'female' trades such as textiles and clothing manufacture.

It was in the spring of 1915 that the government began recruiting women to manufacture munitions, using the services of the pre-war suffragette leader Mrs Emmeline Pankhurst to further the campaign. With the outbreak of war Mrs Pankhurst and her Women's Social and Political Union had abandoned their struggle for the vote in the interests of national solidarity. 'We want to make no bargain to serve our country,' she declared firmly in November 1914. By the summer of the following year she had organized a body of about twenty thousand women to march from Westminster to Blackfriars to announce their willingness to help produce armaments.[14] Meanwhile, despite initial opposition from male workers and their unions (especially the Amalgamated Society of Engineers), arrangements were made under the terms of the Shells and Fuses Agreement for existing trade practices to be relaxed in the munitions industry for the duration of the war. This would allow unskilled males and females to carry out tasks formerly reserved for skilled men. It was followed by what became known as the Treasury Agreement, whereby it was accepted that the 'substitute' labour thus introduced would be paid the same piece rates as the men they were replacing or as skilled male colleagues, providing they performed similar work. No such arrangement applied to time rates, however, and experience was to show that by subdividing the production process and utilizing more machinery, female labour could be used and yet the argument advanced that because they were not carrying out the same work as the men they were therefore not entitled to equal pay. In most cases employers paid them only about 50 to 66 per cent of the male rate and this was done with the tacit approval of the Ministry of Munitions, which had itself negotiated the Treasury Agreement. The Ministry declared that equal pay was 'a social revolution which . . . it is undesirable to attempt during wartime'. Events in the 1920s were to show that it was an experiment which was not to be attempted in peacetime either.

In these circumstances the number of women employed in the metal industries rose from 170,000 in July 1914 to 594,000 four years later, a rise of almost 250 per cent. In transport the increase was from around 18,000 to about 117,000 over the same period, and in banking, finance and commerce, including shop work, from 506,000 to over 934,000. Overall the female labour force probably increased from 4.93 million before the war to 6.19 million by July 1918, an increase of over a quarter.[15] In 1917 the *Labour Gazette* suggested that about one in three of all working women were substituting for men.

Besides these major employment outlets, a host of other occupations were opened up for female substitutes. The government itself recruited thousands of women clerks to staff the new ministries which were being set up in Whitehall, with perhaps 162,000 females employed in that way. Even such tasks as window cleaning, plumbing and electrical work were taken up, to say nothing of posts as signalmen and porters on the railways. 'Practically nothing came amiss to them,' wrote the feminist Ray Strachey enthusiastically, 'and, though on some of the heavier work, such as cleaning boilers, it took three women to do the work of two men, in many other trades the proportion was reversed.'[16] For duties such as meter-reading for the gas industry, they were generally considered more suitable than their male counterparts, despite being restricted by their employers to visiting only 66 per cent of the houses formerly covered by the men.[17]

As women took up their new posts they were often greeted with suspicion by both employers and male colleagues, the latter seeing them as cheap labour who would undermine the status and financial security of hitherto all-male occupations. This remained the case even when growing numbers of women began to join trade unions. Indeed, the Amalgamated Society of Engineers firmly refused to allow them membership, although other male bastions were breached, notably the National Union of Railwaymen and the Electrical Trades Union, in 1915 and 1916 respectively.[18] By 1917 310 trade unions had women members

Women working on aircraft woodwork in the pattern shop at the Instructional Factory at Loughborough Technical College during the war. (Loughborough University of Technology Archives)

(compared to 204 in 1912), but the bulk of females were still in the textile unions, as they had been before the war.[19]

Centres of engineering excellence, such as Loughborough Technical College, opened instructional factories under the aegis of the Ministry of Munitions to train male and female labour in a variety of trades, including shell turning, tool setting, fitting, electric welding, and all classes of foundry practice. For the simpler kinds of work, the period of training was usually about two or three weeks, but for the more skilled operations it might extend to six months.[20]

Once they entered permanent employment, however, some of the women encountered overt hostility. A tool fitter had her drawer nailed up by a male colleague on one occasion, and had oil poured over its contents through a crack on another. An employee in an engineering firm remembered being dismissed because she had hit a man who repeatedly spat chewed tobacco in her pocket.[21] But more common was the response experienced by a middle-class volunteer, Naomi Loughnan, who worked in a munitions factory. 'Engineering mankind', she wrote ruefully,

is possessed of the unshakable opinion that no woman can have . . . mechanical sense. . . . As long as we do exactly what we are told and do not attempt to use our brains, we give entire satisfaction, and are treated as nice, good children. Any swerving from the easy path prepared for us by our males arouses the most scathing contempt.[22]

She also detected an 'undercurrent of jealousy' when it was suggested that females could do the work as well as men. That wounded both their pride and their sense that as family breadwinners they should earn more than any women counterparts. For this reason, most preferred to have women excluded from 'men's work' altogether rather than allow them to be given equal pay. Joan Williams, herself a munitions worker, sympathized with their situation: 'they were torn between not wanting the women to undercut them, and yet hating them to earn as much'.[23]

So while the popular press and government ministers praised the patriotism and the skills of the new female recruits, at a deeper level many male workers continued to express opposition. 'I have to bear with a woman for twelve hours a day and I will not bear with women for twenty-four,' was the ungracious response of one skilled worker when faced with the arrival of female colleagues.[24] Such reactions were a sobering indication that the wider employment opportunities offered to women were very much 'for the duration' of the war only. As early as April 1916 the *Sussex Daily News* put forward what was to be the common view when it declared that although it would cause dislocation after the war when these 'many women workers . . . return to domestic life . . . this dislocation will be trifling compared with the results which could follow their retention in any considerable numbers'.[25] A similar 'back to home and hearth' attitude was adopted by the leading woman trade unionist, Mary Macarthur, when she admitted that although women had done 'some wonderful work, . . . a baby is more wonderful than a machine-gun. I believe that the hand that rocks the cradle will still be a power when the other is only a hateful memory.'[26]

*Women unloading coke from the foundry at Palmers Shipbuilding Co. Ltd, Hebburn-on-Tyne.
(Trustees of the Imperial War Museum, London)*

The additional female labour needed both to substitute for men who had joined up and to meet the demands of war production was recruited from four principal sources. Firstly, there were former servants, who seized the chance to leave the restraints and poor pay associated with residential domestic employment. In all, the number of female servants shrank by nearly 400,000 over the war years.[27] Secondly, there were many working-class married women who responded to appeals to return to employment perhaps on patriotic grounds or because they and their children were unable to live on the military separation allowance awarded when their husband enlisted. In other cases, widows like Mrs Scowcroft in Bury returned to work when their husbands were killed at the front.

Married women provided a particularly important source of extra labour, comprising about 40 per cent of the total female work force by 1918, compared with just over 14 per cent in 1911.[28] Prior to 1914 they had been encouraged to believe that their proper station was as wives and mothers in the home. Only among the poorest families or in specialized areas of production, such as the cotton industry, was there much employment of married women before the war.

But with the outbreak of hostilities the situation was transformed. In Leeds, where in 1911 only 15 per cent of women workers in the town's four principal engineering firms were married, that figure had risen to 44 per cent by 1918.[29] Married women were also relatively popular with male colleagues, who saw their recruitment as a purely temporary measure which would terminate when the war itself ended.

Employers were less enthusiastic, complaining of poor timekeeping and a greater willingness to change jobs than among male counterparts, unless they were restricted by government regulations. In the woollen and worsted industry it was claimed that married women lost 30 per cent more time than the men, while there were 40 per cent more changes in female personnel than in male workers during a twelve-month period. One representative of the Yorkshire and Lancashire manufacturers observed sourly: 'They stay away . . . for what are, from the point of view of the employer, trivial reasons. A day's washing may be a very serious thing for a woman, but to stay away and leave her machine idle for a day's wash does not appear to be anything but trivial to her employer.'[30] He did not mention that the comparatively low wages earned by women woollen weavers prevented their employing domestic assistance to look after their family when they were at work, as was done in sectors of the cotton industry. There was also a failure to recognize that many of the women had the added responsibility of coping with household finances and family problems on their own, while their husbands were away.

A third source of extra labour was provided by young girls who were encouraged to leave school at an early age in order to begin working. In some cases, under parental pressure, that meant taking up war work because of its higher wages. Mrs Beatrice Ashworth, who began her working life in 1916 in a Manchester shirt factory at the age of 14, remembered having to leave, against her will, to enter a cotton mill when her father joined up in 1918. She was one of twelve children and her mother could not manage on the father's separation allowance. As a result of the move Beatrice's weekly wage increased from 12s. to 18s. She had to rise at 5.15 a.m. in order to walk to work by 6 a.m.:

> I was only little for me age. . . . And . . . this woman that taught me, she swore at me . . . and I was frightened of the machinery, but she made a winder out of me. And the next week her got me on piece work and I earned 30 shillings. . . . This was better than me mother and father had ever earned.[31]

Finally, there were the middle- and upper-class volunteers who took up war work out of a sense of adventure or of patriotic duty. Despite accounts of 'ladies of fine breeding' running the lathes in munitions factories or pouring deadly TNT into shell cases, and despite Caroline Playne's comment that it 'became a disgrace' for a middle-class woman to remain at home, the number of such workers was always relatively small.[32] And when they did enter factories they were not always welcomed by working-class colleagues. One such volunteer, Monica Cosens, described her initial reservations about the 'vulgar little hussies' with whom she had to work. Later she came to recognize their good-heartedness and the hard work they carried out, often becoming shadow-eyed and pale in the process. Nevertheless, whenever a new middle-class recruit arrived there was an immediate feeling of defiance in the air.

> One girl will put out her tongue at the unconscious worker's back, another will deride her with an admiring crowd about her, while a third will do everything she can to worry the novice, by borrowing her crowbar and not bothering to return it, and when it is claimed with diffidence, will treat the inquirer with scornful silence and a look of contempt which sets the others around her giggling.[33]

Only when they realized that the 'lidy' meant to play the game and not to patronize them did they offer the hand of friendship.

Naomi Loughnan, another middle-class volunteer, was less tolerant than Monica Cosens, complaining that the girls lacked interest in their work 'because of the undeveloped state of their imaginations'. She admitted that they often carried on when their eyes were 'swollen with weeping for sweethearts and brothers whose names are among the killed and wounded':

> yet they do not definitely connect the work they are doing with the trenches. One girl, with a face growing sadder and paler as the days went by because no news came from France of her 'boy' who was missing, when gently urged to work harder . . . answered, with angry indignation: 'Why should I work any harder? My mother is satisfied with what I takes home of a Saturday.'[34]

Loughnan ignored the fact that while she was working by her own choice, her working-class colleagues had no such option. They must keep on whether they liked it or not in order to earn a living.

Many of the munitions workers were also condemned for their bold behaviour and their noisy and boisterous conduct. One woman admitted to finding 'rather upsetting to one's old-fashioned idea of a "woman's place"' her encounters with groups of girls and women walking 'arm in arm and singing "It's a long way to Tipperary"'.[35] In Manchester, Stella Davies described how the girls who worked in explosives factories – known as 'canaries', because the work imparted a yellow hue to their complexion – were criticized for the high wages they earned and the high jinks they got up to in their free time. Many wore expensive seal-skin coats, and their morals were said to be 'no better than they ought to be', for 'seal-skin coats, hitherto almost unknown among the respectable working-class, could only be bought, it was believed, with "the wages of sin"'.[36]

On a wider basis, there were attacks on female sexuality and alleged promiscuity. 'Some women,' wrote Mrs Alec-Tweedie in 1918, '. . . became hysterical with war. They went out like cats on the tiles and shrieked madly. They wanted to mate. Anything would do.'[37] There were fears that those with venereal disease would infect young soldiers, when they hung around military camps. In December 1917 a letter to *The Times* referred to women as 'sexual freelances' who 'stalked through the land, vampires upon the nation's health, distributing and perpetuating among our young manhood diseases which institute a national calamity'.[38] Such exaggerated reactions were part of the turmoil created by the war and by the recruitment of women into unfamiliar occupations and roles.

Yet despite the formidable increase in female employment during these years, even in 1918 the majority of women were still not working outside the home. In 1921, when the population census revealed there were 15.7 million females aged 12 and above in England and Wales, the total female labour force in July 1918 for the United Kingdom as a whole (including those working on their own account or as employers) was put at 7.3 million.[39] However, those who remained at home were also influenced by patriotic fervour, with much emphasis placed upon their importance in looking after home and family. In 1917 the *Win the War Cookery Book* observed encouragingly:

> The British fighting line shifts and extends and now *you* are in it. The struggle is not only on land and sea; it is in *your* larder, *your* kitchen and *your* dining room. Every meal *you* serve is now literally a battle.

And while working-class wives were deluged with recipes for scalloped parsnips, barley rissoles, bean fritters and bread made from potatoes, wealthy householders were urged to leave cheaper products for the poor: 'the true patriot who can afford it will eat asparagus not potatoes'.[40] Even newspaper advertisements caught the mood. Potential consumers of 'Paisley Flour' were advised that:

> Once it was an extravagance to eat cakes instead of bread but the war has made it a patriotic duty now, because we can use flour substitutes in cakes and so save wheat flour and bread. . . . It is a duty to bake at home. It is also an economy that helps to win the war.[41]

Alongside this there was concern about preserving the health of mothers and babies at a time when huge numbers of the nation's young men were being killed and maimed on the battlefield. 'To provide the conditions which render a strong and healthy family life possible to all is the first interest of the State, since the family is the foundation stone of the social system,' declared a report issued jointly by employers and trade unions in Bristol during March 1918.[42] As a consequence of these attitudes there was a strengthening of the pre-war emphasis on the importance of women's role as wives and mothers, and an attempt to reduce child mortality rates by creating a network of infant welfare centres, and by the appointment of health visitors to advise mothers on the care of their babies. The number of infant welfare centres more than tripled during the war period, from 350 in 1914 to 1,290 in 1918, while the total of health visitors more than doubled. There were campaigns such as the National Baby Week, launched in 1917, and Lord Plunkett's Babies of the Empire Society, which sought to promote infant health by encouraging breast-feeding and providing nurses trained for welfare work.[43] Even illegitimate children were targeted. Their significance increased during the war years, as their share of total births rose from 4.2 per cent in 1914 to 6.3 per cent in 1918. In that year over 41,000 babies were born outside

The cult of maternity: mother and baby show in around 1918 at Boscombe, Hampshire. (The author)

wedlock. Yet, at the same time, the infant mortality rate for illegitimate children was more than double that for legitimate babies.[44] Public opinion was particularly sensitive to the waste of life these figures represented at a time when so many young, fit men were being killed on the battlefield.

It was in these circumstances that the National Council for the Unmarried Mother and Her Child was set up in the spring of 1918, to press for reform of the existing Bastardy and Affiliation Orders legislation and to secure suitable accommodation, including hostels with day nurseries, to enable mother and baby to live together while the mother continued at work.[45] Pressure was exerted to increase the maximum maintenance allowance payable through a court affiliation order from 5s. a week (a figure first established in 1872), and this succeeded in 1918 when the maximum was doubled to 10s. The National Council sought to give help without the usual overtones of moral condemnation associated with illegitimacy. As one activist put it, every effort should be made to ensure that the mothers, 'both for the children's sake and for their own, should be saved from the degradation which too often follows a single lapse from virtue'. No longer ought they to be forced into the workhouse or stigmatized as immoral. 'Very many of the men . . . have already redeemed their fault by giving their lives for their country . . . but let it be frankly acknowledged that the women are no more blameworthy than the men.'[46]

In a similar spirit the Maternity and Child Welfare Act of 1918 widened local authority powers to assist expectant and nursing mothers and children by providing home helps, lying-in homes, food, crèches and day nurseries, as well as

NATIONAL   COUNCIL   FOR   THE
UNMARRIED MOTHER & HER CHILD

MATERNITY
WARD

ANNUAL
REPORT.

May 31st, 1921.

FOURPENCE.

FRIENDLESS
HOMELESS

117,   Piccadilly,
London, W. 1.

Telephone—GROSVENOR 1482

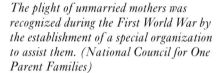

The plight of unmarried mothers was recognized during the First World War by the establishment of a special organization to assist them. (National Council for One Parent Families)

hospital treatment for children under five.[47] These services were to be extended during the 1920s, particularly in London, where by the early 1930s over 90 per cent of the metropolitan boroughs were providing milk and food to needy expectant and nursing mothers, and 61 per cent were offering convalescent home treatment. Stepney, for example, despite being one of the poorest boroughs in London had a relatively good maternal mortality record largely as a result of the welfare facilities it provided for the mothers.[48] By 1918 Birmingham, too, had established five maternity feeding centres to cater for malnourished nursing and expectant mothers, and other services followed in the next few years. In 1920, for example, a maternity home was opened with 185 beds, followed in 1921 by another with 79 beds. From 1920 home helps were employed to carry out cooking and cleaning during a mother's confinement, and local welfare centres were opened to give dental treatment and advice on infant welfare. As a consequence of these initiatives and of slum clearance programmes, the infant mortality rate in Birmingham fell sharply in the 1920s.[49]

The First World War, then, affected the lives of women in many different ways. On the one hand it enabled upper- and middle-class women to extend the scope of their pre-war charitable and voluntary duties and, at the same time, to experience new spheres of employment and responsibility which some were reluctant to relinquish when the war ended. Even leading socialites like Lady Londonderry felt a depressing lack of purpose in their lives when their wartime efforts came to an end. In Lady Londonderry's case this followed the disbandment of the Women's Legion.[50]

In many cases, working-class women left domestic service and other traditionally 'female' occupations to take up posts in munitions factories or in a wide range of 'male' occupations, such as building and transport. There was a sharp rise in the number of those working in shops and offices – thereby providing a pointer to the growth areas of female employment during the 1920s. Even if the new recruits rarely received equal pay with male colleagues doing the same work, the wages they earned and the status they enjoyed were far higher than women had secured before 1914. Yet the old emphasis on the importance of the female role as wife and mother remained, with various campaigns to promote infant welfare and to emphasize that women who remained in the home, caring for their family, were also playing a vital part in the war effort. At the same time they had to cope with the nagging anxiety of never knowing whether their menfolk would return from the front or, if they did, whether they would be able to work again. Mrs Alice Dickinson's mother was not alone in having to work in a Burnley mill during the 1920s to help support the family because her husband, a miner, had been too badly injured in the war to take up his old trade again. Instead he became a general labourer in a tram depot.[51] Mrs Ethel Cleary's mother went to work on her father's smallholding when her husband was killed in 1918, leaving her with three children, the eldest of whom was only ten.[52]

Even when the war was over newspapers regularly carried appeals from women whose menfolk had been posted missing and about whom they could obtain no information. In March 1919 Mrs Harrison of Bury wrote to the *Bury Times* asking 'if any returned soldier could give information regarding her son Private Herbert Harrison, 2nd/5th Lancashire Fusiliers, who was reported missing France, November 20, 1917'. Another enquiry was asking for news of Private Airton of the 9th Battalion; his wife had died about the time he went missing two years before, leaving four children to be cared for by their grandparents.[53]

When the Armistice was finally signed in November 1918 it was greeted with widespread rejoicing. In the mood of euphoria thus induced, sexual encounters took place between perfect strangers in parks, shop doorways and alleys. In Oxford a woman paraded up and down the Cornmarket, 'waving a flag, with her skirts kilted up to her naked middle', to the cheers of Army and Air cadets quartered in the colleges. In a bizarre touch, the owner of a Richmond tearoom was even fined £5 4s. for allowing kissing and cuddling between male customers and herself and her waitresses to take place on the day after Armistice Day. In her defence it was claimed that although a 'certain amount of larking' had taken place, 'on that day kissing and cuddling went on all over London, even in the streets'.[54] But the presiding magistrate was not impressed, calling it a 'very bad case'.

The wealthy played their part, too. Cynthia Curzon, whose father was a member of the War Cabinet, celebrated Armistice night with friends at the Ritz hotel, 'draped in a Union Jack and singing patriotic songs'. Later that night, according to her sister, 'she tore round Trafalgar Square with the great crowd setting light to old cars and trucks to the horror of [her] father'.[55]

Some women seized the opportunity of the arrival of peace to return to their pre-war roles as full-time mistresses of the household or leisured daughters at home. But for those who had wider ambitions the prospects rapidly became bleak.

Under the terms of wartime agreements (culminating in the 1918 Restoration of Pre-war Practices Act), women were expected to vacate those posts which they were occupying as substitutes for men. Any who did not respond speedily were condemned. The press, which had lauded female patriotism during the hostilities, now wrote of the 'Limpets of the War Office' who were hanging on to jobs that should be made available to demobilized soldiers.[56] Even sympathetic commentators could see no solution for redundant office workers but the traditional sphere of matrimony:

> They were all engaged on an understanding that their posts were to be temporary, and they have no legal claim . . . and no legitimate grievance if they have to leave when the man who used to do the work returns. To do them justice, they are not making a grievance of the undoubted hardship which has arisen. The hardship is that after four years of city life and experience during which these girls earned good money . . . they now have to return home as family burdens with no immediate prospect of a similarly active life for some time to come. For many the situation will be solved by the lottery of marriage. . . .
> The real difficulty arises in the case of the woman who is neither brilliant nor foolish but just a steady, accurate, painstaking person of the ledger-keeping type who has carried on just as well as the man she replaced did before the war. Often she is plain and unattractive and perhaps not so young as she once was. . . . I feel that every effort ought to be made to keep these women in the counting-houses of great public companies, and to find more manly work, preferably of an outdoor nature, for the men back from the front whose places have been kept open.[57]

Irene Clephane also commented on the change in public mood between 1918 and 1919: 'From being the saviours of the nation, women in employment were degraded in the . . . press to the position of ruthless self-seekers depriving men and their dependants of a livelihood . . .; all of them became, in many people's minds, objects of opprobrium.'[58] The feminist Ray Strachey wrote bitterly of the way in which it was assumed that all women had a man to support them and that if they went on working 'it was from a sort of deliberate wickedness':

> The . . . very same people who had been heroines and the saviours of their country a few months before were now parasites, blacklegs and limpets. Employers were implored to turn them out as passionately as they had been implored to employ them and their last weeks in their wartime jobs were made miserable by the jeers and taunts of their fellow workers.[59]

Even before the end of 1918, partly as a result of Russia's withdrawal from the war and the consequent decline in demand for some forms of munitions and for military uniforms, female unemployment had begun to rise. Already in November 1918 there had been a march from Woolwich and other London districts to Westminster to demand action to provide work or maintenance for those made

Women working on Southwark capstan lathes in the general machine shop at the Instructional Factory at Loughborough Technical College. (Loughborough University of Technology Archives)

redundant, and a Right to Work campaign was launched by one of the leading women's trade unions, the National Federation of Women Workers. As a result of the war its membership had jumped from 10,000 in December 1914 to about 80,000 four years later, and most of these new members were engaged in the munitions and metalworking trades.[60]

The government responded by offering all demobilized workers an out-of-work donation or 'dole' to tide them over until they could find fresh employment. Those entitled to the benefit had to have been contributors under the Health Insurance Scheme before 25 August 1918, or to have proof of employment before that date if they were aged under 18 or over 70. The donation was 20s. a week for women, to last for thirteen weeks, after which it would drop to 15s. for a further thirteen weeks.[61] In the event, because of the massive dislocations of the war and its aftermath, this non-contributory scheme was continued under various guises until the end of 1919. The following year a new Unemployment Insurance Act was introduced to cover all manual workers except agricultural workers and domestic servants, and all non-manual workers earning less than £250 per annum. The omission of domestic servants, allegedly because they did not experience prolonged unemployment, was of particular importance to women, who made up the vast majority of the domestic work force.

For those laid off it was a bitter pill to swallow. Sometimes they were replaced not by adult males but by still cheaper boy labour: 'they threw us on the slag heap,' declared one woman bitterly. 'Things were bad after the war, very, very bad,' remembered another.[62] By March 1919 just over half a million women were officially recorded as unemployed, but the true number was undoubtedly much higher, since labour exchanges were required to 'exercise "extreme strictness"' when accepting female applicants for unemployment benefit. They were expected to eliminate any applicant whose right seemed doubtful.[63] And although those refused had a right of appeal against the decision, few were successful. In many districts it was said that the chairmen of the investigatory courts cross-examined the women 'as if they were criminals'. Another aspect of the problem was that those offered work by the exchanges, no matter how low the pay or unsatisfactory the working conditions, could be excluded from benefit if they refused. One girl was disallowed because she refused to accept domestic work at 8s. 6d. a week, for hours extending from 7 a.m. to 5.30 p.m. A soldier's wife lost her benefit when she refused to take work at 8s. a week, the week in this case amounting to seven days at 10½ hours a day. In a third case a woman who rejected an offer of clerical work away from home on the grounds that she had a delicate widowed mother to support, was disallowed even though she expressed willingness to take any clerical work offered near home. It was argued that she should have accepted the offer and made arrangements to move home rather than remain on out-of-work donation indefinitely.[64]

Some women were able to return to traditional 'female' employments in textiles, laundrywork and catering, often taking with them their wartime membership of trade unions. Interestingly, women's trade union membership reached a peak in 1920 of 1,342,000 – about a quarter of the female labour force – compared to 433,679 in 1914 and 1,209,271 in 1918.[65] Only with the downturn in trade in the summer of 1920, particularly in the textile industry, did membership slump, falling by about 470,000 in the next two years.

But for most of the female unemployed, the main outlet was in domestic service. Despite their reluctance to return to the regimentation and low wages which all too often accompanied residential domestic employment, more and more were forced to do so. As Gail Braybon points out, placements of maids through the labour exchanges remained 'low from November 1918 to February 1919, then shot up, so that they were 40 per cent higher in the succeeding six months than they had been during the corresponding period in 1918'.[66] Even the Ministry of Labour itself recognized the problem, when it noted in January 1919 that the lifting of military restrictions on the coast meant that holiday resorts would enjoy a good season. 'This should result in the increased employment of large numbers of women, as many who object to private domestic service readily accept work in crowded boarding houses and similar establishments.'[67]

To add to the pressures there was a powerful press campaign claiming that women in receipt of the out-of-work donation were merely enjoying a holiday on the dole. Typical was a report in the *Western Mail* of 20 January 1919, under the headline 'Out-of-Work Money. Munitions Grant Open to Abuse':

Thousands of young women went from the South Wales area to the large munitions districts. Now they have returned and claimed the donations, and unless new industries are established or old industries are extended and developed these women cannot possibly be absorbed, and the time is thus approaching when they must realize that domestic service, which they were originally largely engaged in, must again be their main source of livelihood. . . . Seaside places and other holiday centres throughout the country are said to be now reaping a harvest from young women who are out for a good time on their savings as munitions workers and on their donations. . . . It is recognized that the donation scheme is a temporary measure, but economists fear that its adoption has already interfered very prejudicially with the normal conditions that govern the absorption of available labour in industry.

The need for women to return to service and the drawing up of schemes to encourage them to do so were to be continuing themes during the 1920s. Indeed, when the Ministry of Labour, in cooperation with the Central Committee on Women's Employment, instituted training courses between 1920 and 1922, although they prepared a few women for teaching, nursing and cookery posts, the largest number were trained for domestic service, with 10,000 so instructed during that period. Two years later, with the Ministry of Labour now in sole control of the scheme, the total of women who had completed homecraft, homemaker and home training courses had risen to 23,058, with a further 2,012 undergoing training. By contrast, just 352 had completed clerical courses and 145 had received vocational training.[68]

In these circumstances it is not surprising that at the 1921 census of population a quarter of female workers were engaged in domestic service or charring, while over 2 per cent more were working as laundresses and washerwomen.[69] Married women, who had played such a crucial role in the war effort, saw their role sharply cut back. In 1921 they made up about 13.7 per cent of the total female work force, compared with perhaps 40 per cent during the peak of the war years, and 14.2 per cent in 1911.

However, the war did more than influence women's working lives. It had profound psychological implications as well, especially for those who had lost husbands or sweethearts in the hostilities, or who were having to come to terms with menfolk physically and mentally scarred by their experiences. Some turned to spiritualism in the hope of making contact with their dead husband or son, and professional mediums set up in business in most of the larger towns during the early 1920s. Among those who consulted them was Maggie Hobhouse, who tried to get in touch with her youngest and favourite son, who was killed at Ypres. Later she visited the battleground, where she 'almost felt his spirit by me, telling me how little the mortal remains should mean to us . . . it may be that no proof can be had. But it is curious that most people who look into it are more or less converted to the spiritualist hypothesis.'[70]

Another victim of the war was Vera Brittain, daughter of a Staffordshire paper manufacturer. She had interrupted her studies at Somerville College, Oxford, to work as a VAD in England and later in France. During the conflict she had lost her fiancé, her only brother, and two close friends, and when she resumed her career at Oxford in 1919 she was a very different person from the young undergraduate of four years earlier. On the verge of a nervous breakdown, she suffered severe attacks of migraine and was unable to sleep. 'I suffered for months from the delusion that my face was disfigured,' she confessed later. 'It always looked disfigured when I saw it in the glass, until I got into a state where I almost screamed if I went into a room where there was a mirror.'[71] Only gradually, and with the help of her friend and fellow undergraduate Winifred Holtby, did the wounds heal and she was able to recover her equilibrium.

The loss of around three-quarters of a million young men on the battlefield (to say nothing of many thousands more who were seriously maimed), inevitably affected the gender balance of the population. By 1921 there were over 1.7 million more females aged 12 and above in England and Wales than there were males, an imbalance about half a million greater than in 1911. The position was particularly acute among those aged 20 to 35. For a number of widows and single women, therefore, there seemed little prospect of marriage. At the same time many younger women who had been earning their living and taking their own decisions during the war were determined to make an independent way in the world during the years that followed. After the Armistice among large numbers of former war-workers there was an emphasis on youth and freedom, which found expression in the wearing of make-up, the smoking of cigarettes, and a passion for dancing and the cinema. Skirts were shorter, frocks lighter and simpler in design, and hair was cut short. Whereas before the war a well-rounded 'feminine' figure had been the ideal, in the early 1920s it was a slim, boyish shape which became the aim of the fashion-conscious. This was the era of the 'flapper' – 'a comradely, sporting, active young woman, who would ride pillion on the "flapper-bracket" of a motorcycle' and who scandalized her elders by her free and easy behaviour. As one fashion historian has pointed out, in order to achieve the desired shape of an immature male, breasts were reduced by the wearing of compressors, the waist and buttocks were flattened into a cylinder, and the hair cut to 'masculine proportions. At the same time exposure of the legs and arms gave the appearance of extreme youth at the sacrifice of their erotic properties.'[72] The object was to suggest boyish athleticism.

The mood did not last, however, and as memories of the war faded in the later 1920s more feminine fashions again came to the fore. There was also a wider acceptance of the importance of women's traditional role as wives and mothers. Already in 1919 and 1920 the marriage rate had moved sharply upwards – in 1920 the rate of 20.2 marriages per 1,000 of the population was higher than in any pre-war year – and although in the middle of the decade it fell back, marriage remained relatively popular. Despite the devastation of the war, therefore, many women were marrying.[73] Only among those in their late thirties and above was the gender imbalance still sufficiently serious in 1931 to make spinsterhood a likely fate.

There were, of course, gains from the war years as well as losses. The granting of the franchise to women in 1918 after many years of struggle was one obvious example. But it formed part of a package which included complete adult male suffrage, whereas only women over thirty could vote. In addition, they or their husband, if they were married, had to be a householder or to have some property qualification. Daughters living at home, domestic servants, and the younger women who had played a major part in the munitions factories and other war work were still excluded. In such circumstances, the pious hope of Mrs Fawcett, a leading pre-war suffragist, that the 'moral character' of the nation would be improved by the influx of women voters proved impossibly optimistic. 'It seems to me perfectly certain that the relations between the sexes will improve,' she declared, ' . . . and . . . domestic happiness will get more and more strength the more women's political power is brought to bear on legislation.'

In reality throughout the 1920s women's influence on legislation remained small, not least because of the tiny numbers of women MPs. The maximum registered was in 1929, when fourteen were elected. Indeed, although under a separate Act of 1918 women were able to stand for election to Parliament from the age of 21, in the general election held in December of that year only one woman was successful, although seventeen had stood as candidates.[74] The solitary victor was a Sinn Fein candidate, Countess Constance Markievicz, who had been imprisoned for her part in the Dublin Easter Rising and had contested the election from Holloway prison. Like other members of her party she refused to take her seat at Westminster, and it was left to Lady Astor to become the first woman to enter the Commons when she won her husband's old seat in Plymouth at a by-election in 1919. Despite her innate self-confidence, even she found the experience an ordeal, with some male MPs displaying extreme hostility, and with the hopes of thousands of other women resting upon her. As she recalled ruefully, her correspondence was extremely large, ranging between 1,000 and 1,200 letters a week, a high proportion of which came from women all over the country. In Parliament, Lady Astor devoted much of her attention to subjects affecting the welfare of women and children.[75] But she admitted to feelings of guilt that the first female to sit at Westminster should be someone who had played little part in the pre-1914 franchise struggle.

Of importance in widening the opportunities of professional women was the 1919 Sex Disqualification (Removal) Act which at first sight seemed to open up a range of occupations from which women had been hitherto excluded. Entry to the legal profession had been a particular aim of feminists for many years and following the passage of the 1919 Act a number of women began to study with a view to practising as barristers, while a smaller number, mainly of those having some family connection, became articled to solicitors. Already in the 1921 population census twenty female barristers and seventeen solicitors were recorded, although progress during the rest of the 1920s remained modest.[76] Women were also able to become members of professional bodies like the Chartered Accountants and the Royal Society which previously they had been unable to join either on gender grounds or because they lacked the appropriate qualifications and experience.[77] In March 1921 the *Woman Engineer*, journal of the Women's Engineering Society, proudly reported that one of its members had recently become an Associate of the Institution of Automobile Engineers and three more had been admitted to the Society of Technical Engineers. It claimed that so great was the wish of pioneer women engineers to join the appropriate professional institutions and societies that it was going to publish lists of relevant bodies, together with details of the qualifications necessary to achieve the various grades of membership.[78]

However, the 1919 Act was unable to remove personal prejudice and during the subsequent years of economic depression women found themselves squeezed out of many of the occupations they wished to enter. This was reinforced by the fact that in some professions, such as teaching, the Civil Service, and even medicine, it became increasingly common to bar married women from employment. In such cases females had to choose between a career and celibacy, or marriage and redundancy. As one of the pioneer women engineers commented sadly, there had been opposition in every profession that had been opened to women, and

> the newer industries are going to be just as hard a proposition. . . . When machinery first came into our factories men broke it up! They have learnt better by now so far as machines are concerned and we can only hope that time will show them what a great help to the community women's labour can be.[79]

More encouraging was the fact that the 1919 Sex Disqualification legislation opened the way for the appointment of female magistrates and members of juries. One of the first women Justices of the Peace was Mrs Ada J. Summers of Stalybridge, who also served as mayor of the town between 1919 and 1921. She was the widow of a local ironmaster and had been involved in a number of charitable activities before she became a magistrate. At her death in January 1944 the town's newspaper described her as 'Stalybridge's Lady Bountiful'.[80] Another early appointment was that of Miss Gertrude Tuckwell, a leading trade unionist, while in January 1920 Mrs Lloyd George, wife of the Prime Minister, became the first Welshwoman to be placed on the Commission of the Peace.[81] Although these were at first more of symbolic importance than anything else – even in 1930 there were only about two thousand females among the twenty-three thousand JPs in England and Wales – they did emphasize the political progress made by women since 1914.[82]

Giving rise to greater controversy was the selection of females for jury service. According to the *Oxford Chronicle* at the Winter Assizes of 1920/1 almost as much interest was taken in the role of women on juries as in the cases heard. Special correspondents from the daily press attended to describe their reactions, especially when murder cases were involved. 'The woman in the jury box has . . . shared the limelight with the prisoners at the bar of justice.' However, when the first female jurors appeared in the Divorce Court in January 1921 there were protests that such sordid matters would offend their sensibilities. The *Western Mail* argued that barristers who had to drag disclosures from witnesses and to discuss at length the 'details of immorality and crime' could be expected 'ere long to make a formal complaint that their task is impeded by the presence of women in the jury-box, and that the efficiency of the administration of the law is seriously impaired'. The paper admitted that since women had been admitted 'to the privilege of full citizenship' they ought to assume all the duties of that citizenship, but such a view was fallacious in two respects:

LADY MAGISTRATE. "Officer, *who* is the constable that will keep on bringing in those dreadful ruffians?"

Punch *mocking the first lady magistrates.*

In the first place the civic duty of military defence cannot be undertaken by women; and in the second place no amount of logic as to rights and their corresponding duties can be permitted to becloud an issue of practicability and common sense. The Criminal business of the courts of justice is tainted at almost every sitting by the hearing of cases which no decent woman would care to handle, and which no woman ought to be called upon to handle.[83]

Feminists responded angrily to these strictures, urging women to resist pressures to retire from jury service because of objections from a few judges and barristers. As Mrs E.M. Hubback, Parliamentary Secretary of the National Union of Societies for Equal Citizenship, firmly informed the *Western Mail*, in all the discussions over female jurors in divorce cases, or in those involving assaults upon small children, it was seemingly forgotten that the victims were often women and girls. 'It is in precisely such cases that the need for women as jurors is greatest.'[84] Public opinion took a similar view and the furore died away.

In bringing about these changes there is little doubt that the war itself, and women's part in it, had played an important role. In the midst of the conflict some opponents of women's suffrage had commented sourly upon the enthusiasm they had shown for the war effort:

> They sew and knit comforts for the soldiers, . . . with such a perpetual running accompaniment of suffragist self-laudation that they might as well embroider the sacred name of Mrs Pankhurst or Mrs Fawcett on every sock and every muffler, so as to give notice . . . that Suffragism alone has the trademark of thoughtful and benevolent patriotism.[85]

Even H.H. Asquith, the then Prime Minister and a long-standing critic of female enfranchisement, admitted reluctantly in August 1916 that women's overall contribution had been too important to be ignored: 'when the war comes to an end . . . and when the process of industrial reconstruction has to be set on foot, have not the women a special claim to be heard on the many questions which will arise directly affecting their interests? . . . I say quite frankly that I cannot deny that claim.'[86] Nevertheless, almost two more years were to elapse before the franchise bill reached the statute book and, as we have seen, it fell far short of the straightforward adult suffrage given to men at the same time. Not until 1928 did females achieve full equality.

Despite the hopes of many women at the time of the Armistice that their economic and political emancipation was at hand, therefore, experience over the following decade was to show the limitations of what had been achieved. Progress in some spheres was matched by disappointment and defeat in others. As Adelaide Anderson, the principal female factory inspector, commented gloomily, from the vantage of 1921 it was hard 'to recall the full measure of pride expressed by the nation in what the women did for it in time of need'. Then factory workers had realized, 'some with astonishment – that they were entitled to high praise, and to hold a new confidence in themselves'. But as memories of the war faded, the Restoration of Pre-war Practices legislation closed most of the expected new avenues of employment, and when the economic tide turned in the summer of 1920, rising unemployment obscured their former achievements.[87]

By January 1922 there were 370,000 females out of work out of a total of 3,209,000 women covered by the Unemployment Insurance Acts; among them were 36,000 unemployed in the textile industries, 19,000 in the distributive trades and 17,000 in the manufacture of food and drink.[88] Although the economy then revived, throughout the 1920s many working women, like their male counterparts, were haunted by economic uncertainty and the fear of losing their job.

CHAPTER 2

The Social Élite

Single women . . . and young married women filled their lives with a round of social engagements. . . . I found that, unless I was going to live a very solitary life, it was necessary to dine out nearly every evening, lunch out every day, and go to the country most weekends. . . . One played golf during the day with another woman, or lunched alone with a friend. . . . A great many clothes were necessary. . . . Appropriate clothes could not be bought ready-made . . . but were chosen from models and made individually. One needed clothes for London and clothes for the country, since these were not . . . interchangeable.

Frances Donaldson, *Child of the Twenties* (1959), pp. 133–4.

When peace came there was a wish among the majority of women in all classes of society to put the sorrows and fears of the preceding four years behind them and to return to their pre-war way of life. Some, admittedly, lamented the loss of opportunity to exercise their abilities and skills in the way they had done between 1914 and 1918, but most desired only to resume their customary daily round. Of none was that more true than of the social élite. As the *Daily Mail* acidly observed in February 1920: 'the social butterfly type has probably never been so prevalent as at present. It comprises the frivolous, scantily clad "jazzing flapper", irresponsible and undisciplined.'[1] Although numerous families still mourned the death of a husband, son, or fiancé, there was a deep relief that the slaughter had at last ended and a wish to resume such remembered pleasures as dancing, racing, hunting and foreign travel. Within months of the Armistice St Moritz had again become popular for skating and skiing, although later Mürren vied with it in popularity. For those seeking a warmer climate, the Riviera, Egypt and North Africa beckoned during the winter months.[2]

Even the outbreak of an epidemic of Spanish influenza, which ravaged Europe and killed nearly a quarter of a million people in the United Kingdom alone during 1918 and 1919, could not dampen the mood of optimism. Already in January 1919 the *New Statesman* was commenting on the number of 'shoots' that had been arranged, and the way in which plans were in hand for the refitting of yachts, the purchase of new motor cars, and the resumption of hunting.[3] 'Eve' in *The Tatler* described how the most determined pleasure-seekers were 'wangling' places on the overcrowded trains going to the South of France. She also drew

Winter sports at Mürren, Switzerland, early in 1921. (The Tatler, *9 February 1921)*

attention to the London scene, where night-clubs were 'opening up in rows' and dressmakers were dizzy with orders for dance frocks:

> [T]here's already talk of a . . . Russian Ballet season – the debs, you see, must see a little life, and there's nothing like opera and ballet for starting things off with the properly glittery and sensuous and romantic air.[4]

'Eve' also mentioned the darker side of High Society life, with its 'dope parties' where cocaine, opium and heroin were passed around. Drug-taking had grown up under the pressure of the war and it was to persist in certain circles throughout the 1920s. 'They're by no means the working nobodies – our drug-takers,' wrote 'Eve'. 'Ten pounds for a sniff or two can't be afforded by the poor or the "middle" classes.'[5] Later, Noel Coward's play *The Vortex* was to shock theatre audiences by making drug-taking a major theme.

But for most of the young, dancing and party-going became the main objects in life. Loelia Ponsonby, later the third wife of the Duke of Westminster, claimed that London was 'dancing mad':

> It seemed we couldn't have enough of it. We still had *thés dansants*, a custom which had grown up during the war. One was asked for four o'clock and arrived about five with a partner. . . . Supported by nothing but tea or coffee (a glass of sherry would have turned it into an orgy) we foxtrotted tirelessly till it was time to dash home and change into evening dress for a real dance.
>
> One would have thought that that was enough dancing for anybody, but no. Dancing was more than a craze, it had become a sort of mystical religion. If by chance there was not a *thé dansant*, we foregathered with our girl-friends and as soon as tea was swallowed, wound up the gramophone, put on a record and began practising new steps. At weekends it was the same. Usually there was a

The 'dance craze' as depicted by the society magazine Eve *in February 1927.*

Do you "Stomp?"...   *the new dance step*

room where the carpet was permanently rolled up and we would all start shuffling round together and the hostess would know she need do nothing further to amuse us.[6]

The Prince of Wales shared the craze and by the middle of the decade could often be seen with his close friend Mrs Dudley Ward, practising the Charleston early in the mornings at the Café de Paris. On one occasion he kept a band playing for an hour and a half without a break while he one-stepped and Charlestoned with her.[7] Even at Friday to Monday country-house parties during the winter months it was usual for guests to begin dancing to a gramophone almost as soon as they arrived. Later they scurried upstairs to dress for dinner, and then there would be a drive of several miles to a Hunt Ball, where they danced until the early hours.[8]

Many younger unmarried girls welcomed these country-house weekends for their informality, and their opportunity for flirtation and practical joking. Apple-pie beds with a bunch of holly at the foot, or pillows covered with flour, were favourite tricks, according to Barbara Cartland, while the more spirited male guests would pursue their female companions with a soda-syphon.[9]

Yet for the débutante, in London at least, certain conventions had to be observed. The wealthy heiress Edwina Ashley, who came out in 1920, was one who chafed at the restrictions placed upon her. Etiquette required that she did not engage in a private conversation with a man unless she was dancing with him or sitting next to him at dinner. But when she stayed in the country with her friends, for tennis, croquet, shooting, fishing, sailing and golf parties, everything was more relaxed. No undesirable outsiders were invited and the balanced mixture of outdoor pursuits, indoor games, well-cooked meals and comfortable surroundings proved conducive to matchmaking without any danger of unsuitable liaisons being formed.[10]

Despite the declining incomes of some old-established landed families, arising from higher taxation, agricultural depression and a fall in rental incomes, many continued to live in luxury, surrounded by large numbers of retainers. They were joined by the war-profiteers, who edged their way into society by paying for the privilege, and by pre-war plutocrats such as Lady Wernher – later Lady Ludlow – the widow of the financier and South African diamond magnate, Sir Julius Wernher. When Lady Ludlow arranged musical evenings at Bath House, her London mansion, everything was on a lavish scale. The stairs and drawing-rooms were adorned with banks of flowers brought from Luton Hoo, her country residence. Sometimes up to four hundred guests would be invited for entertainments that commenced at 10.30 p.m. and were preceded by a dinner party for fifty. In order to secure the services of the best performers she was prepared to pay up to a thousand guineas a night in fees.[11] After her marriage to Lord Ludlow not only was her lingerie embroidered with coronets, to indicate her

Edwina Ashley and (on the right) Lord Louis Mountbatten at a shooting party at Polesden Lacey, Surrey, home of the leading socialite, Mrs Ronnie Greville. The party took place in October 1921 and in the following summer Edwina and Lord Louis were married. (The Tatler, 16 October 1921)

new and more elevated social status, but she ordered another Rolls-Royce in her favourite colour, purple, with a coronet on it.[12] 'Eve' in *The Tatler* reflected the chagrin felt by some of the older established families at this ostentatious display by the 'new rich' when she commented acidly that there was no need to worry about keeping down expenditure or paying 'the perfectly *fearful* taxation or anything dull like that when you're the fortunate mistress of Bath House *and* Luton Hoo and now of two more great country places as well as a second town house in Portland Place'.[13]

Similar opulence applied at Trent Park, the country home of the handsome, enigmatic multi-millionaire and MP, Sir Philip Sassoon. Here guests were supplied with 'every published newspaper' when they were called in the morning. And at a dinner party attended by Barbara Cartland at another grand house, the thirty guests ate off gold plates.[14]

In London, the new black American jazz bands were all the rage in hotels, restaurants, night-clubs and at private parties. Jazz in the early 1920s meant 'heavily punctuated, relentless rhythm, with drums, rattles, bells, whistles, hooters and twanging banjoes'.[15] 'All of a sudden everything black was the rage,' notes Georgina Howell, 'black and white decor, Babangi masks, heads wrapped up in turbans, bracelets up the whole arm, jazz and all Negro dances, particularly the Charleston.'[16]

It was characteristic of social life at that date that when Loelia Ponsonby met the Duke of Westminster, her future husband, for the first time in 1929, they danced at the Café de Paris until it closed at 2 a.m. Then, with a party of friends, she was invited to continue the entertainment at the Duke's London home, Bourdon House:

> When we arrived there we found not only a band unpacking their instruments, but Hutch, the coloured cabaret singer, whom everybody wanted at their parties. . . . Even more Arabian Nightish, a lavish supper was laid out in the dining-room, complete with waiters hovering round.
>
> To this day I have no idea how this conjuring trick was accomplished. All I know is that it was a wildly successful party, the more so as it was so miraculously unexpected.[17]

Fancy dress balls were particularly fashionable, with much time and money devoted to devising suitable costumes. One year there was a craze for wearing masks and for dressing up as children, but there were many other fads and fancies. In his novel *Vile Bodies* Evelyn Waugh wrote of:

> Masked parties, Savage parties, Victorian parties, Greek parties, Wild West parties, Russian parties, Circus parties, parties where one had to dress as somebody else, almost naked parties in St John's Wood, parties in . . . night-clubs, in windmills and swimming baths.[18]

A swimming-pool party given by Brian Howard and Loelia's cousin, Elizabeth Ponsonby, at St George's Baths, had a jazz band in attendance and the guests

Fancy dress parties were very popular in the 1920s. In 1927 Cadbury's issued a costume leaflet advising readers how to make costumes representing 'Dairy Milk', 'Mayfair' and 'Bournville Cocoa', three of their brands. (Cadbury Ltd, Bournville)

danced in bathing costumes. The *Sunday Chronicle* made disapproving mention of the 'great astonishment' caused by the fact that 'a large number of society women were dancing in bathing dresses to the music of a Negro band at a "swim and dance" gathering organized by some of Mayfair's Bright Young People'.[19] The principal cause for complaint seemed to be that the band was black and the half-naked female dancers were white.

Cecil Beaton remembered attending another party, given by Mrs Guinness, where the guests were so numerous that some were overflowing into the street: 'all the people one had ever known or ever seen – up and down the big staircase, in the ballroom, along the corridors'.[20] Hostesses often did not know each guest personally and when in 1928 Lady Ellesmere tried to re-establish pre-war standards of exclusivity by turning out four uninvited guests from a ball at Bridgewater House, her gesture proved ineffective. It subsequently emerged that there had been three hundred people at the party whom she did not know and, without exception, public opinion came down on the side of the gatecrashers.[21]

It was part of this ceaseless search for diversion and amusement that led Loelia Ponsonby and her brother Gaspard to invent the 'bottle party', whereby guests brought their own food and drink. For the chronically impoverished young Ponsonbys it was a simple and inexpensive way of entertaining and it became immediately popular.[22] 'Bottle parties' were soon an established part of the social scene.

Loelia, with her friends the Jungman sisters and Lady Eleanor Smith, was also a ringleader in some of the exploits of the high-spirited Bright Young People. They invented a new kind of paper-chase, zig-zagging about London on buses and underground trains, leaving clues behind as they went. This subsequently developed into an adult version of the treasure hunt, with motor cars replacing public transport. Participants assembled at midnight at an agreed venue, with sometimes as many as fifty couples taking part. There were no traffic lights and they were able to race madly through the empty streets, regardless of those who were trying to get some sleep. On one occasion they were sent to the Hovis bread factory on the Embankment where they were given a loaf with the clue baked in the middle. On another, Lord Beaverbrook printed a fake *Evening Standard* with the clue hidden among an item of imaginary news. At the end the participants met together in the early hours of the morning. Light-hearted accusations of cheating were exchanged as everyone claimed the pool, to which all the players had contributed at the start. According to Loelia,

> It was all extremely jocular but as, when the fields became enormous, the prize was sometimes in the neighbourhood of £100, the atmosphere was, in reality, pretty tense. . . . Any wild party, Bohemian rag or large scale practical joke which took place in the West End between 1924 and 1930 was supposed to have been perpetrated by these Bright Young People. . . . Eventually every sort of person, from tiny tots upwards, were having treasure hunts and we lost interest in them.[23]

This was also the era of the flamboyant American-born hostesses like Lady Cunard, whose estranged daughter Nancy earned notoriety through her affair with a black jazz musician, and Mrs Laura Corrigan, who was introduced into society by the Marchioness of Londonderry. Mrs Corrigan was the wealthy widow of a steel magnate. She was extremely snobbish, very generous, and above all, indefatigable in her pursuit of social success. Stories of her vulgarity and malapropisms abounded, but her lavish parties, her originality and her expensive presents to favoured guests ensured success. Friends whom she especially wished to please might find a gold Cartier lighter or compact by their plates, her practice being to give the most costly objects to the most important and aristocratic of the guests. 'One must always be kind to the poor,' commented her rival, Lady Cunard, acidly. 'It's only Mrs Corrigan who's kind to the rich.'[24]

Even philanthropy offered ingenious hostesses an opportunity to shine. In one week in December 1919, 'Eve' of *The Tatler* reported a charity sale organized by Lady Egerton at Belgrave Square to help Russian charities. 'Here for three days all the available Russian princesses and grand duchesses are stall-holding, as well as Lady Linlithgow, young Lady Curzon, Lady Mainwaring, Lady Greville, Mrs Ralph Peto, and Mrs Burdon Muller, who is again having her antique stall.' Then there was a bazaar at Claridge's in aid of the Mission to Seamen, 'for which Katherine, Duchess of Westminster and Lady Chesterfield are both presidents', and a charity ball in aid of the Cambridge Mission at the Hyde Park Hotel.[25]

Restaurant life received a major boost from 1921 when the new Licensing Act relaxed some of the wartime restrictions on the serving of alcohol. Now drinks could be sold until midnight in London, providing food was ordered at the same time. But for many pleasure-seekers that concession was insufficient. They wanted to drink into the early hours and they turned to night-clubs to gratify their wishes. Some of these were respectable and took care to remove bottles and drinks from the tables at the legal hour. But in scores of others their sole concession to legality was to confirm their status by 'signing on' new members at the door. Then they flouted the law by serving alcohol after hours, thereby provoking periodic police raids. One of the smartest clubs, the Kit-Kat, was raided the night after the Prince of Wales had dined there, and regular guests at the exclusive Chez Victor were shocked when Victor was convicted of breaking the licensing regulations and was imprisoned. Another leading night-club owner, Mrs Kate Meyrick, was imprisoned on five occasions for various offences. But she was unrepentant:

> Nothing fascinates me more than to see people throw off the cares of their daily existence and abandon themselves for a few short hours to the call of pure pleasure. . . . Bright lights, music, gaiety and laughter and beauty and brilliance – these are the things which all through my experience have to me spelt Life. . . . In my clubs I have found, as nowhere else, that joy of living at highest pressure.[26]

Mrs Meyrick took the precaution of running several clubs at the same time, so that if one were raided and closed down, the others could continue, even if she herself were in prison. The fines which were levied were more than compensated for by the profits which could be made. 'Champagne cost me on an average 12s. 6d. per bottle,' she admitted later. 'During licensed hours I sold it for 22s. 6d. to 30s. and after legal hours at 30s. to £2 per bottle. For beer I paid 4½d. per bottle, and sold it for 8d. during permitted hours and anything up to 1s. 6d. afterwards.'[27] Nor did her brushes with the law harm her daughters' matrimonial prospects. Three of them married into the peerage, with May marrying Lord Kinnoull, the racing motorist, Dorothy, Lord de Clifford, and Gwendoline, the Earl of Craven.[28]

For débutantes in their first Season, many of the pre-war rituals were revived. Chaperones were still required for formal occasions in town and even on shopping expeditions it was customary for young unmarried women to be accompanied by a maid if there were no other suitable companion. There were walks in Hyde Park to meet friends and rides in Rotten Row, perhaps on a horse hired from a livery stable. On Sunday morning there was 'church parade' after morning service, when the middle-aged and the more sedate met in the Park, sitting in rows on green chairs, or walking up and down gossiping with their friends. On weekday afternoons, calls and card-dropping still went on, although not as intensively as in the Edwardian era. And there were visits to art exhibitions, the theatre, and the cinema. By 1921, according to Barbara Cartland, everybody had become 'movie mad'.[29]

Nancy Mitford, eldest daughter of Lord Redesdale, remembered being told when she came out that there were certain streets in London where it was not proper for her to walk. Sloane Street, for example, was acceptable, but Jermyn Street was not. However, when she and her friend Mary Milnes-Gaskell could get away with it, they escaped from parental surveillance, ostensibly to visit Nancy's brother, Tom, at Eton, but in reality to meet clandestinely with young male friends, for tea. 'I was sorry not to see you the other day when I left strawberries on you,' wrote Nancy to her brother on one occasion, 'but Mary & I were meeting two Oxford chaps in Rowlands at 4.30 & then had to come straight back! Don't tell anyone, I mean about us meeting them.' These harmless escapades came to an end when they were spotted in Oxford on their way to take tea with one of their friends. As a consequence Nancy was severely reprimanded by her parents and banned from attending some balls to which she had been invited. 'There has been a hell of a row,' she told her brother. Lord and Lady Redesdale had been 'absolutely horrified, they thought it was the *most* awful thing to have done etc!' Nancy and her friend both had to promise never to behave in such a fashion again.[30]

Quieter pastimes included embroidery, playing the pianoforte, and, in the country, gardening. After her marriage to the Duke of Westminster the former Loelia Ponsonby found some compensation for the turbulence of their relationship by working in the gardens on their various estates.[31]

Marriage was still the main object of a girl's life (even though many débutantes were surprisingly ignorant of the facts of life).[32] Hence those who did not make an appropriate match felt they were failures. This was true of Frances Donaldson and her sister. Sometimes when the 'marriage hysteria' reached a peak their parents would take them off to the Riviera, in the belief that in new surroundings they might be more successful. But once there, they found themselves meeting the same people they already knew in London:

> my sister and I, knowing that the object was to bring home a young man, had our permanent sense of humiliation and ineptitude heightened to a point that made me believe . . . that I hated travel.[33]

On the Riviera, Frances exchanged golfing lessons in Regent's Park for the attentions of a professional tennis coach on the hotel court. Her sister, less adventurous, merely went shopping with their mother. They swapped the night-clubs of London for those of Cannes.[34]

For girls with few academic pretensions and, often enough, scant practical knowledge of managing a household, marriage was the only long-term career they or their parents could envisage. Admittedly, some earned pin-money by pursuing minor commercial ventures. Poppy Baring, a close friend of Prince George, opened 'Poppy', a dress shop, while Barbara Cartland had a brief and unsuccessful career running a hat shop before she turned to writing. Paula Gellibrand, who later married the ace racing driver, the Marquis de Casa Maury, was the first 'lady' to become a model, working for the exclusive dress firm of Reville. Others, such as Lord Birkenhead's daughter, Lady Eleanor Smith, and Nancy Cunard, dabbled in journalism as well as writing books. In Lady Eleanor's case this meant producing women's gossip columns for an evening newspaper and working as a film critic, while Nancy Cunard sent occasional contributions to *Vogue* from her Paris base.[35] Nancy Mitford, too, turned to journalism when she found it difficult to make ends meet on her annual allowance of £125. This had to cover clothes, laundry bills, travel and tips to other people's servants. She began by contributing anonymous paragraphs of gossip to one of the society magazines and once managed to pay her train fare to Scotland to stay with a friend by photographing the party for *The Tatler*. From these ventures she advanced to providing occasional signed articles for *Vogue* and in 1930 was commissioned to write a weekly column for the *Lady*, at five guineas a week. To celebrate she went out and bought herself 'a divine coral tiara'.[36]

The most successful of the amateur 'entrepreneurs' during the 1920s was Lady Diana Cooper, a daughter of the Duke of Rutland. After her marriage to the diplomat Alfred Duff Cooper in 1919, she quickly realized that she must earn money if they were to maintain their comfortable lifestyle; that included employing a staff of five servants to minister to their wants. As she admitted disarmingly: 'Money had to be spun from somewhere.'[37] In 1921 she became editress of a new English edition of the French magazine *Femina*, even though she knew nothing about editing and most of her contributions to the magazine were written by her husband. She was also a regular contributor to the *Daily Mail* and the *Daily Express* and appeared in *The Tatler* modelling hats for Ascot. But it was as an actress that she was to achieve her greatest fame and fortune, starring in two films at the beginning of the 1920s and then, in 1923, agreeing to appear in New York in Max Reinhardt's stage spectacular, *The Miracle*. She had long believed that money was to be made in America if she only had the nerve to seek it, and this seemed her opportunity. Initially she was to be paid $1,500 a week, but this was subsequently increased. She was also able to boost her earnings in other ways, for example by investing in property in Florida. A testimonial for Pond's cold cream brought in $1,000 and a signature at the end of an article for the Hearst Press secured as much again. She continued to perform in *The Miracle* until May 1924, when she came back to England for a few months' rest, before returning for a lengthy American tour. She repeated this for three successive autumns and winters to enthusiastic audiences and considerable profit. She also appeared in *The Miracle* in Europe, taking part in the Salzburg festival of 1925 and in a longer European tour two years later.[38]

But few other women could match either Lady Diana's good looks or her ingenuity and self-confidence. In fact, for unmarried girls there was considerable family opposition to any suggestion that they should become professional actresses. The Countess of Warwick was horrified when Mercy, her youngest child, appeared on the West End stage. She was even more appalled when, at the age of 21, Lady Mercy announced that she was to marry a divorced theatrical producer.[39] They, in their turn, were divorced eight years later, in 1933.

For most girls, however, marriage to a suitable spouse and reliance on him for financial support was the only option. As Lady Phyllis MacRae noted, it would have been considered 'very caddish to get a job when there was so much unemployment. You had a home, you had money, you had everything you needed; it would have been very wrong to take anyone's job.'[40]

The Countess of Warwick in 1924. During the 'twenties she was an enthusiastic, if erratic, supporter of the Labour Party and in 1923 she unsuccessfully contested the Warwick and Leamington constituency on behalf of the Party. Her Essex home, Easton Lodge, was used as a venue for Labour Party and trade union meetings. (From: Frances, Countess of Warwick, Life's Ebb and Flow *(1929))*

Marriage also offered freedom to engage in an independent life away from parental supervision, and to enjoy agreeable flirtations with eligible young men when the opportunity offered, in a way that was impossible for a single woman who valued her reputation. Edwina Mountbatten, the former Edwina Ashley, was one who embarked on a series of extra-marital affairs soon after her marriage in 1922. Among her admirers in the middle of the decade was the wealthy American Laddie Sanford, who accompanied her to the theatre and escorted her to night-clubs and other venues when her husband went home to bed. After his return to the United States, he was succeeded by Mike Wardell, manager of the *Evening Standard*. Wardell was a good-looking member of Lord Beaverbrook's circle and while Lord Louis Mountbatten pursued his career as a naval officer in Portsmouth, Edwina remained at her luxurious London home, Brook House. Entries in her diary indicate her active social life: 'Dined at the Ritz with Mike . . . after went to *Thy Name is Woman* and later to the Café de Paris', or 'Dined at home with Mike . . . to *Tip-Toes* and afterwards the Embassy and Little Club.' By the autumn of 1926 things were becoming 'hectic'.[41]

Perhaps not surprisingly, under the pressure of this exhausting round, Edwina's health began to suffer and there were repeated complaints of digestive disorders, gynaecological problems, and neuralgia in her diary at this time. Her refusal to wear spectacles because she thought them unbecoming also caused persistent eyestrain, and on several occasions she caused consternation by fainting at dinner.

However, not all spouses were as indulgent towards their wives' vagaries as Lord Louis Mountbatten appears to have been. Lady Trevelyan's daughter remembered the problems her mother faced when she had to bring her household accounts to her husband for vetting. 'I don't know how often that was, whether it was once a month or once a week, but it was always dreadful.' The difficulties arose because of Lady Trevelyan's inability to manage things economically.[42] Even worse was the plight of Loelia Westminster. On her honeymoon she discovered her husband's bewildering swings of mood, from pleasant companion to raging madman. 'My every action was watched and criticized, my words misinterpreted and derided, my plans sabotaged. On the other hand, Benny's every passing whim had to be obeyed as if it were a divine command.' After five years of marriage they separated. They were divorced in 1947.[43]

Some of the more spirited unmarried girls reacted to their parents' strictures concerning their behaviour by deliberately setting out to shock. Despite the disapproval of their elders, they drank cocktails, smoked in public, and adopted the American fashion of wearing lipstick, rouge, nail varnish and mascara. Barbara Cartland remembered older relatives being 'deeply shocked' because she and her friends powdered their noses and painted their lips in a way that before the war would have been expected only from actresses and prostitutes. She wrote of herself at this time as having fair hair 'fluffed over the ears, . . . red lips, subject of much criticism and many arguments, and a clear skin helped by a chalk-white face powder. There were only three shades obtainable, dead white, yellow and almost brown!'[44]

In 1922 the beauty business was boosted when *Vogue* ran its first articles on health farms and electrical massage. As slimness became the fashion, much emphasis was placed on dieting and vigorous exercise. If dancing and tennis did not achieve the desired boyish shape, then tablets and potions were consumed and there were physical jerks first thing in the morning. For the desperate or the most determined there were 'cures' at Baden-Baden, or trips to the Riviera where instruction was given by a 'dazzling "professor" of physical fitness'.[45] The popular flat-chested look was achieved by wearing special 'flatteners' to strap breasts down – sometimes to their permanent damage.[46] Lightweight elastic girdles were worn in place of the old-fashioned stiff whalebone corsets of pre-war days. 'Men won't dance with you if you're all laced up,' was the comment of an American girl visiting London.[47] Skirts grew progressively shorter, starting from a point just above the ankle in 1919 and moving to the knee in 1926. They remained at around that level until 1928, when they began to drop a little.[48] At about that time a more feminine outline also began to replace the boyish figure which had been the ideal for most of the decade, once the famous designer Coco Chanel had put 'rich and aristocratic women' in brief, simple, jersey frocks and necklaces of glass beads.[49]

For those members of the smart set who could afford a motor car, it became 'a new hallmark of chic' to dispense with a chauffeur and to drive oneself. Cars encouraged much flitting about from place to place in search of pleasure and there was also a sense of freedom in driving at speed. Edwina Mountbatten was

Advertisement for a Wolseley car in June 1926. (The Tatler)

one enthusiastic driver but her recklessness – and perhaps her poor eyesight – led to frequent accidents. According to her biographer, she or her chauffeur managed to dent, bump or graze shop-fronts, buses, trams and passing motor cars two or three times a week.[50] Lady Cranborne was another fast and dangerous driver. 'Many's the narrow squeak I've had in a car with her ladyship,' remembered her maid Rosina Harrison. On one occasion she hit an oncoming Rolls-Royce driven by Lord Wimborne and forced it into a ditch.[51]

On a very different note, in 1928 Mrs Diana Strickland created a considerable stir when she crossed Africa from Dakar on the West Coast to Massawa on the Red Sea, driving a 'Star' motor car. She started off with a mechanic and a companion, but early in the journey the mechanic became ill and had to return home and the companion died of blackwater fever. Undaunted, Mrs Strickland finished the journey alone, guided by a compass, driving for hundreds of miles across the rocky desert and bush, sometimes fording rivers and digging the car out of mud and sand when it became bogged down. She had previously crossed Africa on foot with a party, and had also led a big-game shooting expedition in East Africa.[52]

Flying, too, became a popular pastime among some of the most daring. In 1929 Lady Bailey was awarded the Britannia Trophy by the Royal Aero Club for her feat in flying 18,000 miles from England to South Africa and back. The Duchess of Bedford, who only began to have flying lessons in 1928, at the age of 62, a year later took part in a flight to India.[53]

It was this mixture of patriotism, bravado and desire for excitement that led some members of High Society to volunteer to help keep essential services running during the General Strike at the beginning of May 1926. Barbara Cartland carried messages to parts of London she had never visited before, and Loelia Ponsonby and her mother worked in a canteen at Paddington station. Others volunteered to look after the cart-horses at the Great Western Railway goods yard or drove vehicles for the Red Cross.[54] Edwina Mountbatten gave lifts to office girls trying to get to work, as well as making tea and cooking sausages for volunteer lorry drivers at the YMCA canteen in Hyde Park. Later she helped on the switchboard at the *Express* offices, and found the whole experience exhausting.[55] Lady Howard de Walden opened a canteen in her garage to feed undergraduates from Oxford and Cambridge, who had come to London to enrol as special constables, and there were many other initiatives.[56]

Few of these women thought about the causes of the strike or the dire poverty of the mining families who were at its heart. For many it was just another adventure, and when it was over they returned to their accustomed social round with a sense of self-satisfaction. 'Quite frankly, my friends and I were amused by the novelty and excitement of the strike,' wrote Loelia Ponsonby, 'and it was over before it had time to pall.'[57] Only a few, like Barbara Cartland, were aware of the deeper social malaise which it exemplified. For her and those who thought like her it was 'a moment when we ceased to be young and carefree and thoughtless . . . [and] we began to grow up. . . . We developed a social conscience and became aware of the charities which needed our help.[58] But many others saw the defeat of the General Strike as a necessary and salutary lesson to the lower orders, to keep them in their place.

Miss Quilter, daughter of Lady Quilter, lending a hand with the catering for strike-breaking volunteers in Hyde Park during the 1926 General Strike. (Western Mail, *14 May 1926)*

With the dispute over, the formal rituals of the débutantes were resumed. Because of the strike, the Courts, where they made their curtsies to the king and queen, were postponed from May to the first half of June. However, *The Tatler* rejoiced that things were quickly returning to normal:

> our London Season, which after all makes money circulate and gives employment to thousands of workers, is going to pick itself up again just as satisfactorily as all the various trades and organizations have already done. But what a reshuffling of dates, and what a lot of fixtures to be squeezed in in the shortened time. . . . The unusually large number of *débutantes*, who had begun to feel rather anxious about their first Season, will be none the worse for the job of work they put in during the strike, even if it did mean ten-hour night shifts . . . at the various canteens.[59]

The *Western Mail* also commented on their elaborate gowns, with silver and gold lace extensively used, 'many ladies making a special point of choosing those that were made in Nottingham,' presumably in an effort to boost the town's lace trade.[60] As before the war, those to be presented had to wear trains, although, as a gesture of economy, these were now only to trail 18 inches on the ground. Also to be worn was a head-dress made of three small white ostrich feathers and a wisp of tulle. This latter was not very suitable for the shingled and bobbed hairstyles then fashionable, while the trains looked out of place when combined with the current vogue for short skirts.

Lesley Lewis, who was presented by her aunt in 1927, at the age of 18, remembered having several fittings with a French dressmaker, who afterwards inserted in *The Times* 'your name, her name and what you wore. My dress was white chiffon over a pink slip and as skirts were then very short and waists very

AT THEIR MAJESTIES' COURTS LAST WEEK.

LADY DUNEDIN   SIR KYNASTON AND LADY STUDD   MISS PATRICIA SMILEY

Presentations at the first Courts of the 1926 Season, in early June. Lady Dunedin presented her god-daughter; Lady Studd was presented by Susan, Duchess of Somerset; and Miss Patricia Smiley, the daughter of Sir John and Lady Smiley, was presented by her mother. (The Tatler, 16 June 1926)

long, the belt area was round my hips and I had great difficulty in not showing my knees. To my shoulders was attached a separate silver lamé train which in due course was frugally turned into another dress.' Like the other girls she was made to practise with a table cloth to learn how to curtsey without getting entangled in the train, and 'to move off crabwise so as neither to turn my back on the royal couple nor fall flat on the carpet'. She carried a borrowed white feather fan and wore white kid gloves above the elbow, together with silver brocade shoes with straps across the instep. Her aunt wore grey and all the diamonds she owned or could borrow from her nearest relatives. According to Lesley, this was one of the last Courts when motor cars were allowed to queue up in the Mall instead of waiting in the Palace quadrangle. 'The milling East End crowds were good-naturedly enjoying the show and their forthright comments were kindly, but times were hard . . . for the urban poor in about 1927 and the display seemed tactless.'[61]

The presentation itself was soon over. Once the débutante had reached the head of the queue, she handed her invitation card to an official. He shouted out her name, before tossing the card into what Loelia Ponsonby described as 'a rather common-looking little wastepaper basket'; 'one advanced along the red carpet, stopped and made two curtsies to the King and Queen who were sitting on a low dais surrounded by numerous relations, and then walked on'.[62]

Loelia herself was presented by her mother in 1925, when Lady Ponsonby also sponsored another débutante, whose mother had been divorced and so was unable to appear at Buckingham Palace. This ban on divorcées attending Court continued throughout the decade despite the sharp increase in marriage breakdown which was taking place. The annual total of divorce decrees advanced from 1,600 in 1919 to 3,100 in 1920; it then fell back a little before reaching 4,000 in 1928 and 3,600 in 1930.[63] After 1926 the annual total never fell below three thousand and it was the social élite who were especially likely to be involved because they were able to afford the considerable cost which divorce still entailed.

Barbara Cartland blamed the war for many of the breakdowns. After the 'emotional urgency' of marrying a man who might be killed in a few weeks, the fact that so many bridegrooms came back created unforeseen difficulties. One of her friends, who had married a VC, found him completely different when he was out of uniform. 'I couldn't believe it was the same man!' she complained. 'I'm not really a snob, but he did look awful!' She promptly left him.[64] Similarly, Nancy Cunard, who had married a handsome young Army officer in November 1916, confessed to him in January 1919 that she could not go on with the marriage. Eventually a legal separation was arranged and the two were divorced in 1925.[65]

In 1923 the Matrimonial Causes Act equalized the position of men and women seeking to end their marriage by making adultery by either party a sufficient reason for divorce. Previously a woman bringing a petition had also been required to prove cruelty or desertion.[66] This change doubtless contributed to the upsurge in divorce petitions by wives in the 1920s, as did the generally more relaxed and light-hearted attitude towards marriage as a whole. '"Duchesses do not divorce",' reported the society magazine *Eve*, tongue in cheek, ' . . . but in these days it has come to pass that one pauses to remember which duchess has divorced or which as yet endureth.'[67] In the post-war period the divorcées included the Duchess of Marlborough and two Duchesses of Westminster. In 1927 Mildred, Lady Gosford gave evidence in a divorce court that her husband had neglected her from the beginning of their marriage in 1910. They were divorced in 1928 and he promptly remarried.[68]

Meanwhile, for women of all ages fashion was a major preoccupation, with Paris regarded as the pace-setter. Those such as Loelia Ponsonby and her mother who were unable to afford the leading designers, studied *Vogue* and then had the desired garment made up by a 'little woman round the corner'. Even Lady Cranborne, who did attend the Paris fashion shows with her maid, Rosina Harrison, was not averse to Rosina running up modified copies for her when they returned home.[69]

Despite the problem of getting servants after the war, resident domestics were still customary among the families of the social élite, and in the wealthiest households, large staffs were employed. At Luton Hoo when there were important house parties, especially for the pheasant shoots, as many as a dozen people worked in the kitchens alone, while at the Astors' Cliveden in 1928 there were eleven male servants, including a butler and a chef, and twenty females, as well as a substantial outdoor staff for the gardens. During the week, when the Astors were in London, most of the servants moved with them to their town house, 4 St James's Square, but at weekends there were often house parties at Cliveden. 'I do not know which was more pleasant: to appear at tea-time in winter when the tea was set in the centre hall before the big fire, or in summer, when it was laid out, with infinite detail, under a pavilion roof at the end of the broad terrace,' wrote one appreciative guest of his visits to Cliveden.[70] Another, who had spent Christmas 1924 there, was even more flattering to his hostess:

> What a wonderful party it was . . . [at] Cliveden, where . . . you entertain all who are distinguished and distinguish the rest by entertaining them. . . . What is really so charming about it, and so helpful, is your own personality and the sincerity and simplicity of your works and ways.[71]

Yet although Lady Astor presided over these gatherings with undoubted skill and energy, as a busy Member of Parliament and a leading socialite she was inevitably very dependent on her staff to ensure the smooth running of the household.

A surviving estimate of expenditure for the three-month period from 1 April to 30 June 1918 gives an idea of the cost of running the Astors' two main establishments. During this period their London house account amounted to £597, and that for Cliveden to £865. Out of those totals £336 and £380, respectively, were expended on wages, while fuel, electric light and gas cost £124 and £217, respectively. A further £496 was spent on the kitchen account in London and £894 on that at Cliveden, with £475 and £675, respectively, spent on food. The nursery account, by contrast, was a relatively modest £240, of which £90 was accounted for by the wages of the nurses and governess. A further £60 went on school fees.[72]

Once an efficient servant had been recruited, Lady Astor was reluctant to lose him or her. The butler, Mr Lee, first came to the house as a footman in 1912 and remained with the family until the Astors' connection with Cliveden ended in the 1960s, and her last lady's maid remained with her from the late 1920s until her death. In 1929 she was so anxious to retain the services of her head laundrymaid at Cliveden that she not only promised to install a new, electrically powered, hand laundry but to allow the maid to select her own assistants. In addition, she was to have a week's holiday in Paris, at Lady Astor's expense.[73] However, her efforts in the same year to retain her then lady's maid, Mrs Vidler, proved unsuccessful. Not only did she offer to increase the maid's wages to £80 a year but to provide her with a helper, so that much of the 'running about' would be done for her:

> You can't think what it is like with the children's holidays starting [wrote Lady Astor plaintively] and . . . I have no one to look after me, especially with all my new clothes coming, which I feel may be ruined; and I do not want things to get into disorder again.[74]

But Mrs Vidler was adamant that the work was too much for her, and after trying other maids in quick succession, Lady Astor at last offered the position to her daughter's maid, Rosina Harrison, who had previously worked for Lady Cranborne. With some hesitation, Rosina accepted, aware that her new employer was an exacting taskmistress. 'She generally got through five sets of clothes in a day,' Miss Harrison remembered:

> This required from me a deal of organizing, pressing, cleaning and repairing. Also there were perpetual messages to be run or delivered, shopping to be done either on my own or with her ladyship, and dressmaking or copying. I made most of her ladyship's things.[75]

Among other duties she had to collect her employer's jewels from the bank, and return them after use.[76] Working for Lady Astor meant having to concentrate on that particular role for eighteen hours a day seven days a week, but despite this the two women got on well.

Few wives in High Society took their maternal duties very seriously, considering it their main responsibility to run their household efficiently and to act as a skilful hostess for their husband. Even before the war most upper-class families had practised birth control, once the all-important heir had been secured, and that continued in the inter-war period, at a time when, as we shall see in a later chapter, contraception was spreading to the lower orders as well.[77] Hence *Vogue*'s comment of 1929 that the nursery, like the kitchen, should be run by the servants: 'The entire domestic bliss of the young mother's home is balanced on the all-important corner-stone of the Nannie,' was its conclusion.[78]

Lady Cranborne was singled out by her maid, Rosina Harrison, as an unusually loving and devoted mother.

> I say this because in my experience it was rare with the upper classes. Children I think were neglected – not where food, clothing or material things were concerned, but over the one thing that is perhaps more important . . . real love.[79]

Lady Cranborne's concern for her children was in marked contrast to the attitude of Edwina Mountbatten. After her first baby was born in February 1924, she promptly handed the little girl over to the care of the nanny and concentrated on her own recovery. Three weeks after the birth she was ready for her first outing, and within a month, mother and child were separated. 'Too sad, parting,' noted Edwina in her diary, ' . . . took Nurse Nisbit [her maternity nurse] to the Movies.' Significantly, although she had scores of photographs of herself and her friends engaging in various sporting and social activities in 1924, there were only nine of her daughter in the first months of her life. As her biographer delicately expresses it, 'Edwina consigned her daughter to experts, as her own mother had done, until the child had acquired a clearer identity.'[80] However, the evidence suggests that even when the little girl was growing up her mother paid her scant attention.[81]

Lady Cynthia Mosley adopted a similar approach towards her children, devoting herself primarily to the interests of her husband. When her daughter was born in February 1921 she was speedily handed over to the nanny, who had been Lady Cynthia's own nursemaid. In the summer of 1921, while nanny and the baby went to Devon, the Mosleys were in Scotland; in 1922 nanny and baby were on the Norfolk coast, while the Mosleys went to Venice. And when a son was born in June 1923, the same practice was followed. In August Sir Oswald and Lady Cynthia travelled to Venice, leaving the two children in the care of the nursery staff. Even when the little boy became seriously ill, they did not return and it was the nanny who, on her own initiative, took him to London to consult a specialist. Her action saved his life.[82]

Later, as the children grew up, a governess would be employed, at least until they were old enough to go to school. One girl noted wryly that there were three people in her home – governess, nanny and, presumably, nurserymaid – who were employed so that her parents need have 'as little as possible to do with us'. The Hon. Ursula Wyndham remembered her parents as being fully occupied with their own interests: 'it did not enter their heads to include their children in any of them and thus ease our eventual emergence into grown-up life'.[83]

The main qualifications for a governess were that she should be able to keep the children quiet, happy and fully occupied. Hence the bitter comment of another girl that her governess had been engaged solely because she was a disciplinarian. Her educational qualifications were of little account. Indeed, Daphne Finch-Hatton, a daughter of the Earl of Winchilsea, claimed to have learned no maths at all from Miss Plank, her governess, who came in 1925. But this did not matter because Daphne's parents did not consider mathematics necessary for girls. 'My main memory of Miss Plank is not of anything she taught me but of being taken for long boring walks, dragging the dogs on leads.'[84] Sometimes, as with Lady Astor's children, a temporary governess would be recruited during the holidays, perhaps because the children had returned temporarily from boarding-school or because the regular governess was on vacation.[85]

After her ordinary education had been completed, a daughter might be sent to a finishing school in France or Switzerland, or perhaps, like Nancy Mitford, she would be despatched on a cultural tour of Europe. Nancy went with four friends on a trip to Paris, Florence and Venice organized by the headmistress of a school in Queen's Gate formerly attended by one of the girls. For the first time Nancy learnt to appreciate pictures, especially the works of Raphael, Botticelli and Lippi. 'I find to my horror that there are lovely pictures in London, Italian ones & lots of good ones,' she told her mother, 'I have only ever been to the Tate Gallery. This must be remedied! Marjorie knows the National Gallery by heart. I don't think it is too late to devellop [sic] a taste in pictures at 17, do you?'[86]

So far this chapter has concentrated on the glamorous aspects of daily life for the wives and daughters of the social élite in the post-war world. But that by no means represented the whole story. In particular there were serious economic difficulties arising from wartime inflation, heavier taxation and, in the early 1920s, declining incomes. Some sought to compensate for these – or to meet death duties – by selling land and other possessions. In the spring of 1921 *The Tatler* lamented the changes which were taking place, as 'another sign . . . of the impoverished state of . . . the world':

> Positively everybody is selling everything they can lay hands on, and what really puzzles . . . is where on earth the buyers come from. The Duke of Portland, Lord Savile, and Lord Manvers have just sold their mining rights, and I suppose that's only the thin end of the wedge. . . . And all the big historic places being let and sold – Gwydyr Castle; Devonshire House . . . ; Stowe House, that belongs to Baroness Kinloss, whose eldest son, the clergyman Master of Kinloss, married the blacksmith's daughter a year ago. And libraries and pictures and art treasures all going, too. Soon there'll be no sign at all of the glories and traditions of the *ancien régime*, and the only people who'll have money will be the New Rich and the Americans. . . . But I haven't even now got to the end of the house-letting business. The Rutlands have still got the Arlington Street place on their hands, but I hear that Lady Yarborough has let hers a few doors off . . . for a year to a rich American woman much given to entertaining.[87]

During the years immediately before and after the First World War about six to eight million acres, or 25 per cent of the land of England, was sold by the nobility and gentry. In Wales and Scotland the proportion was nearer 33 per cent. Sales of non-landed property included the disposal of silver, furniture and paintings by the Duke of Hamilton for nearly a quarter of a million pounds, and of the contents of Hornby Castle, including its Canalettos, by the Duke of Leeds for £85,000. Even in the mid-1920s, when the land market stagnated, the sales of art treasures continued, with Lord Brownlow selling pictures from his Ashridge and Carlton House Terrace residences for £120,000 and Lady Desborough disposing of a valuable painting of the Madonna to the American collector Andrew Mellon, for $875,000.[88]

Elsewhere families economized by vacating large residences for smaller houses. Some leased their estates as an alternative to sale, with those properties having good sporting prospects most in demand. In December 1928, for example, Kedleston Hall, Derbyshire, was offered with fishing rights and 6,000 acres of shooting, while Levens Hall, Westmorland, was available for letting with 1,814 acres of shooting, 1½ miles of salmon and trout fishing, and a grouse moor of 5,200 acres.[89]

The Duke and Duchess of Atholl not only let their castle, Blair Atholl, to an American but in 1928 felt obliged to sell land, the best of the family jewellery, and the lease of a corner house in Eaton Place, which had been acquired some years before. They moved to a smaller London property in the less prestigious location of Elm Park Gardens.[90]

By 1926 the Dowager Countess of Airlie had likewise given up her flat in Ashley Gardens to move into furnished rooms in Clarges Street. The property belonged to an 'amiable colonial spinster' and was staffed by a man and wife who worked as butler and cook, and a daily housemaid:

I had a sitting-room and a large bedroom, a bathroom and a passage fitted with wardrobe, shelves and hanging cupboards, and a small bedroom for my maid. All this for 8½ guineas, including light, attendance and washing of household linen. My maid's board was 30s. a week. . . . My own meals cost 2s. for breakfast, 3s. for luncheon, 1s. for tea with buttered toast and cakes and 3s. 6d. for dinner. When I wanted more variety I went to a little restaurant called 'The Shepherd's Pie' where I got an excellent three-course luncheon for 2s. 6d. Thus I was able to live comparatively cheaply – which was a necessity – for as usual I had overspent.[91]

Reductions in domestic staff were other alternatives. In 1929 the head laundrymaid at Plas Newydd, home of Lord and Lady Anglesey, wrote to Lady Astor, for whom she had once worked, asking if there were a vacancy for herself and her husband, as reductions were under way in the Angleseys' household:

the place at present seems very disturbed (I suppose when reductions are made & wages cut down it is always so). Lord and Lady Anglesey have both been very nice to us . . . & even though my husband lost his house carpentering job, I have to have all understanding. I quite see with all the work going on to one side of the house . . . & the necessity for economy, it perhaps could not be otherwise, but of course it does away with that feeling of 'Security of Tenure' . . . & naturally one feels it may happen again.[92]

However, Lady Astor had no vacancies, and so they had to make the best of things.

Finally, if all else failed, an owner might decide to demolish an unwanted and expensive house. This was the solution adopted by the Earl and Countess of Wemyss for Amisfield, one of their Scottish mansions, while Gosford, another Scottish property, was run as an hotel for a time by the Earl and his mistress. The family's third seat – Stanway in the Cotswolds – was let during the summer months to the well-known author and playwright, J.M. Barrie, whose secretary, Lady Cynthia Asquith, was a daughter of the Earl and Countess.[93]

For those members of the social élite dependent on dividend incomes a further blow came with the stock-market crash in the autumn of 1929. In Britain this was initially associated with the collapse of a complex network of enterprises set up by the company promoter and speculator, Clarence Hatry. By the use of sometimes fraudulent means, Hatry built up an empire which lost private investors an estimated £15m when it crashed. Hatry himself was eventually imprisoned, but some of those caught up in his machinations – such as the Marquess of Winchester – were ruined both financially and in reputation. Eventually the Marquess was made bankrupt and was obliged to live abroad.[94] He had married for the second time in January 1925, his first wife having died the preceding December.

Noel Coward caught the mood of apprehension which followed the stock-market crash, with its threat to the financial security of many of society's leaders:

Children of the Ritz
Children of the Ritz
Sleek and civilized
Fretfully surprised
Though Mr Molyneux has gowned us
The world is tumbling around us
Without a sou
What can we do?
We'll soon be begging for a crust
We can't survive
And keep alive
Without the darling Bankers' Trust.[95]

Meanwhile, although most upper-class women played some part in the busy social round associated with London and with country-house weekends, many also carried out traditional philanthropic duties upon the family estate. At Ickworth Lady Phyllis Hervey, daughter of the 4th Marquess of Bristol, remembered being expected to do 'a lot of voluntary work. You might be a secretary or chairman of the Women's Institute or the Red Cross; you might run the Girl Guides and Boy Scouts.'[96] Likewise Ulla, Lady Hyde Parker, who married in 1931, recalled being drawn into the life of the village as soon as she moved to Melford Hall:

I hardly knew what the Women's Institute was at the age of 22, but I was made President. I had to be Vice-President of the Conservatives at Sudbury. . . . I was President of the mental hospital in Colchester, which didn't really involve much: I had simply to get people from all over the area to give money. . . . In those days, everything was private. I was Chairman of the District Nursing Association, and the district nurse used to come and see me. I remember her saying, 'We can't let Mrs So-and-So have another baby like the last one: she was just lying there at the top of the stairs and the other children looking on'.[97]

Lady Hyde Parker was encouraged by her mother-in-law to buy as much as possible from the local shops. 'One went down to the village, but one didn't go into the shop: one sat in the car and the shopman came out in a morning coat. There was a grocer's, and a little draper's alongside it. If one went into the shop to look at anything, the shop girl would curtsy, and the village children, too.'

Some of these women held strong religious beliefs and played an active role in the life of the local church. In the case of Lady Astor, this involved a deep commitment to Christian Science. Each morning she would read a Christian Science lesson and during that period gave orders that she was not to be interrupted except for the most urgent of telephone calls.[98] In her zeal she sought to convert her friends and seems to have had success with a number. One of them, Mrs Wintringham, a former fellow MP, wrote in November 1929, thanking 'dearest Nancy . . . for leading me to C.S. & then for all the crumbs of kindness – (often a loaf) – you shew me.'[99]

Lady Astor, the first woman to take her seat in the House of Commons, being introduced into Parliament by the Prime Minister, David Lloyd George, and a former Prime Minister, Arthur Balfour, on 1 December 1919. (University of Reading Archives).

Elsewhere, as with Consuelo Marlborough, the estranged wife of the 9th Duke of Marlborough, these philanthropic preoccupations might lead to involvement in local government. In Consuelo's case that meant serving on the London County Council from 1917 until she left to live in Paris early in the 1920s. During her period on the Council she turned her attention to the slum housing of South London and was also able to obtain a playground for the children of North Southwark, the district which she represented.[100]

After the passage of the Sex Disqualification (Removal) Act of 1919, women were appointed to the magistracy and this was another sphere in which the wives and daughters of the social élite became involved. In April 1921 *The Tatler* referred to the 'rapidly increasing number of lady JPs' and by the end of the decade titled magistrates included Lady Mount in Berkshire, Lady Slesser and Lady Susan Trueman in Buckinghamshire, and Viscountess Harcourt in Oxfordshire.

Finally, a number of the first female Members of Parliament (especially among the Conservatives) were recruited from the aristocracy and gentry. They included not only Lady Astor, the first woman to take her seat in the House of Commons, but the Duchess of Atholl, the first woman MP in Scotland, and Lady Iveagh, elected to her husband's former seat in 1927 at a by-election, when he succeeded to the title. In 1930 she became Joint Deputy Chairman of the Conservative and Unionist Party Organization. Lady Vera Terrington briefly represented High Wycombe for the Liberals in 1923–4, and Lady Cynthia Mosley, daughter of Lord Curzon and wife of Sir Oswald Mosley (himself a leading political figure), represented Stoke for the Labour Party from 1929 until 1931, when she retired. During the 1929 campaign she was derided by opponents as a 'Dollar Princess' both on account of the wealth she had inherited from her American maternal grandfather and her own elegant and expensive appearance. She was also pregnant at the time, but none of this was allowed to interfere with her determined and competent electioneering. She doubled the Labour vote from 13,000 to 26,000, raised the turnout from 75 to 81 per cent, and was elected with a majority of almost 8,000.[101] Unfortunately the stress of campaigning took its toll and she suffered a miscarriage shortly after.[102]

So, ironically, it was in their traditional roles as social leaders, hostesses, and dispensers of charity to the poor and needy, that most upper-class women were to achieve prominence in the 1920s. The main difference from their position before 1914 was the greater personal freedom most of them enjoyed, especially after marriage, and the fact that those who wished to pursue a career were able to do so. However, it is significant that when Harold Macmillan came to assess Lady Astor's contribution to politics in general and the Conservative party in particular he should consider that prominent political hostesses like Lady Londonderry and Lady Salisbury exercised more influence than she did through her membership of the House of Commons. In the end, despite her devotion to her public duties, it was at Cliveden, surrounded by her friends, that she shone. 'She had . . . a greater genius for friendship than for Parliamentary life,' was Macmillan's conclusion. Interestingly, the Duchess of Atholl, of whose abilities he thought highly, was credited with having a 'masculine mind'.[103] These comments were made in 1975; such gender prejudices were still more powerful and pervasive half a century earlier.

CHAPTER 3

Middle-class Wives and Daughters

Could she [Muriel Hammond] stay there at Miller's Rise to 'help her mother' indefinitely? She knew that her mother had never wanted help. Always the hope had been that she would marry. To this end alone had she been trained and cared for; and now she sat, meal after meal, between her mother and her father. She knew that they found her presence secretly humiliating. . . . The thing that mattered in Marshington was neither service nor love but marriage, marriage respectable and unequivocal, marriage financially sound, eugenically advisable, and socially correct.

Winifred Holtby, *The Crowded Street* (1981 edn) pp. 225–6.
(The novel was first published in 1924).

During the 1920s the term 'middle-class' covered a very broad spectrum of the population. It applied not merely to social expectations but to income and standing in the community as well. The lifestyle of a prosperous professional or business family differed widely from that of a clerk or a shopkeeper or a clergyman's widow, clinging precariously to the fringes of gentility and desperately anxious to maintain due distance from those lower down the scale.

The variations in finances and rank were reflected in personal relationships. Each grouping had its own 'exclusion rituals and status ideology', which were designed to preserve its identity.[1] Hence a professional man's widow in reduced circumstances was unlikely to make friends with an elementary school teacher, even though she might invite her to tea from time to time. Likewise the daughter of a veterinary surgeon or a doctor with

pretensions to being county, would not go out dancing with the articled clerk. The unmarried sisters who kept the tea-shop might sit down with the florist or the dressmaker, but hardly with the butcher's wife or the greengrocer's.[2]

Office girls 'from the insecure pinnacle of a typewriter desk' looked down upon shop girls because of their association with 'trade' and members of the

Middle-class girls began to enter offices on an increasing scale during the 1920s. Female clerks in the Cost Office at Cadbury's chocolate factory, Bournville. (Cadbury Ltd, Bournville)

older professions found little in common with clerks in banks and insurance offices.

The rituals associated with such attitudes were carefully described in the books on etiquette published during the decade. Their aim was to protect their readers from the humiliation of a social gaffe. Thus *Etiquette for Women. A Book of Modern Manners and Customs*, first published in 1928, covered such topics as the leaving of visiting cards, the paying of calls, table manners, and 'Little Courtesies that Count', much as its Edwardian predecessors might have done. The author admitted that calls and card-leaving were less formal than had once been the case and advised all newcomers to a district to be guided by local custom. They should not take the initiative until they had been visited by older residents. When calls were paid they should take place between 3.30 and 5.30 p.m.: 'No calls of any kind should be made earlier or later than this.'[3] There is a good deal more in a similar vein.

It was a tribute to the importance of these subtle social distinctions that aspiring middle-class mothers sought out genteel private schools for their daughters, in order that they might learn ladylike behaviour and associate with a 'nice class' of girl. Academic study was a secondary consideration. In 1922 *Queen* magazine, in an article on the Wychwood School, Oxford, quoted the case of a mother who had chosen this school for her daughter primarily because its pupils 'behaved like gentlewomen in the streets and public places'.[4] Similarly when the Dunottar School opened in Reigate in 1926 it had a mere handful of pupils and operated in rented accommodation. But its popularity grew rapidly, despite its frequent moves of premises and the fact that it had no facilities for science. Mathematics was divided among the teachers generally and no member of staff was well enough qualified to prepare pupils for university entrance examinations. Nonetheless it appealed to parents who liked to see their daughters in its distinctive royal-blue uniform and who enjoyed the kudos which association with it brought. They preferred it to the local county secondary school, even though this had an excellent scholastic record, since by choosing the latter they would have lost caste.[5]

Of course, not all middle-class families displayed such petty snobbery. In the case of those from a professional background the desire for academic excellence often led parents to select high schools and grammar schools for their offspring, even though some secretly lamented that these had 'lost tone' by accepting poorer scholarship children. Domestic subjects such as needlework and cookery were given low priority in such schools. Academic success was the main goal, with university entrance the pinnacle of ambition and entry to teacher training regarded as an acceptable, although inferior, alternative. Other occupations counted for little. One girl who attended the Park School, Preston, during the 1920s remembered being encouraged to study to become a mathematics mistress, but her parents lacked the will and the means to send her to university, and so she took and passed the Civil Service entrance examination instead. The school took little interest in that, since clerical work was regarded as being of low status. Another girl, who attended a convent school in Preston, likewise recalled office work being dismissed as 'drumming your brains away' on a typewriter.[6]

Those who reached university found both staff and students were drawn largely from among the middle-classes. In 1927 55 per cent of the female academics at Oxford, Cambridge and London whose fathers' occupations are known came from professional homes, and a further 18.5 per cent were from business families.[7] Of the 385 students entering Somerville College, Oxford, during the years 1920 to 1927, most of those whose parental occupation is recorded were from a similar background. More than 5 per cent were the daughters of clergymen, while other parents included senior army officers, doctors, members of the legal profession, and university professors.[8]

Partly because of their background, but also to maintain a high moral reputation and to encourage concentration on academic work, discipline for female university students was strict. Even women at Bedford and the other non-residential London colleges had to observe a number of rules on dress and conduct, although they did enjoy greater freedom than their Oxford and Cambridge counterparts. At Bedford, students had to wear stockings and hats when they were in the vicinity of the college, though they were exempt from the chaperonage rules that applied at Oxford at that time. They were also permitted to stay out until midnight, whereas at Oxford for much of the decade, women students had to be in by 10.30 p.m. This often meant leaving the theatre before the end of a play. Also remembered as a bone of contention at Oxford was the need to have a chaperon when female students went on the river. However, at least from 1923 females were allowed to join political and other mixed clubs, even though these often met in men's colleges. 'Soon the schoolgirlish evening assemblies for tea or cocoa in students' rooms agreeably gave way to sherry parties with men,' noted Vera Brittain, with satisfaction.[9]

Yet while these careful gradations of rank and conduct were being observed in middle-class circles, there was a growing acceptance among many, and especially among professional families, that unmarried daughters and sisters needed to be able to earn their own living. This represented a radical shift in outlook compared with the pre-war position, and in bringing it about three important influences can be identified. The first was financial. Although the number of salaried workers increased by around 33 per cent between 1920 and 1938, many men in the established professions saw their income eroded by wartime inflation, higher taxes and, during the last years of the 1920s, by a sharp fall in investment earnings. Salary cuts were experienced during the recession years, especially by those in the clerical sector. Although prices began to fall sharply from the early 1920s, many fathers felt they could not afford to maintain idle daughters at home in the way they might once have expected to do. Where they did so, as in one bank official's family in Burton-on-Trent, then the sons of the family had to contribute towards maintaining their sisters at home, even when some of the sons had themselves married.[10] The girls, meanwhile, were given no choice in the matter, and seem to have accepted it meekly.

A second factor, however, was the attitude of many of the women themselves, especially where they had been able to work and enjoy an independent income during the war. They were reluctant to return to the sterile and narrow 'dutiful daughter' routine at home. Lady Rhondda, herself the daughter of a major coal-owner, was not alone in finding 'drawing-room life' demeaning, with its 'appalling social convention of talking for talking's sake'.[11] By 1920, following her father's death, she had become a director of thirty-four companies and subsequently claimed that in the business world she had scarcely ever met a colleague whom she did not find likeable.[12]

The income which working women earned gave them a sense of self-worth which those dependent on a parental allowance could never attain. At its worst, the life of a spinster in the family home could degenerate into being little better than that of a superior domestic. Radclyffe Hall, on a visit to a Devon resort in 1921, commented sadly on the sight of an old lady being waited upon by an ageing daughter: 'ghastly to see these unmarried daughters who are just unpaid servants', and the old people 'sucking the life out of them like octopi'.[13]

The third factor encouraging middle-class female employment was the loss of so many men on the battlefield. This meant that a number of women, especially those who were in their mid-twenties and above, would probably never marry. They therefore had to be able to support themselves. The feminist Mrs W.L. Courtney, in an article on 'The Right to Work', published in *Good Housekeeping* in 1922, drew attention to the problems which daughters from comfortable backgrounds faced when in middle life the death of parents led to their being 'thrown on their own resources, untrained, inadequately provided for, objects of pity, if not of charity'. During the war a number of 'desperate cases of poverty' had come to light amongst 'just those women, daughters of professional men, well born, well nurtured, but left without professional training, only able at best to earn the pittance due to the amateur'.[14] *Eve*, another magazine for the upper- and middle-classes, also referred to the large numbers of elderly spinsters who congregated at such resorts as Bath, Bournemouth, Cheltenham and Torquay and whose principal interest in life was probably a niece or nephew, 'the only living, breathing thing which helps [them] to keep a hold on life'.[15] But perhaps the harshest judgement on the fate of unwanted spinsters was made by Rosaline Masson in the feminist journal, *Time and Tide*. She described the nation's domestic life as being built upon a

> substratum of obscure martyrdoms . . . until the family home is broken up by death. And then the luxurious, hospitable family home belches forth dismayed spinsters into an unsympathetic world, to wander about as aimlessly, and seek cover as nervously, as do the woodlice when the flower-pot is lifted.[16]

The low esteem in which unmarried women were held was strengthened during the 1920s by the work of a growing body of sexologists, including Havelock Ellis. His seven-volume work *The Psychology of Sex* was completed between 1897 and 1927, and in it he argued that women's sexuality needed to be recognized and fulfilled through heterosexual relationships. These views were reinforced by the findings of Sigmund Freud, whose theories were interpreted as encouraging men and women to rid themselves of damaging sexual repressions.[17] The writer Winifred Holtby, herself a spinster, commented sourly that as a result of this women everywhere were being advised to enjoy the full cycle of sexual experience 'or they would become riddled with complexes like a rotting fruit'.[18] A recent commentator has been still more critical in her conclusions concerning the so-called 'sexual revolution' of the 1920s. She sees it not as a way of opening up to men and women 'the possibility of sexual choice' but of 'narrowing women's options to the role of complements to men in the act of sexual intercourse'.[19] Inevitably those females who refused motherhood in order to continue with their work or study were castigated by many of the psychiatrists and sexologists.[20] Such theories harmed single women not merely because they implied that spinsters, deprived of normal sexual fulfilment, would become embittered and frustrated, but because they made them appear social deviants. In 1923 the Catholic writer A.M. Ludovici saw them as representing 'a body of human beings who are not leading natural lives, and whose fundamental instincts are able to find no normal expression or satisfaction'.[21] Four years later Charlotte Haldane, wife of the Cambridge biologist J.B.S. Haldane, echoed these sentiments when she claimed that single women were usually genetically inferior, and lamented that females who were 'biologically superfluous' were 'nowadays socially and politically influential members of the community'.[22] In these sweeping assertions she included not only many leading feminists but school teachers and most other middle-class professionals.[23]

Another aspect of the debate on spinsters arose from the increasing awareness of lesbianism. As early as 1921 an attempt was made in the Commons to make it illegal, in the way that homosexuality had been since the mid-1880s. One MP claimed that the wife of a friend had been led astray 'by the wiles of one abandoned female, who had pursued [her]'; a second claimed that lesbianism stopped childbirth 'because it is a well-known fact that any woman who indulges in this vice will have nothing whatever to do with the other sex. It debauches young girls, and it produces . . . insanity.'[24] Yet, despite these and similar arguments, and a vote in favour of the proposal, the government refused to act. Lesbian practices remained lawful, and there were self-advertised circles in London where the women could meet one another.[25] Not until the appearance in 1928 of Radclyffe Hall's novel *The Well of Loneliness*, which had a lesbian theme, did the subject give rise to widespread public controversy. Within months of publication the book was declared obscene by the courts, amidst a blaze of publicity.[26] 'I would rather give a healthy boy or girl a phial of prussic acid than this novel,' was the reaction of the *Sunday Express*.[27] In such a climate, friendships between women became 'suspect', and this added to the difficulties of the unmarried who were living together for economic and companionate reasons.

Nonetheless, in spite of these prejudices, growing numbers of middle-class women were taking up paid employment in a variety of fields, ranging from teaching, medicine and the Civil Service to social work, librarianship and clerical duties. Some obtained positions in exclusive dress shops, while a few opted for more unusual occupations. Among them was the Oxford graduate Hilda Matheson, who in 1927 moved from being Lady Astor's political secretary to a post as 'Head of Talks' at the fledgling British Broadcasting Corporation.[28] The journal *Women's Employment* also reported on the successful recruitment of females by travel firms. The pioneers included the Wayfarers' Travel Agency, whose branches in Paris and New York were managed by females. In the former city the niece of a 'well-known English Bishop' was at the helm and, as a woman, was well qualified to advise female clients who went to the French capital to buy clothes. Prior to her appointment she had taught French at a prestigious girls' school in England. Nearly all the company's tour leaders were also women. One, the daughter of a prominent Mayfair physician, escorted parties to the Carpathian mountains.[29]

For those less adventurous, *Women's Employment* gave information on the pros and cons of such careers as running a millinery business, taking a post as a lady gardener, and running a dance studio. The latter was considered a particularly rewarding occupation: 'there is very little monotony, as each hour, in all probability, you have a different step to teach, and the exercise alone, for a teacher, keeps her fit and young'.[30] Even the journal of the Girls' Friendly Society offered genteel guidance to middle-class girls on how to follow a 'Profession at Home', perhaps by opening a tea-garden at a country cottage or becoming a 'jobbing gardener'.[31]

One woman who took up employment during the 1920s after a wartime stint in a munitions factory was the writer Noel Streatfeild. She had always had a secret ambition to go on the stage but when she suggested this to her clergyman father he was taken aback. The theatre had long had a dubious reputation and, as such, was unlikely to appeal to an elderly Eastbourne cleric. But he realized that his finances were overstretched and that he could not afford to support his daughters at home until they married, even if he wished. So he agreed to Noel's request, paying her fees at the Academy of Dramatic Art in London and making her a small allowance of £50 a year. When the course ended in April 1920 she found herself without a job, and only with difficulty obtained a temporary post as a chorus girl in a touring company.[32] This was hardly the kind of theatrical career she and her family had had in mind. Throughout the 1920s she pursued an uncertain course, getting employment where she could – including working periodically as a model for clothes – and keeping many of the details hidden from her relations. Only at the very end of the decade, after her father's death, did she turn to writing novels, thereby securing modest fame and a reasonable income.

But for some women, the economic uncertainties of the decade were far more serious than for Noel Streatfeild. In 1926 Helen Brook's father lost all his money when the art gallery he ran had to be sold. Within months the family moved from comparative comfort to poverty. Their home had to be given up and her father was so humiliated by the débâcle that he simply disappeared. Helen's mother had already left him, and it was an aunt who came to the rescue. Helen herself, devoid of training and qualifications, became a waitress in a Lyons tea-shop, a post she held, albeit without enthusiasm, until her marriage in 1928 to the leading violinist at Covent Garden. Whilst working as a 'nippy' she earned 21s. a week plus tips. 'If you were pretty you got sixpence, and if you weren't so pretty you only got threepence.'[33]

Similarly Esma Berte, the daughter of a chartered accountant, turned to domestic service when her father lost his job. She earned 15s a week, of which she sent home 5s., but ultimately the hard work proved too much for her and she had to leave.[34] For a middle-class girl, employment as a low-status servant was particularly galling.

Then there were women such as the artists Gwen John and Nina Hamnett, who persevered with their careers despite being reduced to dire poverty on many occasions. Nina, the daughter of an army officer, went to France in 1920 after a disastrous wartime marriage and a spell teaching art at the Westminster Technical Institute. But she craved the gaiety and more Bohemian atmosphere of artistic circles in Paris, and once there set up home with a Pole. She became a member of the hard-drinking circle surrounding Nancy Cunard at that time but she also continued to paint Paris street scenes, and exhibited art at the Salon d'Automne. On her return to London in 1926 she illustrated Seymour Leslie's *The Silent Queen* and collaborated with Osbert Sitwell on *The People's Album of London Statues*.[35] According to her biographer, Nina was always a witty and uninhibited personality: 'She played the guitar, sang sea-shanties and recited bawdy poems. She was courted by aristocrats, artists and sailors. She had a generous nature, and would go to great pains to provide alternative guided tours of London or Paris for friends arriving in town.'[36] But above all, she exercised her independence and if that meant sometimes being short of cash, she was prepared to pay the penalty.

Most working daughters of professional or business families led more conventional lives than these examples, however, even if, despite the 1919 Sex Disqualification (Removal) Act they still encountered gender prejudice. This ranged from fixing quotas for the number of women admitted to medical school, to the imposition of marriage bars upon those employed in the Civil Service, banking, and the teaching profession. (These issues are examined in detail in Chapter 6.) Inevitably, feminists such as Vera Brittain railed against an attitude which looked upon a woman's occupation as 'a kind of superior hobby', and argued that married women were successfully holding down posts in social work, advertising and journalism, as well as on the stage. But it was to no avail.[37] Restrictions were maintained and when in 1927 the Married Women (Employment) Bill was brought before the Commons by Sir Robert Newman, MP for Exeter, it was greeted with hostility and derision. In vain its sponsor declared that his intention was not to compel any public authority to employ a woman *because* she was married, but merely 'to confer upon married women the right . . . to work'. One opponent claimed that history had taught that any attempt to place women exactly on 'an equality with men' had accelerated 'the downfall of States and Empires', while another foresaw a time when the mother would go out to work and the father would stay at home to look after the baby. He

Middle-class servant problems are highlighted by this Punch *cartoon of a superior charlady and a dubious employer.*

SUPERIOR CHARLADY (*a recent acquisition*). "I never clean stoves, Ma'am – it ruins me hands for whist-drives."

had 'never expected . . . to have that particular travesty put forward in legislation'.[38] The Bill was decisively defeated.

Significantly, as critics were quick to point out, these prohibitions on wives working were never applied to those engaged in menial manual labour, such as charwomen, laundresses and the like. During the 1920s not only did the number of charwomen increase, to meet the growing demand from middle-class women unable to obtain full-time domestic help, but the proportion who were married rose from around 36 per cent of the total in 1921 to 46 per cent a decade later. The proportion of married servants also rose a little.

Within the university world the role of women remained small. In 1930–1 the proportion of females among the academic staff of the various English universities ranged from 5 per cent at Cambridge and 8 per cent at Sheffield to 21 per cent at London and Nottingham, 22 per cent at Exeter, 24 per cent at Southampton and 29 per cent at Reading. From the mid-1920s there was also a drop in the number of women students at university, from 12,962 in 1923–4 to 12,899 in 1928–9, and that trend continued into the following decade. By contrast the number of male students rose, so that by 1938–9 women comprised just 23 per cent of the university population of Great Britain. In medicine and dentistry the female decline was particularly noticeable, numbers falling from 2,595 in 1921–2 to 1,108 in 1928–9. This was largely due to the policy of exclusion applied to women by the medical schools. But it owed something also to the fact that middle-class parents with limited funds were choosing to educate their sons rather than their daughters. Furthermore, both female academic staff and students often encountered strong gender hostility. This was especially true of Oxford and Cambridge. Although women were accorded full membership of the former university in 1920, it was not until the 1940s that they achieved a similar status at Cambridge. And at Oxford anxiety that females were becoming too numerous led to moves in 1927 to place an upper limit of 840 on their total recruitment. That represented less than a quarter of the number of men, and as one female academic noted with wry amusement: 'The naïveté is beginning to strike one as humorous; the university is overcrowded, women nearly 1:4, cut down the women.'[39]

Symptomatic of the general mood at this time was a cartoon in the Oxford student paper *Isis* during October 1920. This showed a Junior Common Room filled with women, babies, women's magazines, embroidery, and toys. The implication was that a place once devoted to rigorous intellectual exchanges had become dominated by trivial female pursuits.[40] The previous week an anonymous contributor to the magazine had predicted that girls would soon outnumber

and swamp the men! And the logical outcome of such a certainty is that men will go to Cambridge and give woman-ridden Oxford a miss! . . . Men come up to the University for a variety of reasons, but underlying the ulterior objective is the very potent if unconscious desire of making new friends with and having a good time amongst other men.[41]

Throughout the 1920s women's role at all the universities remained unsatisfactory, and only a tiny number were able to achieve professorial standing.[42]

Jane Lewis has drawn attention to the ambiguities and contradictions associated with the position of female professionals in these years. As the number of qualified women increased and it became more common for middle-class girls to work when they left school, so the lines of sexual segregation were ever more closely defended,

> a pattern exacerbated rather than explained by the economic depression. Ideas regarding the proper role of married women . . . lay behind the introduction of the marriage bar, which assumed that all married women could be treated as a reserve army of labour because of the primary responsibility to home and family and because they could be expected to rely on their husbands for financial support. This view was more rigidly enforced in the case of professional women, who were the daughters and potential wives of the men implementing the marriage bar, and whose roles were the more rigidly prescribed.[43]

Yet, ironically, it was precisely from the ranks of the middle-classes that most of the feminists were drawn who were to challenge these gender prejudices. During the 1920s there were three major organizations concerned with campaigning for female equality. One, the Six Point Group, was established in 1921 with the aim of removing 'all artificial barriers' to women's progress. It was initiated by Lady Rhondda and its immediate objectives included the passage of reforming legislation to deal with cases of child assault; to improve the position of the unmarried mother and her child; to benefit widowed mothers; to achieve equal rights of guardianship between fathers and mothers; to secure equal opportunity for men and women in the Civil Service; and to obtain equal pay for male and female teachers. Its egalitarian principles appealed to many traditional feminists who had earlier campaigned for women's suffrage. Winifred Holtby, herself a supporter of the Six Point Group from a younger generation, admitted that its motto of 'Equality First' and its concentration on aspects of national life where sex differentiation still prevailed, might seem negative and backward-looking. But, to her, that was erroneous. 'Old Feminism' was concerned with the 'primary importance of the human being'.[44]

The leader of the rival National Union of Societies for Equal Citizenship (NUSEC) was Eleanor Rathbone, who served as President from 1919 – the year of its formation out of earlier suffrage organizations – until 1928. Eleanor was born into an eminent Liverpool family, her father being a noted philanthropist and Liberal MP for the city. From an early stage she had helped him with his social research and when he died she took over much of his public work, becoming the first woman councillor in Liverpool in 1909 and also an active supporter of women's suffrage.[45] In the post-war years she became a strong advocate of 'New Feminism', which put forward policies designed to meet the special needs of working-class women as wives and mothers, rather than merely to achieve general equality between the sexes. That led critics to accuse her and NUSEC of acquiescing in the traditional gender divisions of society, but in practice she never lost sight of the need for greater social justice for women in the work place. In 1927 NUSEC gave support to the Married Women (Employment) Bill although, as we have seen, without success.[46] In 1926 a new pressure group – the Open Door Council – appeared. Its main purpose was to ensure that women were free to work and to be protected as workers *on the same terms* as men, rather than merely on grounds of their sex. It sought to secure for females, irrespective of marriage or motherhood, the right to choose whether or not they should take up paid employment.[47] On a number of issues the Six Point Group and the Open Door Council campaigned together.[48] All three organizations were critical of 'parasitic' middle-class women who depended on their family for support. Lady Rhondda, in particular, was scathing in her condemnation of wives who lacked all vitality and engaged in vapid conversation: 'what a world in which a whole class of human beings is condemned to a life which turns the majority of them into devitalized bores . . . the kept wife has no raison d'être as a person.'[49]

Yet despite such strictures and the pressures exerted by feminists in the employment field, there were still many girls who stayed at home 'helping mother' and carrying out appropriate social and charitable duties – these last being scornfully dismissed by Lady Rhondda as 'slumming'.[50] In 1931 17 per cent of all single girls aged 18–29 in England and Wales declared no occupation to the census enumerator, and among the age group 25–29, it was over 18 per cent. Most were probably from a middle- or upper-class background.

Sometimes, as in the case of the Holtby family, one daughter would remain at home while another pursued a career. Hence the future writer Winifred Holtby followed her wartime service in Queen Mary's Army Auxiliary Corps with a period at Oxford University. After graduating, she and her close friend Vera Brittain began working as journalists, lecturers and part-time teachers. But Winifred's elder sister, Grace, stayed at home until she was 'rescued' from spinsterdom by marriage to a widowed doctor several years her senior. As Winifred and Vera agreed, whatever the doctor's deficiencies, 'the man who brought her the only vocation she desired would have no disadvantages in her eyes'.[51]

The career of Amy Johnson, the daughter of a Hull fish importer, was a variation on the theme in that she was given the option of staying at home with her mother to learn housewifery skills when she left school. But she longed for wider horizons and after much discussion it was agreed that she should attend Sheffield University. There she had an undistinguished academic career and followed it with a short secretarial course, before entering an office.[52] From this she moved to a number of other jobs, to the consternation of her family, before she obtained a secure but humdrum post in a solicitor's office in London. Soon after she linked up with a girl she had known at Sheffield University and they shared lodgings, 'or rather, a variety of lodgings for, in my restlessness, I took her along with me in my constant changes'.[53] Sometimes Amy chose one of the special women's hostels which were being set up for middle-class working girls living away from home in a number of towns and cities. At other times she and her friend lived in rooms. But within a year or two she was able to gratify her secret desire to fly and subsequently became one of the most famous women pilots of her day. She was also the first woman to gain the Air Ministry's ground engineer's licence.

Amy Johnson was a woman of determination and ability, but it is significant that her father never suggested that she should join his business, as would doubtless have been the case had she been a boy. It was this aspect of sex discrimination which particularly irked Lady Rhondda. In an article in *Good Housekeeping* in 1923 she argued that until the average businessman brought his daughter into the office 'as naturally as he now brings his son, the business woman who desires to work up from the ranks will not get a fair chance'.[54] According to Lady Rhondda, during the decade after the First World War there were a mere 300 females among Britain's 27,000 company directors, and most of them were associated with small undertakings, often connected with the dress trade.

Her sentiments were echoed by Vera Brittain, another feminist daughter of a businessman. In her book *Lady into Woman*, she described an 'enterprising Surrey fishmonger' who had caused considerable amusement in the 1920s by registering his business under the title of Marment and Daughter. 'Such a variation on the time-honoured style "and Son" was then still inconceivable to most British fathers.' Instead they burdened their womenfolk with 'small duties and petty economies'.[55]

And this, in fact, strikes at the heart of the middle-class woman's dilemma during the 1920s. Despite the increased scope of female employment, the prevailing philosophy remained that marriage was a woman's true vocation. *Good Housekeeping* caught the general mood in its January 1929 article on 'The Best Job for a Girl'. Its male author claimed that no matter how fulfilling a girl's professional career might be or how well paid, she

> ought to keep the idea of getting married *in the front of her head*. No woman who merely has achieved success in a business career ever is happy. The feminine nature craves masculine love and affection. Buried somewhere in each woman's heart is the desire for a home of her own – and for children. . . . No girl can take a course in life against nature and find happiness and contentment. The happiest women in the world are those who cheerfully fulfil their natural destiny and get husbands and homes of their own, with children in them.[56]

In this connection it is significant that of the twenty pieces of legislation enacted between 1918 and 1927 and designed to improve the status of women, almost all were concerned with enhancing their position as wives and mothers.[57]

The women's magazines which proliferated during the decade took up the propaganda in favour of marriage and maternity with particular enthusiasm. Their columns were filled with advice on how to keep a husband happy and children healthy, once those essential adjuncts to female existence had been acquired. *Wife and Home*, in its first issue in 1929 exemplified the twin preoccupations with domesticity and child rearing. 'In these pages,' the editor assured readers, ' . . . you will learn all that you need to know to make you a perfect wife and mother. If you are a real homemaker you will never fall short of your man's belief in you, and *Wife and Home* is planned to help you to make his dream of the perfect wife a reality.' In addition, every 'true woman' longed to hold her own baby in her arms and the magazine promised to

> sweep aside all the anxieties and fears of the young mother-to-be; the beautiful baby pictures and photographs will fill her mind with lovely thoughts so that the months of waiting become the most precious she has ever known.[58]

Among the articles published in this first issue was advice from Dr Josephine Baker on 'how King Baby should progress along the Royal Road to Health and Happiness'. Readers were reminded that the 'career of the home-maker is the finest in the world'.

A similar note was struck by *Woman's Pictorial*. This ran a weekly two-page spread of advice to mothers on bringing up their babies. It was produced by the matron of the Mothercraft Training Society, and photographs were published of 'Better Babies', who had been brought up on the Society's principles. The magazine exhorted readers not to miss 'these pages of vital importance to mothers'.[59]

Good Housekeeping, an American home monthly whose first English edition appeared in 1922, was broader in its approach and less sentimental in its language. But it, too, was anxious to remind its middle-class purchasers that housewives were the 'craft-workers of today'. Although it claimed to be concerned with

Swimming costumes advertised by Debenham & Freebody in June 1923. (Time and Tide)

taking the drudgery out of housework, the high standards it set and its encouragement to women to apply scientific principles to the running of their home were likely to increase the pressure rather than eliminate it. A model kitchen was fitted up on the magazine's premises where the cookery editor could test all her recipes before they were printed in the magazine.[60] In 1924 it set up the Good Housekeeping Institute to serve as a practical testing station for all kinds of domestic appliances, and to recommend suitable products to readers. Certificates of Approval were issued for those goods which passed its rigorous tests, and the Good Housekeeping Seal of Guarantee became synonymous with reliability and high quality in the minds of female consumers.[61]

Home dressmaking was also encouraged by the magazines, with advertisements and features describing the latest fashions and how to follow them at modest cost. Among the advertisements appearing in the first issue of *Woman and Home* in November 1926 was an insertion by Clark's Threads, Embroideries, and Cottons, suggesting that diligent dressmakers could

> add guineas to the appearance of [their] clothes. Hand embroidery is the last word in smartness this season. Coats, sports suits, afternoon and evening gowns all depend for their effect on exquisitely coloured embroidery . . .

The 'Gold Fleece Knitting Machine' advertisement in the same issue suggested that £3 per week could be earned by 'knitting at your own fireside. If you buy a Gold Fleece Knitting Machine you will be able to turn out an amazing quantity of stockings, socks, children's woollies, etc. Many women, finding a ready sale for their output, are now earning as much as £1 per day.' In this case, the advertiser was subtly linking the cult of domesticity with the desire of women to achieve a high level of skill in the arts of housewifery and, if possible, to have an income of their own without abandoning the respectability of being a 'wife at home'.

Other advertisements sought to stimulate the middle-class woman's sense of competitiveness with her friends and neighbours, at a time when it was becoming increasingly difficult to recruit domestic servants. One such was for an electric refrigerator made by Frigidaire. It showed a husband and wife relaxing after the last guest had departed following an evening's entertainment:

> you are left with the memory of your dinner party. A treasured memory – for you realize how much your faithful Frigidaire has contributed to your guests' content. . . . You will gain a reputation as a wonderful hostess; for you know how these things get round. Even now amidst the debris of the table you can visualize the delectable array of delightful desserts and frozen delicacies prepared so easily by Frigidaire.[62]

Efforts to improve the quality of electrical appliances and to expand the scope of electric supply were initiated by the Electrical Association for Women, set up in 1924 with the feminist Caroline Haslett as its first director. Its illustrated magazine, *The Electrical Age for Women*, included articles explaining the benefits to be derived from electricity in the home. It also opened showrooms and

Female employees at the King Street Branch of the Manchester and Liverpool District Bank at the end of the First World War. (National Westminster Bank Group Archives, 20437)

mounted special travelling exhibitions, where various electrical appliances were demonstrated. Although originally based in London it developed branch associations, as well as encouraging electric cooking classes in many schools and colleges.[63]

Marriage and its associated domestic role, therefore, became the goal at which women were encouraged to aim. Yet, equally, a desire to achieve an appropriate lifestyle might lead some engaged couples to postpone their wedding for a few years, perhaps until the prospective bridegroom had achieved a good position in his firm or had obtained a pensionable post, or the bride had saved enough money to buy the furniture. Banks, for example, feared that if staff married too young or when they were earning too low a salary to support their anticipated standard of living, they might get into debt.[64] About 30 was thought a suitable age for a male bank clerk. Hence the case of an engaged couple working at the Hanley Branch of the Manchester and Liverpool District Bank. The future bride had worked there since the First World War, mostly as a ledger clerk, and during that time her salary had risen from £1 7s. 6d. a week in 1919 to £2 13s. 6d. in 1926, when she resigned to marry a bank colleague. He and his brother also had to support their widowed mother, and this must have added to the young couple's financial pressures. But in accordance with bank policy, she, like all female employees, still had to leave on marriage.[65]

Once a woman *was* married her way of life normally depended on her husband's income and upon the nature of the locality in which they lived.

Proximity to a golf course or a leafy park might bring extra status. But with the housing shortage which followed the First World War many had to settle for less. In Liverpool, 41 per cent of the first post-war council houses built in the city were occupied by middle-class tenants. This was partly because the high cost of their construction meant large rentals, which most working-class families could not afford, and partly because the council was anxious to secure occupiers who would not run up rent arrears. Two tenants who rented houses on the Larkhill Estate, for example, had incomes as high as £11 a week. One was a single lady living on 'private means', who was able to afford the services of a resident maid. Other tenants included a bank manager, master mariners, architects and clerks. One girl brought up in a Liverpool council house at this time was a daughter of the managing director of a furniture company. Each morning a chauffeur-driven car would arrive to take him to work. 'You see we were very comfortably placed. My father always paid for my education, first infants and then juniors and when I was eleven he paid for me to go to Holly Lodge and that was a school for real ladies in those days.'[66]

But for those wives at the bottom of the middle-class earnings scale, living in an urban villa or a small suburban semi-detached, the daily round could become a wearying routine of cleaning, washing, cooking, disputes with the charwoman or maid (if such help could be afforded), care of the children and struggles to make ends meet. Despite the propaganda campaigns of *Good Housekeeping* and the Electrical Association for Women, few were able to afford labour-saving appliances such as vacuum cleaners. Furthermore, it was not until the 1930s that the number of households with electric services increased rapidly, from 18 per cent in 1926 to 32 per cent in 1932 and 65 per cent in 1938.[67]

More relevant in easing the burdens of domesticity were suggestions on how to make household interiors easier to clean. 'Avoid ledges, avoid fretwork, cosy corners and elaborate mouldings,' advised one 1920s magazine; 'have solid balustrades to the stairs if necessary and generally banish all those resting-places for dirt and dust.'[68] Catering problems could be eased by the use of convenience foods, such as canned goods, custard powder, pudding and cake mixes, and jelly crystals.

The fact that families were smaller – clerical and lower middle-class workers generally had the lowest fertility rate of any social class during these years – released wives from the pressures of constant childbearing. But to counterbalance this many had to perform menial tasks which they would once have delegated to servants. As a consequence, some felt they were becoming less the mistress of the household than its drudge. Leonora Eyles described the unhappiness of the wives of young professional men whose incomes were relatively low, and yet who were expected to keep up appearances at a time when women were being pressed to achieve ever higher standards in the home. According to Mrs Eyles, the fact that a maid demanded wages equal to about a sixth of a husband's salary put such assistance out of the question, especially when in order to keep their children in the same social class as themselves parents felt they must send them

to good schools, buy them good clothes, keep a certain standard of beauty and order in their homes; to do this on the young professional man's salary is a work

A Hoover vacuum cleaner in use in a middle-class home, c. 1930. Electrical appliances were beginning to be used as substitutes for domestic servants. (Hoover)

of extreme difficulty and heroism; to do it and keep a maid at the same time is impossible.[69]

One former kindergarten mistress whom Mrs Eyles knew and who before marriage had been able to 'dress nicely' and go on continental holidays, found herself tied to the home, caring for three children and too weary at the end of the day to engage in an intelligent conversation with her husband, as she had once done. Nor had she time to read, and 'her music has gone – you can't play the piano with fingers sore and rough through cleaning floors and grates and vegetables'.[70]

In other cases, as with Mrs Ruth Quick, the wife of a Nonconformist minister, a young school-leaver might be engaged as a maid from 9 a.m. until tea-time to assist with the housework and with looking after the babies. Mrs Quick agreed to train her for 'more advanced domestic work later on' and paid her 6s. a week for 6 days' labour: 'but her mother was satisfied with this. After about a year she took a better post. I had several girls to train.'[71] She also employed a washerwoman once a week; she came for three hours and was paid 2s. for lighting the boiler fire in the wash-house, laundering the clothes and hanging them out.

Some women, unable to employ servants, used shopping as a surrogate status symbol. They would tell their friends they were arranging a 'fitting' at the tailor's or dressmaker's, and they would display a gracious manner of conscious condescension to the milkman. Transactions with the butcher or the grocer might become 'a mode of receiving respect'. Visits to genteel tea-shops, whose numbers increased in this period, could be considered as part of the same process.[72] In other cases, despite the exhortations to wives to achieve higher standards in housekeeping and to adopt scientific methods in managing the home, there were a few women who 'made it a point of honour' to cook badly. They were reluctantly doing their own domestic chores, and to have read recipe-books and produced attractive meals would have signalled acceptance of the servitude to which they were unwillingly bound.

Those living in the newly built suburbs, away from family and friends, and with husbands leaving for work early in the morning and returning late in the evening, were often lonely. For them a visit to the shops became the major event of the day, and a number suffered from what was called 'housewife's neurosis'. One victim was Edith Broadway, who before her marriage in 1928 had been a millinery designer. She and her husband, a cashier with an oil company, moved to a large three-bedroomed house in Essex, but Edith was frustrated by the sheer monotony of her daily life. Each morning her husband left at 6.30 a.m. and did not return until 7 p.m.:

What do you do with yourself when you've done all the housework and the things that you've got to do and there's nothing and nobody, when you've been used to a life full of people? . . . I was allocated a certain amount for housekeeping . . . I had been earning about twice the amount that my husband was earning but . . . [he] wanted me to be . . . dependent on him . . . I can remember the tears falling into the sink when I was doing the washing. . . . You see, I was creative and housework isn't very creative.[73]

When she suggested returning to work, under her maiden name – 'they wouldn't take you if you were married' – her husband threatened to give up his own job. She was not sure whether he meant it, and so she meekly submitted and continued her depressing daily round. The well-known desire of the middle classes to 'keep themselves to themselves' added to the sense of isolation of these young wives.

Anna Wickham, who did break away from a similarly narrow existence, described in verse the cramping nature of this dull respectability:

> I married a man of the Croydon class
> When I was 22
> And I vex him and he bores me
> Till we don't know what to do!
> It isn't good form in the Croydon class
> To say you love your wife
> So I spend my days with the tradesman's books
> And I pray for the end of life . . .
>
> But every man of the Croydon class
> Lives in terror of joy and speech,
> 'Words are betrayers', 'joys are brief'
> The maxims their wise ones teach
> And for all my labour of love and life
> I shall be clothed and fed
> And they'll give me an orderly funeral
> When I'm still enough to be dead.[74]

Even for more affluent wives, who could afford domestic help, frustrations remained. Strict segregation between servant and mistress was hard to achieve within the confines of the small villas which were being constructed in this period. Tensions arose, too, between maids resentful of the petty controls of servant life and employers who were anxious to keep their distance from their staff. A woman who worked as a maid in Paignton recalled bitterly the lack of consideration she was shown. 'Why did they have to treat us as though we were less than human?'[75] Another girl, employed by a doctor's family in Cheadle, remembered that although her mistress and the daughters of the family were 'very nice people', they were also 'very patronizing . . . I'm a lady and you're a maid, sort of thing'.[76] On one occasion she was reprimanded for singing while she cleaned the bathroom, but the most serious problem arose when she had her hair bobbed. She had asked her mother's permission beforehand but when she took her mistress's tea in the next morning, the latter's shock was apparent. She sat bolt upright in bed, and as soon as she came down for breakfast she called her maid into the library and shut the door:

> she was in a raging temper and she wasn't normally . . . they could be very cutting and very sarcastic . . . but always in a very gentle voice – but this time . . .

she said 'Now you look what you are, a common little slavey'. . . . I just turned round and walked out of the room. . . . Anyway after breakfast she called me in again and she apologized . . . but . . . I never felt the same about her again.[77]

More fortunate was Rose Luttrell, who lived at Box in Wiltshire. She was a bank manager's wife and had a staff of six servants. She took little part in running the house beyond seeing the cook in the morning and ordering the meals for the day. Her time was spent in gardening, writing letters, walking, visiting friends, and playing with the children when she felt so inclined. She also suffered from migraine attacks, which her rather aimless existence may have encouraged. In 1923 she learned to drive a car and would then take the nanny and her children for picnics.[78]

Mrs Thompson, the wife of a director of an iron company, likewise left the management of her Stalybridge home to the housekeeper-cum-parlour maid, Mrs Humphries, a widow. The latter lived in the house with her young son and was assisted by her step-daughter and a sister-in-law, who came in daily, and by a washerwoman.[79] Mrs Thompson, meanwhile, occupied herself with the Mothers' Union, church fêtes, various charities, and membership of the No More War peace movement – later the Peace Pledge Union. Her daughter remembered 'banners being made of hessian or sheeting and painted with slogans for marches and demonstrations'. One of the charities with which her mother was involved supplied clothes and food parcels to poor families. Mrs Thompson repaired and made many of the clothes herself, especially the baby wear. She was particularly adept at running up small dresses from old woollen stockings! 'The upper leg made the skirt, and the lower parts the yoke and sleeves.'[80]

Even women in such relatively comfortable circumstances as these were concerned to restrict the size of their families. A decline in the middle-class birth-rate had been apparent before the war and after 1918 it became more obvious. It was a trend encouraged by the writings and propaganda of Dr Marie Stopes, who embarked upon her campaign to promote planned parenthood at the end of the First World War. In her first two books, *Married Love* and *Wise Parenthood*, she was particularly concerned with advising upper- and middle-class couples on the means to achieve marital sexual fulfilment and also a restricted family. *Wise Parenthood*, for example, suggested wives should routinely insert the cervical cap contraceptive Dr Stopes recommended while they were dressing for dinner. Her birth control message emphasized the importance of happy, healthy and *wanted* babies. It was designed to appeal to women unable to achieve the pregnancies they desired and to those who too easily 'succumbed to undesired ones'.[81] Later Dr Stopes became anxious that at a time when the affluent were limiting their families, the less desirable sectors of the population – 'the diseased, the racially negligent, the thriftless, the careless, . . . the very lowest and worst members of the community' – were producing 'innumerable tens of thousands of stunted, warped and inferior infants'. If they, too, learned to practise contraception, then the

better classes, freed from the cost of the institutions, hospitals, prisons and so on, principally filled by the inferior stock, would be able to afford to enlarge their own families, and at the same time not only to save misery but to multiply a hundredfold the contribution in human life-value to the riches of the State.[82]

In 1921 Dr Stopes established her first birth control clinic in London (a venture discussed in detail in Chapter 5) and in the same year she and her husband set up the Society for Constructive Birth Control. The clinic's notepaper was headed with the motto: 'Joyous and Deliberate Motherhood. A Sure Light in Our Racial Darkness.' In this context the 'undesirables' represented the 'racial darkness' to which she referred.[83] However, her eugenist message to encourage family limitation among the lower orders proved even more popular among the middle-classes, for whom the one- or two-child family was becoming the norm. It was during these years that childbirth came increasingly to be seen as a 'special and momentous event in a woman's life to be planned by the parents', rather than the routine event it had been for many Victorian wives.[84]

But if family planning was one important component of the demographic debate during the 1920s, another was the welfare and survival of mothers and babies. Infant mortality rates were falling, and were already lower in middle-class than in working-class homes. But it was a sobering fact that childbirth was as painful and as dangerous for women from better-off homes as it was for those from the poorer districts. Even in 1932 only 60 per cent of maternity patients at London's Royal Free Hospital were supplied with any form of pain relief, and in 1927 Vera Brittain, giving birth prematurely to her first child in a London nursing home, received no analgesics because of 'a mistake'.[85] Her experiences led her to become a strong campaigner for improved maternity services for all women.

A still greater cause of public outcry was the realization that maternal mortality in some middle-class areas was actually greater than among the working-classes. Thus in Leeds the rate of maternal deaths in the 1920s was about twice as high in middle-class districts as in working-class ones, and in 1931 the maternal mortality level in middle-class Chelsea, at 5.4 per thousand live births, was considerably worse than in impoverished Hackney, where it was 3.2 per thousand.[86] At the 1932 meeting of the Maternal Mortality Committee, an unofficial pressure group which included women from all sectors of society, Mrs A.L. Smith claimed to be speaking for 'mothers of [her] own class, because . . . the death rate is higher in well-to-do neighbourhoods like Hampstead than in the slums of London'.[87] Private nursing homes, which were likely to be patronized by middle-class mothers, had some of the worst death rates of all. Lack of competence among the medical staff was blamed for the poor record.

Rose Luttrell, despite her affluent circumstances, was one sufferer from medical mismanagement. The birth of her first child proved difficult and eventually the doctor, who was her own general practitioner, had to use forceps to aid the delivery. Before this she had been in labour for many hours, and when the delivery eventually took place the baby's skull was injured, while she herself was badly torn. The child died shortly afterwards, and both parents were 'very shattered and upset'.[88] For her next child, born a year later, in 1919, she went into a nursing home, and had no problems. Two further babies followed in 1921 and 1928, and all three youngsters were brought up by a nanny. Rose herself had little to do with any baby once it had been born, except feed it. Only once did she and her husband take the children away for a holiday without the nanny. It was such hard work that they resolved never to repeat the experiment.[89]

On a broader basis, the 1920s was also the era when baby care experts became of major importance and the scientific study of infant needs brought with it a strong emphasis on discipline and regimentation. These new ideas were readily taken up by the middle-classes, and baby-care manuals were produced which warned mothers in dictatorial tones of the importance of adopting a 'scientific' approach towards their infant's upbringing. The leading figure in the movement was a New Zealand doctor, Frederick Truby King, and after his visit to England in 1917 a Mothercraft Training School based on his principles was opened in North London. Although his motto of 'breast fed is best fed' was beneficial, other aspects of his methods were less benign. These included an emphasis on routine and regimentation rather than parental love.[90] Victoria E.M. Bennett's *Health in the Nursery*, published in 1930, typified the general approach:

> It is a good plan to have a graphic timetable . . . posted on the nursery wall, showing the times for food, baths, sleep, etc., and nothing whatever should be allowed to interfere with the routine.[91]

One of Truby King's most enthusiastic British disciples underlined the benefits which would accrue from observing the system's strict system of habit training:

> Self-control, obedience, the recognition of authority, and later, respect for elders are all the outcome of the first year's training.[92]

The instructions were followed most conscientiously by mothers seeking to produce a 'perfect' child, and particularly by those bringing up a first baby. This was true, for example, of Stella Davies, the wife of an industrial chemist in Manchester. Stella had almost died from puerperal fever when her first child was born but once she had recovered she and her husband endeavoured to follow the rules laid down in their Truby King handbook. As she later recalled, with wry amusement at her own naïveté,

> The child was fed by the clock and put outside in his pram in all weathers. My neighbours would shake their heads over him and say, 'Poor little thing, I doubt you'll ever rear him. Dust think it ought to be out in this cowd? Lap it up and take it in t'fire.' They *would* try to kiss him and I would stand in horror thinking of germs. The Truby King handbook advised against kissing babies on hygienic grounds and against cuddling them or fussing over them in any way. A kind but professional aloofness was the attitude at which to aim. This was the hardest to obey of all the rules and it often went by default.[93]

Even the strong-minded Vera Brittain accepted that mothercraft was a science which had to be learnt. For this reason she supported the Chelsea Babies' Club set up, on a fee-paying basis, for middle-class mothers about the time her first child was born in 1927. Later she claimed that but for her 'providential discovery' of this club her frail firstborn might well have succumbed 'to the after-effects of his catastrophic arrival'.[94]

Another aspect of the preoccupation with infant welfare was the continued activity of the National Baby Week Council, whose patron was the queen. During its annual conference in 1923, for example, lectures were given on child welfare and maternity, and visits were arranged to mothercraft schools, nurseries, and hospitals.[95] The Council also organized national mothercraft exhibitions and offered certificates and shields to mothers who entered its competitions for home nursing, the making of children's clothes, and similar projects. So enthusiastic were its supporters that as early as 1921 it had over a million members, and a thousand local committees organized baby shows, pram parades, slide lectures and welfare exhibitions.[96]

But the encouragement given to mothers to devote so much time to child care had its disadvantages. One woman who carefully followed the Truby King feeding schedules found it a time of 'untold agony' for herself and her baby daughter.[97] Stella Davies noted that parents such as herself who sought to pay meticulous attention to cleanliness and the strict adherence to a timetable became 'hag-ridden by anxiety' as they stood over a screaming child 'watching the clock during the last few minutes before the appointed hour for feeding'.[98]

Even the women's magazines of the day, whilst extolling the virtues of maternity, caught something of the prevailing authoritarianism. In *Wife and Home*, Dr Pink advised expectant mothers to keep 'an extra stiff lip' during labour. 'Do you not think that it is cowardly to make the worst of childbirth? Is it not more sporting to make the best of it? . . . If you feel sick, don't talk about it; don't wail about headaches and heartaches, dyspepsia and cramp. . . . Would that not be a real thrill, not only to know that you are a mother, but that you have been a *brave* mother? . . . The greatest help to the woman in labour is to realize that this pain is only *a pain of hours*.'[99]

With medical attitudes like these, to say nothing of the still considerable risks attached to childbirth and the heavy expenditure involved in bringing up a baby, it is not surprising that more and more couples decided to limit their family. As the one- or two-child household became widespread, those with cash to spare preferred to spend it on the education of their existing offspring, or upon holidays away from home, or perhaps on purchasing one of the new consumer durables, such as a motor car or some household appliance. Others elected to take out a mortgage to buy a house, and there was a sharp increase in the number of building society borrowers in Great Britain from 554,000 in 1928 to 720,000 two years later.[100] The property-owning middle-classes were beginning to emerge.

CHAPTER 4

Working Women

The general endeavour to keep women in a depressed condition, and to treat their work as incidental to industry, is still reflected in the number of processes forbidden to them in various trades, in the comparative limitation of opportunities in business, and in the refusal, in the majority of professions, to promote them to higher posts and to employ them after marriage. The General Report of the 1921 Census showed that, as a result of this attitude, women have hitherto tended to stagnate within the lowest grades of any given occupation. In commerce, for instance, three-quarters of the total number of shop-assistants were women, and in the textile industry, which is one of those most favourable to the industrial woman and in which 62 per cent of all the workers are females, 92 per cent of the foremen and overlookers were men.

Vera Brittain, *Women's Work in Modern England* (1928), p. 4.

With the coming of the Armistice in 1918, there was a speedy exodus of women from many of the occupations they had filled with considerable success during the war years. Those who sought to retain their jobs were subjected to strong condemnation, especially from returning ex-servicemen. In 1920 the tramways company in Bristol dismissed its tram girls after vehicles had been attacked by former soldiers, and a year later a correspondent to the *Western Mail* complained of women working on the trams at Newport in Wales:

> every day queues of men visit to register at the Labour Exchanges, many of whom faced death to help to make this a land 'fit for heroes to live in'. I suggest that the women tramworkers should resign in a body to make way for the ex-service men.[1]

Even in the Civil Service there were angry comments about 'hussies' with '3 inches of powder on their faces', who declined to behave in a 'womanly way' by surrendering their jobs to the men.[2] However, under Treasury pressure the number of women in the Civil Service did fall dramatically, from 56 per cent of the total labour force in November 1918 to 42 per cent in July 1919 and 25 per cent by July 1923. It stayed at around that level for the remainder of the 1920s.[3]

Married women were the subject of particular criticism when they continued to work, and it was during these years that a growing number of occupations

This advertisement illustrates the kind of work on which women were employed during the First World War and from which they were increasingly excluded in the post-war world. (Woman Engineer, June 1921)

imposed a marriage bar on their female staff. Typical was the view put forward by the paternalistic chocolate and confectionery manufacturer George Cadbury at Bournville, when he maintained that a married woman's first duty was to her children, and she could not be in two places at once. He also believed that working wives encouraged their husbands to 'loaf about . . . and . . . the poor things invariably came back after childbearing to work long before they were fit'. When asked what a woman should do if her husband were ill or out of work, he did not deny the urgency 'or pathos of the question. But as a good Quaker he pondered . . . deeply over what were the limitations of his own responsibilities.' He concluded that his personal duty lay 'within the vineyard which he was required to tend. If others would only recognize the same principle there would be less unemployment, less sickness and fewer wives seeking to pick up a livelihood.'[4]

At Bournville, female employees had to resign on marriage, although those who had been employed for two years or more were rewarded with a wedding present of a bible, signed by one of the directors, and a small sum of money. At busy times of the year a few might be re-employed to help out, but this was essentially a temporary arrangement.[5]

Also significant at a time of much unemployment and underemployment was the belief that married women should not take jobs which unemployed single girls could do. That led, not surprisingly, to a situation in which 69 per cent of women workers were under the age of 35 and about 30 per cent were under 21. In some businesses the proportion of youngsters was even higher. In 1923 30 per cent of Bournville's 4,623 female employees were under 18, while in parts of the expanding electrical industry 40 to 50 per cent of those at work in 1931 were under 21. In instrument making and assembly, for example, just over half of the female staff were under 21, as were 44 per cent of those in coil winding.[6] In Slough, where a number of new industries were set up between the wars, evidence suggests that employers seeking cheap, unskilled or semi-skilled labour preferred to recruit young people rather than adult women.[7]

Shop work, too, attracted very young workers; indeed, the preponderance of juveniles threatened the job security and the wage rates of adults. Some firms had a policy of dismissing workers when they were 18 or 20 and then recruiting younger replacements, at low wages. As one commentator wryly observed, it was a case of being 'too old at eighteen'.[8] Mature spinsters over 35 in this, as in many other unskilled or semi-skilled occupations, had great difficulty in getting stable employment at all.

Only in textile manufacture and in certain other traditional female jobs, like charring or keeping a lodging house, was there a substantial number of married women regularly working in the 1920s. In other cases wives who had to take a job for family or other reasons might conceal their marital status in order to avoid the hostility of colleagues and the rejection of potential employers. One office worker admitted taking this step in order to give her mother continued financial support after her marriage.

I had a very hard time from some of the other girls who were resentful that I 'was taking a single girl's place', and I tried hard to find other employment

Two winders, aged 14, at Salt's Mill, Saltaire, near Bradford, in 1930. They were responsible for winding the spun yarns ready for the next production process or for storage. Wages were low, at around 10s. for a 55-hour week, but parents were anxious for youngsters to begin earning. (Bradford Heritage Recording Unit)

which took until 1929. To do this I took off my wedding ring and called myself 'Miss Adams'.[9]

It is not surprising, therefore, that the female labour force was not only predominantly young but also single, with around 77 or 78 per cent of women workers unmarried in both 1921 and 1931, compared with 14 per cent married in 1921 and 16 per cent married in 1931. (See Appendix 1.)

A second characteristic of the labour force was the narrow range of occupations in which females were concentrated, with 71.6 per cent of them employed in personal service (especially domestic service), textile and dress manufacture, shop work, and office duties. Even among the relatively small number engaged in the professions (see Chapter 6), a similar 'bunching' occurred, with the vast bulk engaged in teaching and nursing. The only change with the pre-war position was the increased importance of shops and offices as sources of employment, and the declining role of textiles and clothing manufacture, and, to a lesser degree, domestic work.

Some posts were considered more 'respectable' than others, with laundrywork, rag sorting and general labouring regarded as particularly rough and unfeminine. Even within trades, there were distinctions of status, so that in textiles the cardroom workers were considered to occupy the lowest position, while 'in metal working, lacquering girls were . . . the "ladies" and would not eat with the "dippers", whom they regarded as their social inferiors'.[10]

In deciding what occupation to pursue most youngsters were influenced by their parents, particularly their mother. As Mrs Newcombe of Hyde, Cheshire, put it, 'when yer were fourteen yer left school and yer weren't asked what yer wanted'. In her case this meant mill work, 'whether yer liked it or not . . . but anyway yer made the best of it'.[11]

Mrs Ethel Cleary, who was born on the outskirts of Manchester, had a similar memory. Initially she was apprenticed at a confectioner's, but although she loved the work she had to leave because of a skin complaint. While she was visiting the doctor with her mother he suggested she should become a servant, adding that his wife needed a housemaid. Ethel took little part in the subsequent discussion but she knew her mother was desperately poor and 'in those days it was usual to do as you were told . . . I wasn't . . . consulted about it . . . the doctor . . . said, send her into service and that was it'.[12]

In other cases, parents or friends pulled strings so that a daughter might work in the same firm as one of her relatives, or perhaps they used community contacts to get a post. Mrs Windor of Lancaster went to work for a grocer who attended the same church as her parents. Partly because of this link she remained there for ten years, from 1924 to 1934, even though the pay was poor and the hours long:

> He always sulked if you'd had a holiday, and he always sulked if I went anywhere that he'd think I shouldn't go . . . [H]e wanted to rule your life, and you were getting very little for it.[13]

On one occasion she was invited to a school Christmas party but on the evening in question her employer set her to weigh and pack currants after the shop had closed. 'I tried not to let him see me, but I was actually crying. The dance finished at ten o'clock, and I arrived at a quarter to ten. The shop officially closed at seven but he didn't think I should go.' He even insisted that she should wear black stockings, although other girls were wearing fashionable light-coloured ones. She felt ashamed to be seen in them but her mother said, 'Well, you will have to wear them because he wants you to wear them.'

At the paternalistic chocolate manufacturers, Rowntree's of York and Cadbury's of Bournville, the mothers of new employees were encouraged to visit

*Women workers hand-packing assortments of chocolates at Cadbury's Bournville factory in
1925. The two workers nearest the camera were packing Cadbury's Savoy chocolates.
(Cadbury Ltd, Bournville)*

the works. This was not merely to extend hospitality but, as a Cadbury
representative put it, to remind them of 'the value of a mother's advice and
sympathy' when a youngster was just starting out in the world. Both firms, unlike
most others at that time, arranged day continuation classes for junior staff. These
were intended to improve their general education and their domestic skills,
including infant care and home nursing. In addition, the trainees were instructed
in gymnastics and, at Bournville, in swimming as well. 'Punctuality in attendance
at classes is considered as important as punctuality in the factory,' the Cadbury
rulebook declared firmly.[14]

   A third characteristic of female workers during these years was their relatively
low pay and the fact that most were employed on semi-skilled or unskilled tasks,
which often encouraged a poor level of job commitment. In the new electrical
trades, girls took on the most mechanized jobs, such as the manufacture of
batteries, incandescent lamps, and motor accessories. They were recruited

because of their nimble fingers, the speed with which they learned their particular role, their cheapness, and their ability to 'withstand monotony'. Men controlled the technical processes, and females operated the machinery without understanding how it worked or knowing how to maintain or repair it. In making light bulbs, for example, teams of girls each performed one in a series of operations, while the men worked as supervisors and maintenance engineers.[15] As one commentator has put it, 'where there was dull work, there were women' and 'where there was interesting work, there were men'. She was writing about the Civil Service, but her statement was equally applicable to other occupations.[16] Even a government committee examining the distribution of women in industry in 1929 mentioned the growing numbers of females working automatic machines, but added complacently: 'Though this work is, if judged by ordinary standards, dull and monotonous, the women seem to be perfectly contented with it.'[17]

The fact that so many girls were engaged in 'blind alley' occupations was considered unimportant since most would leave after six or seven years to be married, and some moved from job to job still more rapidly. One working-class London girl listed the posts she had held between the ages of 14 and 17. These included three production line jobs in electrical engineering, metal work and a sweet factory; two as a domestic servant; one as a shop assistant; and one as a tea-trolley girl in a factory.[18] Not surprisingly, in such circumstances, the 1931 Census showed that less than $2^{1}/_{2}$ per cent of all female workers were in the 'managerial' category, as compared with over 83 per cent who were operatives.

Despite the hopes aroused by the 1919 Sex Disqualification (Removal) Act, women were routinely paid less than male colleagues who were carrying out similar work. Throughout the 1920s the average earnings of female industrial workers were less than half those of average males; only in textiles did they rise above that level.[19] Apart from the fact that many of the women and girls were younger than their male colleagues, this discrimination was justified on the grounds that the men would probably have to maintain a family. That remained the case even when research indicated that only 52 per cent of industrial male workers had dependents for whom they had to provide, while around 25 per cent of women workers also had dependents whom they supported, be they aged or sick parents or, in the case of widows, young children.[20] Winifred Holtby condemned the ingrained prejudice which helped to perpetuate this situation – and the reluctance of men to take orders, or money, or criticism from females:

> Why are women . . . still debarred from all executive posts in the Civil Service except those rare ones which leave only women under their command? . . . Why are women business directors almost wholly confined to the proprietors of acknowledged 'women's businesses', such as dressmaking or catering? . . . The woman boss is a matter for comic pictures and music-hall jokes and sly banter.[21]

Feminists such as Holtby and her friend Vera Brittain claimed that the continuing inequality was partly the result of protective labour laws. By restricting females from working at night or in certain occupations involving the use of noxious substances like lead (which might adversely affect them as future mothers), these reinforced the gender bias, since employers could claim that the women were unable to work on terms of strict equality with men.[22] But others took the view that 'insuring the race' was all important, by preventing women from being overworked or employed in trades unsuitable for them:

> we would suggest that the only differentiation between men and women which can be justified is such as has its basis in the need of preserving women's powers unimpaired for those primary activities which are connected with the family and the home.[23]

Holtby and Brittain responded by pointing out that the prohibitions on night working did not apply to nursing or domestic service, but merely to manufacturing processes. However, many workers in the protected industries – and particularly women trade union leaders – were not enthusiastic about the need for change. They feared that the loss of legal regulation might worsen the situation without bringing any corresponding benefits in the form of higher pay or more prestigious posts.

They were doubtless reinforced in that belief by the knowledge that in occupations without protection, such as teaching or domestic service, males were still paid more than females. In textile weaving, where male and female piece rates were the same, the men's greater stamina still enabled them to mind more looms than most of their women counterparts and they thus received higher wages. But the position here was complicated by the fact that although the majority of weavers were women, men dominated the supervisory grades. In 1931 over 24 per cent of all male weavers were foremen or overlookers, compared with less than 1 per cent of the women holding similar posts.[24] Likewise in hosiery, another predominantly female occupation, men's pay was nearly double that of the women, partly because they were in charge of a greater number of machines but also because in districts where there was little alternative male employment, as, for example, at Hinckley, Leicestershire, trade union agreements stipulated that certain tasks be reserved for them, even though women were quite capable of carrying them out.[25]

In some occupations, male trade unionists were determined to exclude females from the most skilled and lucrative positions by preventing them from receiving the necessary training. That applied in engineering and printing, among others, and, along with the youth of the female work force, it perhaps helped to account for the low level of female union membership in the 1920s. From a peak of 1,342,000 in 1920, the total fell to 835,000 in 1925 and 731,000 in 1931. Even women organizers in many of the large mixed unions felt discriminated against. As Mary Carlin of the Transport and General Workers' Union declared in 1925, male officials often regarded the organization of women 'as a side-line'.[26]

Nor did the setting up of additional trade boards, under legislation passed in 1918, rectify the pay inequalities. The boards were designed to provide a minimum wage for workers in certain low-paid industries, and originally it was intended to establish sixty of them to cover about three million workers, 70 per cent of whom were women.[27] However, in the face of employers' hostility,

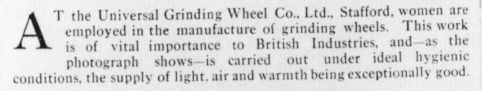

The Making of Grinding Wheels — a new *Industry* for *British women.*

Corner of shaping shop where the wheels are taken from the moulds and are deftly turned into shape by the girl operators.

AT the Universal Grinding Wheel Co., Ltd., Stafford, women are employed in the manufacture of grinding wheels. This work is of vital importance to British Industries, and—as the photograph shows—is carried out under ideal hygienic conditions, the supply of light, air and warmth being exceptionally good.

UNI

Universal Grinding Wheel Co., Ltd. Stafford ———————— England

Women did move into some new areas of mass production in the 1920s. (Advertisement in the Woman Engineer, June 1921*)*

especially in the distributive trades, and of deepening economic recession, that target was abandoned. Typical of the opposition encountered was the claim by the chairman of the Drapers' Chamber of Trade that raising pay to the proposed levels would merely cause more unemployment.[28] As a result of the various pressures, by 1925 only one and a half million workers were covered by boards, and retail distribution remained largely outside the system.

Even with this reduced coverage, about three-quarters of the workers involved were women and girls – a clear confirmation that they were the sector of the labour force receiving the lowest pay. Furthermore, when minimum rates were fixed, they continued to show gender differences. That was partly because of the different work carried out by men and women but it owed something, too, to the traditional belief that men ought to earn more because they had a family to support. In laundry work, while female operatives were paid $6\frac{1}{2}$d. or 7d. an hour, their male counterparts received 1s. $1\frac{1}{2}$d. an hour. Likewise in the manufacture of boot and floor polish, the 7½d. an hour paid to the females was little more than half the 1s. 1½d. paid to the males.[29]

Another difficulty was that in occupations without effective union organization the trade board rates were hard to enforce. This certainly applied in 1926–7, when the High Court established that women drift-net menders had been underpaid by the east coast trawler owners for whom they worked. The employers responded by persuading them to sign an agreement accepting £1 in settlement of their claim for back pay, instead of the £15 to which they were entitled.[30] Little attention was paid to the fact that these women might have family commitments or perhaps had to earn enough to live on. Society persisted in regarding female wages as pin-money. Or as the Fabian socialist Sidney Webb put it, there was a widespread assumption that a female always

> had some kind of family belonging to her, and [could] in times of hardship slip into a corner somewhere and share a crust of bread already being shared by too many of the family mouths, whereas the truth is that many women workers are without relatives, and a great many more have delicate or worn-out parents, or young brothers and sisters, or children to support.[31]

This belief that women could, in the last resort, rely upon someone else to support them was seen with particular clarity in respect of unemployment benefit. After the brief post-war boom had petered out in the autumn of 1920, unemployment levels rose steadily for men and women alike. By January 1921 there were half a million females officially recorded as unemployed, and the Lancashire cotton industry, suffering from a loss of exports, was badly affected. In 1923 it had over 21 per cent of its insured women workers unemployed, compared to 18 per cent of the insured males.[32] In these circumstances, in February 1922 the local committees administering the additional dole or 'uncovenanted' benefits paid to workers not entitled to the normal unemployment benefit, were told to withhold payments from certain types of applicant. These included married women whose partners were in full-time work and single persons living with relatives, provided the family income did not fall below 10s. a week. Although this directive was withdrawn by the minority Labour government in 1924, it was restored by the Conservatives a year later. And significantly, while just 3 per cent of *male* applicants were rejected on income grounds by the committees, no less than 15 per cent of the *females* were.[33] In addition, many women simply ceased to register at the labour exchange as conditions grew more stringent. 'In this way,' comments Martin Pugh, 'they began to lose out in the struggle for scarce resources within a very short time of acquiring the vote.'[34]

One victim of the system was Mrs Naylor of Mossley, who began work as a winder in a cotton mill in 1926 when she was 14. Two years later she lost her job and although she received benefit for a time, she was then disallowed because her father was working and she lived at home:

> every week we used to go out looking for work . . . all round t'mills, I've tramped many a mile. My father . . . kept me 12 months. . . . You might get a

week's work here and a week's work there. . . . It just depended how you were – they could choose. The good workers were kept on and the bad workers – 'you're not wanted this week'. . . . I used to stand in a bunch in t'yard and 'I'll have you and you this week' and you were lucky if you got in.[35]

The hardship and the humiliation of this situation, with youngsters dependent on parents who could not afford to keep them, remained in Mrs Naylor's memory. As she bitterly recalled, she was too poor even to replace her stockings when they were worn out. 'I used to patch them out of others, many a time I've had a knee patched . . . you wouldn't go out with a hole.'

A final aspect of female employment during these years was the importance of regional variations both in the proportion of women who went out to work and the positions they filled. Although domestic service employed more women than any other single occupation in the whole of England and Wales, absorbing around 23 or 24 per cent of the female work force in 1921 and 1931, this was not the case in Lancashire. There only 11 per cent of female workers in 1931 were servants, compared to almost 32 per cent engaged in textile manufacture. In addition, of all females aged 14 and above in the county in that year, 43.2 per cent declared an occupation. In England and Wales as a whole the figure was 34.2 per cent. In Wales itself, however, the situation was again different. Employment in the principality was concentrated in heavy industry (especially coal and steel) which offered little opportunity to women. As a result, in 1931 only 21 per cent of Welsh females aged 14 and above declared an occupation. Of those at work, more than a third were maids. Even then, as we shall see, many would-be servants were forced to leave the principality altogether in order to get a place.

Much the same was true of rural counties like Norfolk and Oxfordshire. Here, too, local jobs were in relatively short supply, at least outside the county towns of Norwich and Oxford, respectively, and of those who did work a third or more were in service. But in Greater London, where nearly 40 per cent of females aged 14 and above claimed an occupation in 1931, the job range was much wider. Although domestic service recruited nearly 23 per cent of the labour force, 12 per cent were engaged in the manufacture of clothing and a further 16.8 per cent worked as clerks and typists, an indication of the importance of administrative posts in the capital. This was a product of the recent expansion of Whitehall ministries and of the fact that many firms in insurance, banking and commerce were merging to create large London-based head offices. In the resultant rationalization and mechanization, male clerks and typists were displaced by cheaper females, who carried out the routine tasks.[36] By 1931 women and girls accounted for 43 per cent of the total clerical work force in London and the five Home Counties.[37] It was a trend that began during the First World War but was destined to continue throughout the inter-war period.

Against this background of a female labour force composed very largely of young, single women, who expected to continue working only until they married, we have now to examine the daily round of some of them.

Despite the reluctance of most girls to take up domestic service, with its low status, poor pay, and restricted leisure time, as we have seen it was household work which proved the decade's biggest single employer of women. As early as 1919 the Ministry of Reconstruction's Report on Domestic Service had concluded that the main reasons for the occupation's unpopularity were the long hours of duty, the lack of companionship, and the loss of standing which it entailed.

The fact cannot be denied that domestic workers are regarded by other workers as belonging to a lower social status. The distinctive dress which they are required to wear marks them out as a class apart, the cap being generally resented. It is sometimes stated that the differentiation in the quality of the food for the dining-room and that for the servants' hall or kitchen is another class distinction which leads to a spirit of bitterness. The custom of addressing domestic workers by their Christian or surname is one of the causes of the superior attitude adopted by workers recruited from the same or even a lower social status. Further, the attitude adopted by the Press and the stage is usually an unfortunate one, as servants are frequently represented as comic or flippant characters, and are held up to ridicule.[38]

The fact that they were not covered by the 1920 Unemployment Insurance Act added to the low esteem in which the job was held. Women who had previously been in insured posts and had then become servants found they were no longer

Edith May Moulding (b. 1901) in service. She became a servant in Pontypridd at the age of 18 but when this photograph was taken she was employed by Mr Howard Williams, shipowner, in Cardiff as an assistant cook. She was one of seven servants and was paid 10s. a month, for hours from 7 a.m. to 9 p.m. She had a half day off every week and a half day on alternate Sundays. She shared a bedroom with two younger maids and was expected to be in bed by 10 p.m. (National Museum of Wales: Welsh Folk Museum)

entitled to the benefits to which they had contributed in their earlier employment. In addition, prior to the 1928 Representation of the People Act, which gave the vote to all women over 21, resident maids were unable to vote. Only women with a property qualification in their own right or whose husband had such a qualification were enfranchised under the 1918 legislation.

The reluctance of unemployed women to become maids at a time when many middle- and upper-class familes were seeking domestic help caused much hostile comment in the Press and elsewhere, just as it had in the immediate aftermath of the war. 'Servants, or the women who register themselves as unemployed servants, prefer to remain unemployed rather than take a wage of £30 a year,' declared the *Western Mail* severely. 'Now that the demand for women's labour in factories is so much reduced, it is surprising that there should be continued unwillingness to give good domestic service for board and a reasonable wage. For the young girl a situation in a small middle-class home with a thoughtful and practical mistress means, in most cases, a training which is a valuable preparation for marriage.'[39] The women themselves were not convinced.

In some cases the problem was eased by an increased recruitment of day servants. At the end of the 1920s around one-third of all the maids employed on Merseyside were non-resident and a similar trend was apparent in London.[40] 'Dailies' were particularly common in one-servant households since employers were glad to be freed from the need to accommodate a maid, with all the extra cost and pressure on space that that involved. At a time when many families were moving into smaller, modern homes or flats these were important considerations. From the servant's point of view this solution had the merit of enabling her to remain in contact with her own home and to enjoy the company of friends out of working hours.

But even for residential servants conditions did improve over the decade. More free time was allowed – usually a half-day per week and one free evening, compared with one day per month off before 1914.[41] Food and accommodation were also better. Although it was still common for young servants in larger households to share a room, more senior staff had a place of their own. The fact that gas had replaced coal for heating and cooking in many homes obviated the need for maids to rise at a very early hour in order to lay fires. This was a point seized upon by gas suppliers in their advertisements. The British Commercial Gas Association, for example, drew attention to what it labelled 'The Servants' Magna Charta':

Freedom from the slavery of carrying coals and laying fires. Freedom from kitchen grates that won't cook. Freedom from cleaning out sooty flues and dusty fireplaces. Freedom for servants to get their work done more quickly and with less drudgery.[42]

Bathrooms with hot and cold running water were found in a growing number of homes, and these removed the need for maids to struggle upstairs with heavy cans of hot water for washing. The use of laundries and other outside providers of services, such as bakers and confectioners, further eliminated tasks formerly carried out in the home.

Nevertheless, domestic work continued to involve much hard and menial labour, especially for younger staff. Mrs Neal of Bath, who entered service in 1918 when she was 14, remembered having to rise at 6.30 a.m. to blacklead the stove. Her next chores were to clean the fireplaces and light the fires, jobs over which she 'shed a good many tears'. She next swept and dusted the dining-room and laid the table for breakfast. After that it was time to prepare breakfast, and to eat her own meal, before the family came down.

I had to carry all food on a dumb waiter which was nearly bigger than myself. . . . After breakfast there was a host of washing up to be done. Then I had four bedrooms to sweep and dust, bathroom, landing and stairs, scrub front door step, polish large hall, then kitchen and scullery. Prepare vegetables for lunch . . . with various other jobs thrown in.

Time for lunch at 1 p.m. Mine was portioned out in the dining-room, which I collected after a ring of the bell, which each [of the children] took it in turn to ring.

After lunch clear table, wash up, leave everything tidy. Get myself ready to be out with the girls [the daughters of the house] at 2 p.m. The lady expected me to dress as a nursemaid. . . . We lived at the seaside. Summer days I had to take the girls to the beach hut and make sure the elder girl did not venture in the sea too far. Tea was set picnic style. . . . Then home for an hour to play in the garden. . . . Bedtime [for the children] 8.30 p.m. in summer, 7 p.m. in winter. I had every other Sunday afternoon and evening off and every Wednesday I used to go to Guides. Any other outing I tentatively asked for was not very well received, sometimes granted, mostly not. I had to be in at 9.30 p.m. and that was my life for the first five years of slavery.[43]

During these years lack of alternative work caused many girls to take up domestic duties because of pressure from the labour exchange, or because they were anxious not to be a burden on their family. 'When I realized in the 1920s that domestic service would have to be my lot, because the depression in the Welsh mining valleys left little else, I was very unhappy,' wrote Mrs Fugill. 'I didn't want to be a servant. I heard of a vacancy as scullery maid at the Monmouth Training College and thought at least I would be serving my own kind and not be serving people with money to buy service.'[44] She started work in 1926 and remained for three years before going to London, where she became a housemaid in St Leonard's Hospital, Shoreditch. Her prime reason for moving was to earn more money, but it meant she had little opportunity to visit her home and family in Wales.

The training schemes set up by the Central Committee on Women's Employment, in association with the Ministry of Labour, also served to channel unemployed women and girls into domestic service. By 1930 thirty-seven non-residential centres were in operation, offering home training courses to about four thousand women a year. Most were located in the depressed areas of the north of England and South Wales, with twelve centres in Durham and Tyneside and twelve in South Wales. Others were opened in the Lanarkshire coalfield and in

Wigan and Workington. In addition there were a few residential centres, some of them – for example, at Market Harborough, Leicestershire and Long Benton, Newcastle upon Tyne – concerned primarily with preparing girls for domestic work in the Dominions.[45] By the end of 1930 almost fifty thousand trainees had passed through the various homecraft, homemaker and home training courses organized by the Central Committee since the beginning of the 1920s. More than five thousand of them had also been provided with uniforms to enable them to take up employment.[46]

Despite the importance attached to these schemes by the Ministry of Labour, they did not always run smoothly. One problem was the securing of suitable places for trainees once they had completed their thirteen-week course. That was particularly true of the youngest recruits. 'The reluctance of parents to let their daughters go far from home is the cause of much of the difficulty experienced in placing [juveniles],' complained one Ministry official. 'In long-distance placing the possibility of putting the trainee in a district where she may have friends or relations should always be kept in mind.'[47]

Just what this meant in practice can be seen from the records of the Ystrad centre in the Rhondda, where fifty-two girls were trained between June 1928, when it opened, and the end of the year. Of these, nine were unable to get places when the courses ended and one was too ill. Of the remaining forty-two, thirteen got employment in London, twenty obtained posts in Wales, in four cases the destination was not noted, and of the remainder, employment was found in places as far afield as Barnstaple, Eastbourne, Bath, Weymouth and Weston-super-Mare.[48] Twenty-nine of the trainees were only 16 when they began their course, and the sense of isolation they must have experienced when they were sent away is easy to imagine. In addition, rates of pay were often poor, with £20 a year (or less than 10s. a week) a common wage; some girls earned as little as 7s. or 8s. a week.[49] In an unfamiliar environment, surrounded by strangers, many found difficulty in settling in, while a number were exploited and ill-treated by employers. 'The problem of Welsh girls coming to London, at times without references, money, or adequate luggage, has engaged our attention for some time past,' declared leaders of the National Vigilance Association in a letter to the *Western Mail* in June 1926. 'Every week, with great regularity, our workers at Paddington assist such girls. We have been greatly impressed by the casual way in which the decision to come to London is in most cases made, and the total absence of any sort of common practical arrangements on the part of the parents.'[50] The Association was concerned with the moral welfare of girls and it gave numerous examples of cases its members had encountered. One involved a young Welsh girl who had arrived at Paddington station expecting to be met by her mistress. Whilst she was waiting a man had approached her and had offered to take her to her destination by omnibus. The girl took fright, however, and he went off. At this stage a National Vigilance Association worker noticed her plight and spoke to her. 'She had no money and was in great distress of mind. A message was sent through to her prospective mistress and the girl was looked after until she arrived.' The police were given a description of the man who had accosted her.[51]

On another occasion, a 16-year-old girl was discovered in tears. She had run away from an unsatisfactory situation but had no money, and was trying to beg the return half of a cheap excursion ticket. The girl was found accommodation until arrangements could be made for her to go home.[52] During 1929 679 girls were helped by the Association at Paddington station alone, and almost another thousand were assisted at other venues. By the early 1930s that annual total had risen to almost five thousand cases.[53]

Sometimes young migrants lost touch with their families because of their inability to write a letter home or because they lacked the cash to purchase notepaper and stamps. In 1930 a mother from Pontypridd wrote to the National Vigilance Association asking for help because she had not heard from her daughter, who was working in Hackney. A caseworker visited the employer and was able to reassure the anxious mother that her daughter was 'very happy & comfortable', and that her mistress regarded her so highly that she was treated as 'one of the family'.[54]

Nevertheless, except for servants working in big and prestigious households, where living conditions were comfortable and staffs large, domestic service remained the least popular form of female employment during the 1920s and the most widespread. By 1931 about 1.3 million women and girls worked as maids in England and Wales, a total which approached the pre-war figure. The only difference was that the rise in the number of households over the intervening period meant that they were spread more thinly among families than had been the case before 1914.

Factory work, despite its hardships, at least had the advantage of a fixed working day, while operatives employed in large groups could enjoy the companionship and camaraderie of their colleagues. 'I was very happy,' remembered one woman of her life as a cotton weaver. 'We had a lot of fun . . . as well as working hard.' Another cotton operative recalled how older workers would play tricks on the raw recruits. 'They used to . . . want a glass hammer and a bucket with a big hole in the bottom – all sorts of silly things they used to send you for. . . . You're green when you start . . . I got wise to them in the end.'[55]

Discipline was strict, however, partly because of the youth of many of the workers but also to ensure the production process proceeded smoothly. Even benevolent employers like Cadbury's had firm rules concerning staff conduct. As might be anticipated in a food manufacturing firm, much emphasis was placed on the importance of hygiene. Each Monday morning operatives had to appear in a clean uniform. This had the merit of ensuring that outer garments coming from homes of dubious cleanliness were kept away from the production area, being stored instead in special dressing rooms. Muslin caps had to be worn as necessary, and senior girls were required to keep their hair close to the head. Juniors must either have plaits or, if their hair was short, they had to wear caps.[56]

Within the Bournville factory, males and females were strictly segregated, and the corridors were so constructed that they did not even meet on their way to and from the workrooms. No girl was allowed to enter a room or office away from her own working area without a pass from her forewoman and in the passages connecting the workplace and the dining-room strict order had to be maintained. There was to be no running, pushing, linking of arms, or reading, and when

Factory workers from Briggs cotton mill, Park Bridge, Lancashire, on a day excursion to Blackpool. With unemployment this kind of companionship disappeared, along with the weekly wage. (Tameside Local Studies Library, Stalybridge)

groups of operatives entered or left a room they had to remain behind their leaders.

Good timekeeping was insisted upon in all factories, with fines or even dismissal the fate of those who offended. Mary Welch, who worked in a leather factory at Hoxton, London, remembered that when she and her friends went out for their luncheon break, they were always careful to be back 'a bit early because if you got in one minute past you'd lose the half hour'. They worked forty-eight hours a week, finishing at 6.30 p.m. on most nights and 7 p.m. on Fridays, 'because the half hour made up forty-eight hours. You'd work right until the last minute and then you'd have to queue up all the way around the room and draw your wages [in] your own time. And every Friday you never knew if you were going to get the sack or not.'[57] Mrs Welch also recalled the unhygienic working conditions:

We'd have to use glue and paste and you had no meal break or any thing, except your hour for lunch. . . . So if you wanted to . . . have a sandwich or the girl

Women working patent cotton underwear machines at the Milanese Hosiery and Textile Co. Ltd, Ilkeston, Derbyshire, at the end of the First World War. (Trustees of the Imperial War Museum, London)

would bring you round a cup of tea, you'd have to eat it with the glue and the paste on your hands, still standing – you could never sit. . . . If you weren't on your bench, the foreman would get the idea that you were in the toilet, and then you'd get timed. He'd send somebody out after you and you'd walk out so sheepish.

You might talk at work, but you'd check to see whether or not he was looking. I've had many a punch in my back to get on with the work.

Textile mills were very noisy on account of the machinery. Within the weaving sheds, workers had to communicate with one another by signals because of the deafening clatter of the looms. There was much short-time working, too, during these years, which hit pay packets. Mrs Emma Kirk, who began weaving at the age of 14½ in 1925, eventually progressed to being in charge of four looms. Then came the depression:

sometimes I'd only have three looms, sometimes I'd only have two. We were waiting for warps you know. And then . . . you were made to stop with one

[loom], you couldn't come home and sometimes I'd only take 5 shillings home.[58]

Another Lancashire weaver remembered the unpleasant smell of the oil used after the looms had been cleaned at the weekend. 'I used to dread Monday mornings.'[59]

During the 1920s women's share of jobs in manufacturing industry declined from 26 per cent to 22 per cent. In 1929 female unemployment in the insured industries was already over 60 per cent of the male rate and by February 1931 the women were suffering more severely than the men in many industries. For example, while 48.4 per cent of female workers were unemployed in cotton, only 45.6 per cent of males were. In pottery the respective figures were 47.2 per cent and 35.5 per cent, and in food manufacturing 21.3 per cent and 11.1 per cent.[60] Many of the unemployed women also missed the company of their fellow workers, as well as the loss of earnings.

The experiences of Maggie Newbery, who worked in the twisting department of a Bradford mill, serve to underline the financial uncertainties of the decade and the seriousness of female unemployment.

Maggie worked for the firm of Unwin's until it closed in 1921:

We were all given a month's notice, we could leave any time as we got other employment. This was not so easy, several mills had closed down, others were on short time. Unwin's doubled our last week's wages. . . . I drew over £5. I stayed till the last week.[61]

Soon afterwards she saw an advertisement for an assistant at Singer's sewing-machine shop in the town and decided to apply. They wanted someone to follow up new sales by visiting the homes of customers and showing them how to use the various attachments on the machines. Although the wage was only £1 5s. a week, out of which she paid her mother 18s. for board and lodging, she decided to take the post. She was happy to leave mill life and, in particular, the need to rise at 6 a.m. each day. She also took sewing cotton to sell to her customers on commission, and this usually brought in an extra 2s. a week.[62]

Life proceeded uneventfully until 1926 when the depression deepened in Bradford and factories were closed because of the miners' strike. In an effort to cut costs Singer's reduced their staff and Maggie was given a week's notice. She had to sign on at the labour exchange and received benefit of 15s. a week. This was less than she had been paying her mother, so she handed over the whole sum and was given 2s. 6d. in return as pocket-money:

I answered all kinds of advertisements but I seemed to be really up against it and the weeks slipped by. I was able to help in the house and I altered dresses and made old ones into new ones or into aprons. We were always making do and mending.

Eventually she noticed an advertisement for probationer nurses at a local mental asylum. 'No previous experience necessary, wages £2 2s. per week, from which

19/- will be deducted for food.' She applied and was successful. 'Then began another phase of my life.'[63]

One of the growth areas of women's work in the 1920s was in retail distribution. But this was an occupation where working conditions varied greatly, with employment in a large department store or major private emporium rated more highly than that in cheaper multiple stores or in corner shops on the fringe of a town. Mrs Windor, who worked in a grocer's shop in Lancaster, remembered that shortly before she left school, Woolworth's opened there, 'but on principle I wouldn't work in Woolworth's. I could have been getting a lot more money than I was getting in the grocer's shop, but because it was a privately owned firm it was a little bit better. It was just snobbery.'[64]

Cicely Colyer of Folkestone similarly took much pride in her three-year apprenticeship at Plummer Roddis, the town's leading drapery store. Apprentices who aspired to be showroom girls there were expected to come from 'good homes'. They were chosen with care and were trained in elocution, deportment and manners as well as in such technical matters as how to distinguish the quality of cloth, how to conduct a fitting, and the proper way to fold clothes. Within these large stores there was a rigid staff hierarchy. Selling was the province of the senior assistants, who were paid on commission for goods purchased. They were helped by the apprentices, who did the packing, found chairs for the customers, ran errands and carried out such daily chores as 'dressing out' counters and display cabinets, and dusting, before the start of the day's business.[65] At the top were the buyers. 'Female buyers wore stunning gowns made of silk moiré with satin trains to demonstrate their status.' The buyers also controlled the price of merchandise. More expensive lines, such as exclusive model gowns, were kept in special glass cases and prices were only quoted on request.[66]

At F. Cape & Co. in Oxford, former assistants remembered the stringent discipline, with gossiping among the staff forbidden. All were very much under the eye of their employers, who had desks in the shop, and the assistants would use code words to warn one another of the approach of a senior member of the firm. They were expected to take pains with their dress and appearance, and all had to wear black. They provided their own clothes, with the lady buyers at Cape's allowed to wear black silk or satin dresses. As in almost all shops at that time, hours were long, from 9 a.m. to 8 p.m. or 10 p.m. on Saturdays.[67] Not until 1928 did the Shop (Hours of Closing) Act lay down that on four days a week stores must be closed by 8 p.m., on one day by 9 p.m., and on the sixth day by 1 p.m.[68]

Many girls chose shop work because it enjoyed a higher status than domestic service or factory employment. The relative cleanliness of the environment and the absence of industrial noise were other attractions, even in less prestigious small shops. The phasing out of the 'living in' system, which had been common before the war, also helped to make the work appealing. However, at some of the large London department stores, like Bourne and Hollingsworth, and John Lewis, the practice still continued, partly because of the difficulty of young workers finding respectable accommodation at prices they could afford. But it was a policy which gave employers great control over their staff. In 1920, when there was a strike at John Lewis's over the issue of trade union recognition, two hundred girls who were 'living in' were given twenty-four hours to leave the hostels. With the union's help they managed to find fresh accommodation, but the firm continued to refuse union recognition, and after six weeks the strike collapsed.[69]

For some women, shop work opened up opportunities to exercise specialist skills. Female hairdressers and beauticians increased rapidly during these years, as fashion-conscious women were recommended to have a permanent wave in order to look their best even when dancing 'the giddiest foxtrot' and 'the craziest jazz'. As early as June 1926, the hairdressing firm of Feminix in Albemarle Street, London, was extolling the merits of Miss Helen Laving, 'admitted to be the most accomplished woman Permanent waver and proved world's Record Speed holder'. Feminix promised 'Women's Service for Women', instead of relying upon male hairdressers, as many of its competitors did.[70] By 1931 there were over 33,000 females working as hairdressers and beauticians in England and Wales, compared with less than 6,000 so employed a decade earlier. Forty-three per cent of the 1931 total were under 21.

However, whatever the attractions of employment in a shop, one doctor at least considered the health of assistants to be worse than that of women and girls engaged in many other occupations. The long hours of standing caused flat feet, varicose veins and inflamed toe joints, and there were widespread problems with dyspepsia and menstrual disorders. The space behind the counter in most shops was so narrow that the assistant had to stand in the same position for almost the whole day. Staff were expected to remain alert and pleasant even when there were no customers, and where seats were provided for them it was rare for these to be used: 'It has been told me over and over again that if any girl does sit down the shopwalker will find some other job for her to do . . . and quite likely she will not have a job next week.'[71]

Large stores usually had staff canteens and other welfare facilities but in smaller shops, meals often had to be taken in the selling area and were, in consequence, interrupted by the need to serve customers. One woman, who was the sole assistant in the shop, 'was found crouching behind the counter taking her meal as unostentatiously as possible from a lower shelf. There were no means of cooking, and no water supply inside the shop.'[72] In other cases meals were eaten in dirty stock rooms.

Girls working in greengrocer's shops were considered to have the hardest work. Apart from having to lift heavy fruit and vegetables, they spent much time sorting the produce, grading it, throwing away sub-standard items, and tidying up, as well as serving.[73] In order to attract passing trade and to keep the greengrocery as fresh as possible, open-fronted shops were common and the girls' health suffered as a result of standing for hours in the cold during the winter months.

Other problems arose from the 'sweated' labour of juveniles in all kinds of shops and the fact that employees over 25 enjoyed little security of tenure. This was especially true of drapery stores, where female staff predominated and there was a widespread use of part-time labour on the busy days of the week, such as Fridays and Saturdays. This led to full-time workers being kept to a minimum. One large firm on Merseyside regularly engaged a hundred or more extra girls at the end of the week. Some were former employees, who had left to be married and were glad to earn a little cash. Others were recruited through employment exchanges from the ranks of the unemployed. If they proved satisfactory they were sent, as and when required, to the same firm on one or two days a week. They worked from about midday to 6.30 p.m., or 8 p.m. on Saturdays, and were paid 4s. 3d. a day, plus two meals. However, in the early 1930s if a girl worked for one day only, excluding her meals she was just 9d. in pocket because 1s. was taken from the 4s. 3d. as her insurance contribution, and a further 2s. 6d. was deducted for each day she worked from her weekly unemployment benefit of 15s. Refusal to take a job, however, would lead to the benefit being stopped altogether. One inducement for a competent girl was that she might be asked to join the permanent staff.[74]

Autocratic employers like the octogenarian John Lewis in Oxford Street added to this sense of insecurity. According to one former employee, he would sometimes take a dislike to a staff member for no reason at all and would go up to him or her 'and ask one or two questions about their length of service with the firm and then would say "You have been here too long. Go to the counting house and get your money."' At other times he would approach an assistant and say: 'I did not engage you.' When she responded that one of the senior staff had appointed her, Lewis would reply, 'He had no right to do so.' The person so engaged would then be dismissed. This happened to a young woman engaged for the 'foreign fancy department. During the first morning there she was accosted by Lewis and told to get her money, which meant only the day's pay.' As she had come from the provinces, the buyer and other members of the staff collected some money to cover her fare home.[75]

Overall there was a rapid increase in the number of retail outlets during the 1920s. These ranged from shops selling ready-made clothes to those offering sweets, cakes and biscuits. Kiosks were opened wherever there was passing pedestrian trade, such as near to railway stations or omnibus termini, and small sweet shops, some of them also stocking toys, were found in many High Street locations.[76] Some women also ran open-air stalls, like the Lambeth moneylender who combined her financial transactions with a business selling watercress, celery and other salad vegetables. Queenie Thomas, who lived in the area, remembered that 'people had to deal off her because she lent them money and some of the old rubbish that she used to serve up to them – all stale stuff. I never had no money off her, but I wouldn't have the stuff. . . . It was a large family of them because she'd got another sister further down the road with a stall.'[77]

Sometimes young millworkers took up part-time shop work in order to supplement their wages. One Bradford girl remembered taking a Saturday afternoon job at Woolworth's when she had finished at the factory:

I'd . . . run home, . . . have my dinner, get washed and changed and be . . . up at Woolworth's for one o'clock. I worked there from one o'clock till nine and it was five shillings. If you were on short time you could ask to go in all day Saturday. It was ten shillings for all day. I went there in the first place because we only got one-and-six spending money, and if we wanted to go dancing, we could only afford to go once. So five shillings was like a fortune.[78]

Waitresses employed in one of the expanding areas of women's employment in the 1920s. (The author)

The growing popularity of eating out led to a proliferation of tea-shops and restaurants, where women were employed as waitresses and kitchen staff. The large department stores, too, began to open cafés, and in the 1931 census, for the first time, a new category of restaurant and refreshment room counter-hands was included, as well as waitresses, washers up and restaurant keepers. At the beginning of the 1930s well over a hundred thousand women and girls were employed in these various categories, most of them working very long hours. Anna Dagnall, who worked in her grandmother's café near the Liverpool docks, recalled that her experiences there encouraged her to join the Labour Party. She was shocked by 'the rough side of life' that she witnessed and 'the outcasts of the First World War' whom she met. 'Young girl as I was, the impression of poverty and injustice was pervasive.'[79]

Wives played a major part in running many of the smaller restaurants and the cheaper eating houses, such as fish and chip shops and pie shops, while tea-shop ownership was regarded as a genteel occupation for spinsters.

Except in the case of the Cooperative stores, few workers joined a trade union. Often, as at the John Lewis store, this was because of employer hostility, but the youth of the labour force and its low pay (which made contributions difficult to afford) were other factors discouraging involvement in the labour movement. Nevertheless, despite all the disadvantages, shop work remained popular. As Gillian Darcy points out, more than any other unskilled or semi-skilled occupation, it offered women contact with people – the human element.[80]

EMPLOYER. "Look at this letter from Messrs. Smith, beautifully typed."
TYPIST. "Um—and the grammar's excellent too."

*Not all typists enjoyed good relations with
their employer as this* Punch *cartoon shows.*

Finally, there was a large expansion in the number of female clerical workers, particularly typists, telephonists and general clerks. Most were young and single, and they rarely held responsible positions. In the Civil Service, for example, the vast majority worked as typists and writing assistants, this last being a clerical grade for women only. The biggest employing department was the Post Office, which recruited 68 per cent of all females in the Civil Service at this time.[81] Yet, despite the often dull and routine nature of many of the tasks they performed, girls welcomed the security and the status which went with government employment. The fact that they had to resign when they married worried very few in these lower grades, since most saw the job merely as a means of filling the interval between leaving school and getting married. When they left to marry they had the added benefit of a gratuity which amounted to one month's pay for each year they had worked, up to a maximum of twelve years. This was in lieu of the pension they would not now receive, and many valued it as a help in setting up their home.[83] Friendships were formed with the girls from the office and they spent a large part of their leisure hours with these friends, going to the cinema or the theatre, attending concerts, and even going on holiday together.[83]

For those working outside the Civil Service, conditions varied according to the size and status of the firm which was employing them. Banks, insurance offices and the public services were more prestigious than industrial companies. One woman who entered an export office in London, after leaving commercial college, remembered being warned by her aunts to steer clear of offices connected with factory premises. She remained with the firm for six years, until she married in 1926. By then she had become secretary to one of the directors. But in her early days as a junior shorthand-typist she had been expected to open letters, make telephone calls, go to the bank, do the filing, make the tea and coffee, and organize the post book. As a secretary, she had a close personal relationship with her boss and enjoyed the responsibilities the job offered her.[84] It was, in fact, this close personal contact with the boss which gave the shorthand-typist or secretary her status within the firm. As Teresa Davy has neatly put it, 'she was . . . associated with authority although she never actually wielded it'.[85]

Most girls attended a commercial college for one or two years before taking up employment. There they learnt basic office skills and were taught to dress demurely, to speak correctly, and to be discreet and tactful. But office work had its darker side. In smaller city offices, a typist might have to share a room with several other girls as part of a pool, or she could be carefully segregated in a small office connected to a warehouse or minor manufacturing or professional enterprise, where she was the only female staff member. Frances Donaldson, an upper middle-class woman who worked for a time in an office, remembered the hardships of some of her humbler colleagues.

> I was shocked by their conditions and touched by their lives. Typists were very badly paid . . . and extremely hard-worked. . . . [The] large pool of ordinary typists were paid twenty-five shillings. Most of them subsisted on buns and coffee or tea, and their clothes were few and poor. They were often treated, in my view, with insufficient courtesy. . . . Typists in offices, living on a pittance, could be kept at work until ten o'clock at night at the whim of the great man [their employer]. For this they got no overtime; sometimes they did not even get thanked.[86]

Despite such disadvantages, however, office work gave girls from an upper working-class or lower middle-class background an entrée into a respectable occupation away from the limitations of manual labour. Although it was not a profession, its educational requirements (usually some secondary schooling or commercial college training) and its emphasis on the importance of discretion and tact, gave it a certain standing. It was also an occupation dominated increasingly by women. After the First World War shorthand-typing was considered a 'cissy job for men'.[87] Yet significantly, the more senior and lucrative managerial and accountancy posts remained the prerogative of men. Even in the mid-1920s there were only ten female chartered accountants, compared to nearly seven and a half thousand males with that qualification.[88] It was an indication of the limitations on women's progress in the office world.

CHAPTER 5

Making Ends Meet: Working-class Family Life

The doorsteps and window-sills of the houses are worn hollow. Once a week, sometimes twice, the women clean them with brown or white rubbing stone: the same with portions of the pavement immediately outside their front doors. . . . [A] married woman could be distinguished from a single by a glance at her facial expression. Marriage scored on their faces a kind of preoccupied, faded, lack-lustre air as though they were constantly being plagued by some problem. As they were. How to get a shilling, and, when obtained, how to make it do the work of two. Though it was not so much a problem as a whole-time occupation to which no salary was attached, not to mention the sideline of risking one's life to give children birth and being responsible for their upbringing afterwards.

Walter Greenwood, *Love on the Dole* (1958 edn), pp. 5, 20–1.
(The novel was first published in 1933.)

The cult of domesticity which so influenced attitudes towards women in middle-class families was applied with equal force to the working classes. Pressure on females to accept their role as full-time managers of a household came from many quarters, even though it was realized that not all would marry, and, of those who did, some at least could not afford to give up outside employment. Nevertheless, it was an ideal at which most women aimed, with the majority of working-class wives considering it a sign of social progress and a symbol of emancipation when they were able to stop working for wages and could rely on their husband for support.[1] In this they differed from their middle-class feminist counterparts, who saw 'freedom' in terms of the right to take up outside work in an occupation of their choice.

Once they had left school working-class girls were normally expected to move into full-time employment, at any rate until they married. During that time they would contribute to household income and thereby ease the family's financial position. In the textile industry, according to Mrs Naylor of Mossley, young workers handed over almost all their pay packet to their mother, only keeping

Washing clothes at the rear of the house,
c. 1930. The laborious nature of the
work is all too clear. (National
Museum of Wales: Welsh Folk
Museum)

about a penny in the shilling for their personal use. Another woman remembered
that up to the time she married she was allowed to keep just 2s. a week from her
wages, the rest being 'tipped . . . up to mother'.[2] As they grew older, a number of
girls resented this arrangement and some insisted on retaining a larger proportion
of their pay. But most youngsters accepted the situation as a normal part of family
life.

Within the home it was the wife's responsibility to do the cooking, cleaning,
washing, shopping, weekly budgeting and other domestic chores upon which the
smooth running of the home depended. 'I married on the understanding that it was
the wife's job to be the careful thrifty housewife and to stay at home to manage the
house to the best of my ability,' declared a Liverpool woman.[3] To be an efficient
manager added to a wife's self-respect. But should she fail, when times were hard,
then she might receive abuse and even physical violence from her husband. 'Many
husbands' threats to beat their wives formed a significant undercurrent in couples'
silences about money,' wrote Ayers and Lambertz of conditions in Liverpool. As a
last resort, if rent arrears had built up, the family might have to do a 'moonlight flit',
perhaps hiring a barrow or a horse and cart to remove their scanty belongings to a
new neighbourhood where they were not known.[4]

Although a husband and children, especially the older girls, might assist with
the domestic chores, only if the mother were dead or incapacitated would

Mother and daughter on baking day at Abercynon. (National Museum of Wales: Welsh Folk Museum)

someone else – probably a daughter or sister – assume those duties on a long-term basis. In Birmingham, Lil Perry, as the oldest child, remembered taking charge of her brothers and sisters when their mother went into hospital for a lengthy stay:

> our kids used to cry for our Mom . . . I nearly killed our Winnie . . . I fed her that bleedin' much I nearly killed her. Farley's rusks and Nestles milk. I used to feed her every ten minutes.[5]

It was with relief that she relinquished her responsibilities when her mother returned home.

In many households incomes were small and uncertain, especially in families affected by the high unemployment of these years or when the head of the household was a widow or a man in casual employment. In those circumstances the skills and ingenuity of the mother were of major importance in ensuring the comfort and security of her family. Much of the work carried out involved heavy physical labour – carrying water, bringing in coal, handling washing, and scrubbing floors. Health was often undermined as a consequence, especially as many women reduced their own food intake in order to give more to their husband and children. Violet Harris in Lambeth suffered from malnutrition during the 1920s when her husband was unemployed: 'many a time I never got . . . a good meal. I always reckon . . . being hungry was something to do with my Ada being born deficient.'[6]

Eleanor Rathbone wrote sadly of the way these sacrifices showed themselves in the women's haggard appearance during early middle age:

> the lines round their mouth and eyes, their complexion and the texture of their skins, . . . the prematurely thinned or whitened hair, the stooping shoulders and dragging gait all seem to testify to an endurance of physical discomfort and weariness so habitual and so habitually repressed that it has become subsconscious.[7]

Among older wives there were the serious effects of repeated pregnancies as well. An eminent obstetrician estimated in 1931 that one in ten of all pregnant women was disabled in some way as a result of childbirth, with anaemia, back pains and various gynaecological problems widespread. Partly for this reason, younger mothers increasingly welcomed the idea of contraception.

It was to ease the lot of these women that 'new feminists' like Eleanor Rathbone campaigned for the payment of family endowments as part of the State's social welfare programme. Such allowances would provide mothers with an independent income to spend on their children instead of their being reliant on the goodwill and earning capacity of their husband, or their own money-making abilities.[8] For Rathbone, this approach also had the advantage of removing one of the arguments against equal pay for women, since it would no longer be possible to claim that men must be paid more because they had a family to support. If the endowment covered a major part of the expense of bringing up children that excuse lost its validity.

During the First World War, certain sections of the Press had emphasized the importance of the female domestic role. After the war those views intensified, with newspapers and magazines including in their 'women's pages' lengthy articles on motherhood and mothercraft. Even left-wing journals like *Labour Woman* devoted much space to baby competitions, housewives' competitions and the importance of 'mothercraft', with a page entitled Motherhood and Mothercraft becoming a regular feature in 1927.[9]

The trade union movement also accepted that women's duties and interests should lie in the domestic sphere, not merely because this would remove a potential source of cheap labour from the market but because it was their rightful place. In 1924 Margaret Bondfield, a leading union activist who was destined to be the first female Cabinet minister, addressed the Independent Labour Party's summer school on the theme 'Woman's Place in the Community'. She told a somewhat sceptical audience that 'woman's greatest opportunity and service was in the home'. Although a number of feminists argued that worthwhile employment was superior to the role of the homemaker, Bondfield rejected this:

> The woman who fulfils the function belonging to her sex, who builds up the life of the family around her, who recognizes the importance of bringing to the service of the home every new development of science, who realizes that her job

Pupils at Wingrave School, Buckinghamshire, in the 1920s. Cookery lessons were organized during the spring term, when a classroom was converted into a kitchen and the peripatetic teacher employed to teach domestic subjects arrived with her equipment. The girls made their pinafores during the previous autumn term. It was part of the general drive to inculcate housewifery skills into the rising generation of working-class females. (Mrs M. Horn)

is to create an environment for every child, and such an influence . . . as to raise the whole line of civilization to a higher place – that woman is doing the greatest work in the world.[10]

Such lofty sentiments must have seemed a world away from the humdrum and arduous realities of life experienced by many of the women in her audience.

The education system also contributed to the general debate, with efforts made to improve the housewifery skills of older girls in elementary schools. In Manchester the number of domestic science teachers employed rose from sixty-four to ninety-nine between 1924 and 1934, and the time girls spent on domestic subjects also increased.[11] Similarly in London around 70,000 girls were receiving instruction in 325 domestic science centres by 1931.[12] Lessons covered not merely basic subjects such as cookery, laundrywork and simple first aid, but hygiene in the home, the repair of broken china, toymaking, and child care. At Bridgend/Penybont Girls' Homemaking Centre in 1922, pupils were taught how to clean felt hats and remove spots from clothing as well as more usual domestic chores. In November and December they also brought in young children to the centre so that they might learn in a practical way how to bath and care for them.[13] Again in 1920, 1921 and 1926, periods of high unemployment and distress in much of industrial Wales, girls at schools in the principality were taught to prepare and serve free dinners to necessitous fellow pupils. At Hannah Street

Girls' School, Barry, meals were provided for over one hundred girls and infants during June 1921. Earlier in that year a party of pupils had been taken to see some nearly completed council houses. The clerk of works pointed out to them the special merits of the semi-detached dwellings, with their labour-saving equipment, open spaces, and improved drainage.[14]

The emphasis on child welfare was seen, too, in the forging of links between schools and nearby clinics. At Penarth, South Wales, senior girls spent an afternoon a week in an infant welfare clinic, and at Darwen, Lancashire, 13- and 14-year-old pupils attended maternity centres to gain practical experience in child rearing, so that they would know how to look after their own children when the time came.[15] Doris Hadfield, who left school at Hyde, Cheshire, in 1926, when she was 14, remembered spending several weeks at a local maternity home. 'Each school in the district had two representatives who would go there for six weeks. . . . We would have one week in the upstairs rooms. Then we would have another week in the kitchens. Then another week in the laundry, and . . . the final tuition came as we were taught how to set the tables and prepare some sort of meal.'[16] The benefit the girls obtained from this instruction appears somewhat

Margaret Rees and her sister on washing day at Abercynon, c. 1920. (National Museum of Wales: Welsh Folk Museum)

problematic. Most seem to have learned their homemaking skills from their mother and to have regarded the school courses as irrelevant. 'We just made little cakes and soups and things like that,' declared a former pupil dismissively.[17]

Against this background of determined domesticity, it is not surprising that Mary Craddock, a Tyneside miner's daughter, born in 1924, should remember the fireside as the centre of activity in her home, with her mother as its presiding deity:

> She was always doing something at the hearth – black-leading the grate, putting dough to rise at the fireside, raking coals under the oven or hanging clothes on the huge clothes-horse, to dry round the fire. . . . Every evening when Father came back from the pit, he'd put his bait tin and flask on the table, then strip to the waist and have his tub-wash in the flickering firelight. Mother would take a scrubbing brush to his back.[18]

According to Mary, her mother rarely went out on social visits. There was too much to do in and around the house, with pit clothes to beat and brush, the 'bait-tin' to prepare, and the shopping to bring in, to say nothing of the usual routine of cleaning, scrubbing and mending. Shopping itself was a major activity in most working-class homes, as women bought in small quantities day by day, partly

Washpowders were beginning to be used on a growing scale. 'I remember that they'd discovered something wonderful, to find this Rinso in the shops,' declared one Welsh woman (Advertisement in Woman and Home, *January 1928)*

because they lacked the funds for large-scale purchases, which would, of course, have been more economical in the long run, and partly because the storage of food in overcrowded homes was difficult. Visiting the shops also provided an opportunity for gossip with neighbours. Customers would take their time as they ordered each item separately, and in the interval they would hold conversations or exchange pleasantries with assistants and fellow customers. One writer labelled the corner shop 'the housewives' club'.[19]

Even in the 1920s few labour-saving appliances were available in the majority of homes. And despite a council house building programme which helped to construct about one and a half million new dwellings between 1920 and 1930, there remained much overcrowding and sub-standard accommodation, especially in the larger industrial towns and in London.[20] In Liverpool, one woman remembered that 'after the war there wasn't any houses for anybody, everybody had to squeeze in with their parents if they weren't lucky enough to get a couple of rooms'. She and her husband and baby shared a house with the husband's parents and brothers and sisters. Eventually when she became pregnant for the second time she was allocated a council property: 'it was like paradise having a home of my own, the quietness and all the space'.[21]

Still greater was the hardship of another woman who began her married life in rooms: 'then my fella fell out of work and we moved in with me mam and her lot. . . . [S]he just had the one room, . . . a cellar, and we all squeezed in. . . . [T]here were eleven of us in one room.'[22] Slum property of this kind was not only badly maintained but it was also infested with vermin.

In such crowded circumstances, privacy was impossible. Neighbours knew each other's business and family quarrels were heard all over the house and even penetrated into the street. Inevitably these conditions, with shared hallways, stairs, doors, wash-houses and lavatories, gave rise to ill-feeling between tenants. Violet Harris, who brought up her children in rooms in Lambeth, remembered having to take the smallest ones with her to the 'damp, dark wash-house to do me bit of washing, so I could keep an eye on them. Everyone in the house used that wash-house. And very often you went after one where they never emptied the copper out or tidied it up.'[23]

As Mary Chamberlain points out, in multi-occupied houses,

how people slept, when they slept, where they slept, what work was done and taken in, which rooms were vacant, who was dirty, who was clean, who was healthy, who was sick, who was in work, who was without . . . all this was common knowledge. . . . Who last cleaned the stairs, used the lavatory, used the wash-house: all were points of potential friction.[24]

At the beginning of the 1930s between 30 and 50 per cent of dwellings in cities like Manchester, Glasgow, Liverpool, Birmingham and Leeds were still classed as slum properties according to the standards of the day.[25] Nonetheless, it was during the twenties that better housing came to be seen as essential if the nation's health and its spirit of citizenship were to be improved. The medical officer of health for Glasgow argued in 1926 that the improvement of dwellings involved not merely their physical condition but the wider reform of working-class lifestyles and behaviour – a form of social engineering. For him, rehousing included the inculcation of better habits, 'encouraging, indeed disciplining, the backward in thrift, self-respect, neighbourliness and house pride, and preventing them from drifting downwards again.'[26] Council housing, by setting higher standards for working-class tenants, would assist women in creating a hygienic and comfortable domestic environment which would prove 'a cosy and inviting home for their menfolk'.[27]

Unfortunately, however well-intentioned the aspirations of the planners and reformers, the high cost of building during the early 1920s and the enormous wartime backlog of demand – estimated at around 800,000 dwellings in the immediate post-war period – meant that few working-class families were able to move into subsidized modern accommodation during the decade. High council house rents, which were sometimes almost double those charged by slum landlords for a small property, meant that the main beneficiaries of the building programme were members of the lower middle-class, such as clerks, shop workers, teachers and the like. Only a minority of working-class families, whose breadwinner had secure and relatively well paid employment, were able to follow suit. Where, as in Liverpool, efforts were made later in the decade to 'build down', by reducing the size of dwellings and economizing by having a bath in the kitchen instead of upstairs, problems still remained. Many of the city's menfolk worked on the docks and were subject to irregular employment. 'When my husband had work we managed alright, mind you it was never easy, there was never anything to spare,' remembered the tenant of one of these cheaper houses. 'When he was laid off, and that happened a lot, him being a docker, when there was no money coming in we just did without. We couldn't afford coal, we would burn old boots, anything to get a bit of heat in the winter, couldn't afford the electric, just had candles and well, food, if they wouldn't give you credit in the shops, you had to go without that too.'[28]

The fact that the new estates were usually a long way from people's place of work was a further deterrent to poorer families, who could not afford the transport costs and perhaps the need to purchase a midday meal in town. A shortage of shops on some estates meant that tenants had to rely on travelling grocers, butchers and bakers, who charged higher prices, or spend longer visiting distant shopping centres.[29] In any case, the councils themselves preferred tenants with steady incomes so as to avoid the risk of arrears.

Prejudice was also displayed in the allocation of houses. The 'Irish labouring classes, with their ever-increasing families, are among the worst destroyers of property,' declared the chief sanitary inspector for Whitstable, while 'the habits of the lower-class Jewry are also filthy'. This cultural assumption that the poor had 'slum habits' worked against the most needy being given council housing.

When tenants moved into a new property they normally needed extra furniture, since their existing posssessions were rarely sufficient to furnish it. Often this was obtained on a hire-purchase system, although some local authorities, including Leeds, Glasgow, Birmingham and certain of the London boroughs, set up furniture supply schemes whereby they bought in bulk and sold without profit. But even on new estates tenants resorted to old methods to make ends meet. On the London County Council's massive Becontree and Dagenham estate in Essex during the 1920s the 9.30 'pawnshop bus' ran from Five Elms to Barking every Monday morning. It was filled with women carrying bundles of goods to pawn. Not until 1931 was a pawnshop opened in Dagenham itself.[30]

But for many wives and mothers there was no alternative. They must live in an overcrowded home, with little opportunity for quiet or privacy. In 1931 7 per cent of the population of England and Wales were living with an average of over two persons to a room, while in Leeds, with its hundreds of back-to-back dwellings, it was over 8 per cent, in Liverpool almost 11 per cent, and in Greater London nearly 9½ per cent. In fact, in Finsbury alone over 10½ per cent of the population were living more than *three* to a room, and the position had actually deteriorated since 1921.[31]

One London woman, a Mrs E., whose husband was constantly in and out of work after his discharge from the Royal Navy, described the misery of living in a single furnished room with her husband and their two children. Because the space was so limited – the room was only 12 ft square – they all had to sleep in one bed. Their water supply was obtained from the bathroom tap, and the combined bathroom and lavatory was shared by five families. Although her husband earned only about £2 5s. a week, he had to keep 10s. of this for his fares, midday meal, tea and cigarettes. Of the remaining £1 15s., 12s. went on rent, 1s. on insurance, 1s. on subscriptions to a clothing club, 1s. on coal, 2s. 6d. on gas for light, while bread and milk took up 2s. 6d. apiece and meat 3s. 6d. This left 9s. for all their other purchases.

> The room I live in is a back room on the second floor . . . I have no convenience for washing, having to boil my clothes on the gas-stove and wash them in the one room which we live and sleep in. I am very discontented, not only for the inconvenience it affords, but due to the fact that the house is overrun with vermin.[32]

In these circumstances families would spend as much time as possible out of doors. The children played in the street, the men went to the public house, if they could afford it, when they were not at work, and both men and women sat outside the door, talking to neighbours or, in the case of the women, doing their sewing during fine weather. But especially where houses were old and insanitary, such as that inhabited by Mrs E., there was a constant battle to be waged against bugs, cockroaches and fleas. Mrs Pearce of Preston remembered that when she had the springs renewed in one of her children's beds she had to take it outside into the yard to clean it with boiling water and paraffin before it was fit to be sent away. When it was returned the repairer told her it was the first time he had mended a bed without bugs in it. Although she was pleased at the implied compliment, Mrs Pearce drily added: 'he didn't know what I did before it went'.[33]

In most households a fire had to be kept in even during the summer months so that meals could be cooked and water boiled. Many homes still had no other form of heating, except perhaps a single gas ring. There were also dwellings which still lacked an indoor water supply and water had to be carried into the house from a communal tap in the yard or street.

Standards of comfort varied not only with the quality and size of the accommodation a family inhabited but with the energy and resourcefulness of the wife. If she were a slattern, then the whole household suffered. But some women were extremely houseproud, competing with one another to have the whitest scrubbed kitchen table, or the crispest lace curtains at the window, or to be the first to hang the washing out to dry. Floors were usually of scrubbed flags or bare boards, but the starkness of rooms could be relieved by linoleum or by pegged rugs, made from the remnants of old coats, and by carefully dusted ornaments and pictures on the walls.

In Wales it was common to have a line above the grate where clothes could be aired, and this, too, was carefully arranged, in case a neighbour called. 'They . . . had to be tidy – their hems all lined up. . . . people would look at it when they came to the house. . . . It was one of the things people would do, look at the clothes on the line,' remembered a woman from Clwyd. Elsewhere, as in the Welsh mining community of Rhyd-y-Car in Merthyr Tydfil, wives would divide off their single living-room. The best furniture, including a chest of drawers, sofa and table, was arranged 'as a showcase down one side of the room away from the working area, and facing the door so that it would be seen first by any visitor'. Mrs Davies, who lived at Rhyd-y-Car during the 1920s, also remembered how she and the other wives saved up to buy a sideboard to replace the chest of drawers, since this was thought more fashionable. With the help of her earnings as a charwoman she and her husband were later able to buy their house for about £50. Other families built sheds in their back garden and used these for additional living accommodation.[34]

At Dorothy Newton's Dukinfield home in Cheshire the chores were carried out by her grandmother, who lived with them. The family spent their time in the kitchen because Dorothy's mother used the front parlour for her dressmaking business. Soon after the little girl's birth in 1924 her father lost his job and although he soon obtained fresh employment it was at a lower wage. Mrs Newton therefore decided to return to work in a factory in order to make ends meet. However, she was a skilled seamstress and she soon realized that she could earn more by staying at home to make clothes full-time than by continuing in the cotton mill. To improve her skills she attended tailoring classes in the evening at Manchester School of Technology and quickly built up an extensive clientele among the better-off wives of Dukinfield and vicinity. From an early stage Dorothy understood that sewing was her mother's first priority.

Beside the fireplace in the living-room was a large cupboard which held all the pots and pans as well as a range of dried goods such as rice, lentils, butter beans, flour, sugar, jams and pickles. It was the medicine store, too, with a wide variety of patent medicines.[35] Grandma Newton was never stuck for a 'cure' and at a time when medical treatment could be expensive, even for families who had joined a doctor's panel or a friendly society, self-medication was a normal part of working-class family life.

Some households were too poor to afford even simple patent remedies and they resorted to concoctions of their own. Elizabeth King, who grew up in Hyde, recalled that her father was a great believer in herbs. He also brewed 'brimstone and treacle for [our] skin . . . And then my mother used to give us a teaspoonful of olive oil every morning. If you had a really bad cold you'd have to hang your head over a bowl and you used to have this poppy head. It was put into the water and the steam would come up. . . . We were rubbed with goose grease for colds.'[36]

Dorothy Newton's grandmother prepared the meals while her mother worked in the sewing room:

> the mincer was used for something or other every day. Grandma would make pies and puddings and brawn for teas and would keep a close eye on whatever was for dinner: broth, cheese and onions, liver and onions, 'pay' soup with a ham bone, steak puddings, potato pies. . . .[37]

Several times a week old Mrs Newton went by tram to nearby Pendleton to help in her sister's greengrocery business. As part payment she brought back some of the discarded produce, and this added variety to the family's diet. Jam was made from soft fruit when it was in season.

Both of Dorothy's parents had to work hard to maintain the household in modest comfort. But the family always had enough to eat, their home was clean if cramped, and the parents' joint earnings were sufficient to enable them to have a holiday away each year and to pay for their daughter to have dancing lessons – something no other child in her street was able to do.[38]

Other mothers, with tighter budgets, bought cheap offal from the butcher or fishmonger, or throwaway items like a pig's head, a sheep's head, a cod's head or a bag of bones, these last being used for soups and stews. Stale cakes and broken biscuits were obtained at cut prices from the baker, and over-ripe fruit and vegetables were secured when they were being almost given away by greengrocers and market traders.[39] If the family had a garden or an allotment, fresh produce could be grown, but in the larger towns that was unlikely and diets became heavily dependent on bread, potatoes, dripping and lard. Beatrice Ashworth recalled her family being sent to a particular shop to buy cheap bacon pieces and cracked eggs. They never had butter, only margarine, and for a long time did not have milk in their tea.[40]

In the poorest districts there would also be shops and stalls selling second-hand clothing and furniture. In Lambeth they were called 'tot stalls' and according to Lily White this was how mothers used to clothe their children. 'All the tot stalls used to do a roaring trade down . . . [Lambeth Walk]. Everybody used to wear second-hand, third-hand, fourth-hand clothes. Get them on the tot stalls.'[41]

Where incomes were particularly low or mothers were poor managers, the situation could become desperate. Maud Rose, who was born in Birmingham in 1912, remembered that her father was unemployed for most of the 1920s. He kept money for drink 'and if our Mom hadn't got any . . . and he'd got money he wouldn't give her more, he'd go and booze it'. As a result the children often relied on the generosity of their next-door neighbour, Mrs C. She was a rather blousy 'semi-prostitute' with dyed hair, but

You wouldn't go hungry not if next door had got any bread . . . the lads in the
street used to play outside her house . . . and all of a sudden one'd be 'ungry.
They thought nothing of dashing into Mrs C.'s house. 'Can we have a piece,
Mrs C.?'

If she had no bread of her own she would send to a neighbour for a loaf and half a
pound of margarine. 'They used to fetch that loaf in her house and her used to
cut that loaf up for them kids.' On occasion, she used her 'immoral' earnings to
pay the rent of needy neighbours.[42]

In other cases the friendship of the poor for one another in these close-knit
communities might show itself by one woman doing washing for a neighbour who
was ill, or giving coal to a family with young children who were without it. That
readiness to lend a helping hand was shown clearly in many mining villages
during the long coal strike of 1926. In that year the men stayed out for seven
months in a vain attempt to stave off further reductions in their already
inadequate wages, and a lengthening of their working day.

Dr Marion Phillips, chief woman officer of the Labour Party and an organizer
of aid for the wives and children of the miners during this bitter dispute, praised
the way in which the women helped those less fortunate than themselves. Some
turned their homes into clothes stores or set up communal soup kitchens or
arranged individual assistance to the most needy on a case by case basis. Through
their work they came across families like that of a wife recently confined who had
virtually no food in the house, or of mothers who were obliged to feed tiny babies
on rice water and meal water because their own milk supply was insufficient.
Thanks to the efforts of the Women's Committee for the Relief of the Miners'
Wives and Children, over £314,000 was raised from the public and various labour
organizations. In addition, food manufacturers were persuaded to donate supplies
of baby food, condensed milk, jam, biscuits and tinned goods free of charge.
Occasionally the volunteers would get clothing and bedding out of pawn, while
pennies were put in gas meters to provide light and fuel for cooking.[43] During the
summer over 2,100 children from mining families were sent to host families,
mostly in the south of England, for a holiday.[44]

Even after the dispute had ended high unemployment and the debts run up
whilst it was in progress meant that help continued to be needed in some areas. At
Maes-yr-haf Settlement in the Rhondda Valley, opened in 1927 with charitable
backing, arrangements were made for local women to produce clothes and rugs
for sale. In addition, sewing groups were organized up and down the valley, and
materials purchased by the Settlement at wholesale prices so that wives could
make their family's clothes cheaply and pay for them on an instalment plan. At
the same time the groups enjoyed companionship and this helped to relieve the
strain of feeding a family on inadequate means and of keeping up morale within
the home.[45]

The difficulties which occurred in the mining communities as a result of the 1926
dispute were on a large scale. Most communal help, however, was given on a smaller,
more localized basis, with neighbours helping neighbours over a difficult patch.

Some women resorted to the pawnshop or the money lender to raise extra funds.

According to Leonora Eyles, while two-fifths of working-class women would rather starve than go to a pawnshop, the remaining three-fifths went there often. They would take freshly laundered clothes or even spare boots and bedding, and would redeem them at the end of the week ready for use.[46] Lil Smith in Hackney remembered her mother regularly pawned the boots her husband kept specially for Saturdays, without his knowledge. Shortly before he wanted them one of the children would be despatched hastily with the relevant ticket and sufficient cash to get them back. They were then taken in again the following week.[47] Some women felt too ashamed to visit the pawnshop in person and they relied on a neighbour going for them, usually for a small commission. Others feared their husband might find out and a family row – or even a beating – would be the result.[48] In Walter Greenwood's novel *Love on the Dole*, set in Manchester during the 1920s, Mrs Nattle performed the role of agent, arriving at the pawnbroker's on one occasion with a basinette loaded with nine suits, a dozen frocks, numerous boots and shoes, three watches and chains and two wedding rings. She was accompanied by two small children who carried additional goods. As she told a neighbour, her round was 'gettin' that big . . . I'll not be able to manage it, soon'.[49]

Buying groceries on credit from the corner shop or clothes on hire purchase from the tally man, as he went from door to door, were other ways in which the more desperate or the feckless kept their family fed and clothed. Many had their personal economies, converting old flour bags into pillow cases and towels, or cutting up worn-out clothing to make patchwork quilts:

> tailors' samples were begged and made into woollen patchwork blankets; brown paper was put between blankets to provide extra warmth in the winter . . . Children went picking on railway banks for pieces of coal.[50]

If times were really hard, the poorest women turned to soup kitchens and charities to supply food, clothing, bedding and Christmas gifts for the children.

In order to boost inadequate family incomes wives might engage in various money-making ventures of their own. In the textile towns this could mean full-time employment in a mill, and then arrangements had to be made for the children to be cared for by a relative or baby minder. In other cases part-time jobs were taken which enabled the women to combine work with caring for their home and family. Some went cleaning for better-off neighbours, while others took in washing or became small-scale traders. In the coal-mining villages of South Wales faggots were prepared for sale by a few women. They were made from liver, lights and pork pieces chopped finely and mixed with onions, breadcrumbs, sage and seasoning. They were always prepared on specific days of the week and regular customers would come along to collect the required number of these forcemeat balls.[51] In Lambeth, one of Violet Harris's fellow tenants would buy beetroot in the market. She then took these home, boiled them in the copper and took them out on Sunday morning to sell in Lambeth Walk.[52]

Elizabeth Roberts also mentioned the case of Mrs Manning, who grew up in a poor area of Lancaster during the twenties. Her mother took in washing but some of their neighbours engaged in a variety of activities:

Mrs A. had this lodging house, and then Mrs H. had the pub. Mrs H. used to brew pop and sell it. Next door to us Mrs P., she used to make apple pies and jam pies, and charge a penny a piece. She used to roast potatoes and make a living like that. There was a shop just a bit lower down. . . . Mrs R., a halfpenny of milk, a halfpenny biscuit, and a halfpenny packet of cocoa. We used often to go in for cocoa and have it for school. . . . There was Mrs H. she used to cut up firewood and sell it in bundles, 3d. or 6d. a bundle.[53]

Sometimes women kept these trading ventures a secret from their husband and neighbours to avoid losing face. A Liverpool woman recalled taking a tram ride to the outskirts of the city, where the Corporation was constructing new houses. There she collected as many waste wood off-cuts as she could carry and then brought them home, where she chopped them up, made them into bundles, and hid the bundles in a shed. The next day she travelled to another part of the city 'where she was not known'. 'My husband would have been mortified if he'd known what I did,' she declared; 'he always boasted what a good manager I was and I wouldn't have wanted people roundabout to know . . . the shame was something terrible.'[54]

One of the commonest ways of earning extra cash, however, was to take in washing. Mrs Martha Ann Hall of Hyde remembered her mother doing this when her father returned home seriously ill as a result of his experiences as a prisoner-of-war during the First World War. He eventually died from the effects but in the meantime his wife helped maintain the family by taking in baskets of clothes for 1s. 6d. a time. Martha and one of the other children used to deliver the heavy loads of clean laundry: 'we had to keep putting [the basket] down and struggling to get it where we had to take it . . . I can . . . remember . . . hating having to knock on the door and ask for the money. It was awful.' If it were a wet day and the clothes had to be dried indoors the unpleasant smell of damp cloth would permeate the entire house and tempers became frayed.[55]

Ivy Summers, the wife of a Grimsby fish splitter, was another of these part-time laundresses. In her case the difficulties were compounded by her frequent pregnancies. She had seven children between 1920 and 1931 and another five thereafter. While she was at work she used to tie her smallest child, who was a few months old, to a chair, laying him on a pillow and fastening him in with a scarf. The next eldest would be seated in the armchair, with something to play with, while she got on with her work, boiling sheets in one bucket and tablecloths in another. Her husband made the children simple toys and when she was working at night he would amuse them, singing and playing the mouth organ.[56]

Even those who did not take in laundry for other families found washing one of the hardest domestic tasks of all. Water had to be heated, clothes boiled and repeatedly rinsed, before being dried and then ironed, which was itself a major operation. The labours of wives in mining communities were particularly arduous. A Dowlais miner claimed the women sometimes cried 'when you brought working trousers home to them, because with the sweat and everything they'd get as hard as iron. They had to patch them. . . . You'd see great lumps of soap by the side of them – they'd push the needle into the soap first. And they had to have a strong needle to do the job as well.'[57]

Weekly bath nights were another headache for mothers. Lil Smith from Hackney remembered the stratagems adopted in her overcrowded home, where she, her parents and five brothers and sisters lived in two small rooms plus a tiny kitchen on the ground floor of a terraced house. Above them was a family of five. The oldest children all slept in one bed, the three girls at the top and the two boys at the bottom, with their feet towards their sisters' faces. The baby slept in a drawer in the parents' room. On Saturday bath nights the children had to share the same water, which was topped up from time to time. There were only two towels and these rapidly got soaked, so the last two children, including Lil, had to dry themselves on their dirty underwear. 'My job was to dry the kids as they came out,' she recalled. 'We had no nighties or pyjamas. We put our clean vest on and went and sat on the bed in the back room.'[58]

The kitchen was too small for the bath tub to stand on the floor, so it was put on the table. To Lil's embarrassment when she was in her teens, this meant that she was visible to the neighbours as she climbed in naked. But her mother allowed no false modesty and reluctantly she entered the 'pale grey soup'. She and the other children also washed their hair in the same water. Then came the laborious task of emptying the bath. Her mother held one end and Lil and her eldest brother grasped the other:

> we used to scramble out, in our vests, to the backyard to empty the water down the drain. . . . Then we come in . . . We [had] a cup of Perkses cocoa . . . and to us kids it was marvellous, 'cos we had condensed milk in it.

That was the only night in the week they had cocoa. Their mother celebrated the completion of the bathing routine with a Guinness, which Lil had fetched previously from the off-licence. It was put 'on the slate', to be paid for the following week.[59]

With such conditions it is not surprising that working-class wives put a bathroom with plenty of hot water at the top of their list of priorities for improved housing. Working-class women's groups, such as the Women's Labour League, made three basic demands for better housing design – an indoor bathroom, a scullery/kitchen for cooking, and a front parlour, where they could display their 'best' furniture and entertain visitors.[60] A Liverpool woman who moved into a council house in 1922 felt 'like the queen' because she had an indoor bathroom instead of having to go down a yard to the privy.[61]

In some households, such as that of Lil Perry, a father might be unemployed for most of the 1920s and yet be unwilling to ask for poor relief. Instead the family depended on the mother's money-making skills. In the case of Lil's mother these included taking in washing, charring, laying out the dead and acting as an unofficial, untrained midwife.[62] She had to endure much physical violence from her husband – something which other wives in deprived areas experienced, especially if the men were heavy drinkers. Lil remembered her mother having a number of 'beltings. Our Nance was born with black eyes, the way he'd belted her. Then her jumped the bedroom winder when her was having Winnie 'cus he was belting her.'[63] Some women retaliated by hitting their husbands when they came home too drunk to defend themselves, or they enlisted the help of grown-up sons to stop the beatings. Extra-marital sexual relations also caused disputes. One wife who discovered her husband was the father of a neighbour's child refused to speak to him any more, even though she remained at home to look after the house and the children.

But if most men accepted it as their duty to hand over the greater part of their wages to their wife, so she could use the money for the benefit of the whole family, widows and deserted wives were without that recourse. Even after the awarding of State widows' pensions in 1925 the small sum involved – just 10s. a week for the woman, 5s. a week for the first child, and 3s. a week for the rest, up to the age of 14 – did little to solve their financial problems. Although little more than a fifth of all widows were recorded as having an occupation in the 1931 Census, a far larger proportion had part-time employment, especially as domestic workers and laundresses.

Marie Stott's widowed mother in Oldham was too poor even to afford an iron, but she was determined that her daughter should be kept clean and tidy. So when the clothes were washed she would put them under the rocking-chair seat and Marie had to rock to and fro to press out the creases. 'Sometimes there would be no Sunday dinner,' but her mother was anxious not to let the neighbours know this. She therefore rattled the pots as if she were preparing a meal, 'because everyone had their doors open, and everybody knew everybody's business'.[64]

Of central importance to the welfare of working-class households was the size of the family and the effect of repeated childbearing on the mother's health. One of the most disturbing features of the 1920s was the way in which at a time when other death rates were falling, maternal mortality continued to increase. Indeed, at a meeting in Westminster in 1928 to discuss the question, one speaker claimed that motherhood was the most 'dangerous occupation' in the country – more so than mining and seafaring.[65] Within the broad national picture there were sharp regional differences in the death rate, and even variations between individual districts within a region. Hence while in England as a whole the puerperal death rate rose from 4.02 per 1,000 live births in 1924–8 to 4.20 per 1,000 live births in 1929–33, in Wales the comparable figures were 5.34 and 5.85, respectively. There were differences, too, between industrial South Wales, where the rate was 5.24 per 1,000 live births between 1924–8 and 5.79 between 1929–33, and the rest of the principality, where the respective figures were 5.68 and 6.01. Interestingly, while Anglesey consistently registered a very high level of maternal mortality throughout the whole period, its rates began to drop between 1929 and 1933, while those in Glamorgan, where the mining industry was in sharp decline, moved upwards. In Wales as a whole maternal deaths increased particularly sharply in 1927, after the long coal strike and its devastating effect on the living standards of many miners' families.[66]

It is difficult to establish why so many *more* mothers were dying as a result of childbirth in the 1920s than had been the case before the First World War. The increase was taking place at a time when the number of welfare clinics was growing, although it must be admitted that these were often more concerned with *infant* welfare than with that of the mother. Antenatal provision increased far more slowly. Even in 1933 there were only 1,417 antenatal clinics in the country, compared with 120 in 1918.[67] In 1930–2 out of nearly three and a half thousand women who died in childbirth more than one in seven had lost her life because of inadequate antenatal care.[68] (See also Appendix 2.)

In areas where the old staple industries were in serious decline and unemployment was high, it would be easy to blame poor nutrition and inferior living conditions for the rising rate. The Ministry of Health's report on maternal deaths in Wales gave partial credence to this when it mentioned the 'excessive' amount of 'ill-health and disability among . . . women' in the principality, which was likely to contribute to the high mortality rate among Welsh mothers. It also drew attention to the poor standards of personal hygiene in many rural areas, while, as elsewhere, the death rate was higher among single women bearing illegitimate children than among those who were married. This was probably because of lack of care during pregnancy and at the confinement.[69] Many unmarried girls sought to conceal their condition as long as possible and continued working, thereby putting further strain on themselves.

This practice of working almost up to the birth of a baby was suggested as a reason for the relatively high maternal mortality in some English textile towns too. Thus in 1924–33, while the average rate for all English county boroughs was 4.24 per 1,000 live births, in Halifax it was 7.05 per 1,000 births and in Oldham, 6.88. Of the ten county boroughs with the highest levels of puerperal mortality at that time, six were textile towns.[70] 'S.B.', herself a mill worker, described the pressures exerted on females at a time of high unemployment. Once a woman became ill she was 'almost afraid of staying off her work long enough to enable her to recover. She reads with fervour the . . . great patent medicine advertisement hoardings, and willingly invests what little money she has in hand to be whipped like a tired horse.'[71] In the weaving districts of north-east Lancashire pregnant women were often dismissed when their child was due and they then had to 'take their chance if they wanted to return to work'.[72] Such policies encouraged mothers to conceal pregnancies where they could. They also gave an incentive to limit family size.[73] For some this might mean resorting to abortion through self-induced miscarriage, which further threatened their health. Marie Stopes, the birth control pioneer, referred bitterly to the 'commercial sharks' who were prepared to sell expensive pills which promised to procure an abortion: 'They sell . . . gold-plated pills sometimes 25/- per box, two guineas, three guineas a box, and women starve their other children and starve themselves to save the money' to buy them.[74]

But it was not only among the working classes that maternal mortality rates were rising. Middle-class women were at risk, too, and there were those who argued that the increased use of doctors rather than midwives at birth was a contributory factor. General practitioners were busy people with many calls on their time and they could rarely wait for the natural process of birth. Instead they began to intervene in the course of labour by using forceps; there were also dangers of cross-infection, as Stella Davies discovered to her cost. She almost died from puerperal fever and she later discovered that the infection had originated with a shepherd's wife who had been treated by the same doctor. That woman did lose her life. In the 1930s the Rochdale medical officer of health condemned as 'little short of murder' the methods used by some local GPs in delivering babies in his area.[75]

In an attempt to reduce maternal deaths attention was paid to restricting the activities of the unofficial, unqualified and untrained midwives or 'handywomen', whose services were still used by some. Often they were older neighbours who would also care for the sick and dying and lay out the dead. Lil Perry's mother fulfilled this dual role in Birmingham, for example.[76] 'Granny Anderson' performed a similar service in the district of South Shields where the sisters Molly B. and Lily N. were brought up:

> if your mother sent you for Granny Anderson, you used to run like the clappers . . . to get to her. And your house had to be spotlessly clean before she'd enter. . . . She used to give you a list of what had to be ready or to hand, like torn sheets, piles of newspapers and boiling water. . . . There was a tap in the yard and a range that you cooked on. We used to have to save the newspapers for her and she'd spread it out around and on the bed. And then torn sheets for draw sheets and pads.[77]

Mrs Anderson presided at the birth and returned to bath the baby for a few days while the mother rested in bed. She also treated neighbours for minor ailments, such as sore throats and colds. Despite her unqualified status she seems to have been a successful midwife. But others were less competent and less scrupulous. Edie M., who used handywomen for her confinements, later confessed that she had had 'some dodgy looking after. But you didn't pay them much for the ten days.'[78]

Under the Midwives Act of 1910 it was already illegal for women who were not certified midwives to attend mothers in childbirth 'habitually and for gain', except under the direction of a medical practitioner. Despite this, a number continued to work in the poorer districts. In 1926, in an attempt to eliminate them once and for all, a new Act was passed laying down that uncertified women who attended at a birth had to satisfy a court that the attention they had given had been on account of 'sudden or urgent necessity'. Those found guilty of breaking the law could be fined the then substantial sum of £10.[79] Even then a few continued to practise surreptitiously but by the 1930s the era of the handywoman was coming to an end.

Yet if anxiety over the growing incidence of maternal deaths was one aspect of working-class family life in the 1920s, another, equally striking, development was the decline in the birth rate itself. This fell from a peak of 25.5 per 1,000 of the population in 1920 to 18.2 per 1,000 in 1925 and 16.3 per 1,000 in 1929 and 1930. By then the one- or two-child family was spreading from the middle-classes to those well down the social scale.

Commentators disagree as to the causes of this change. Some argue that parents wished to limit the size of their family on economic grounds, preferring instead to save up to purchase certain of the new consumer goods which were coming on the market, or perhaps they wished to do their best for their existing offspring by giving them a better education. This was particularly important in families where the wife did not go out to work.[80] Others have seen it as an expression of feminine independence, as women become less willing to put their body at the disposal of their husband, and perhaps undermine their health in the process. One Barrow woman who had had two babies within eighteen months at the end of the First World War felt she could not go through the ordeal again, and she had no more children.[81] But another woman, a friend of Leonora Eyles, was less fortunate. Her husband refused to consider contraception, arguing that he was 'entitled' to sexual relations when he chose and without the use of any protective device. As a result, by the time she was in her mid-thirties his wife had had nine children during fifteen years of married life. She pleaded with her husband not to give her any more babies, but he claimed that 'he'd have consumption if we took any precautions. He said that's what always gives men consumption.'[82]

According to Mrs Eyles, it was common for wives to admit that they would not 'mind married life . . . if it wasn't for bedtime'.[83] The fear of pregnancy, especially when there was already a large family, caused an 'unbearable nervous distress when bedtime came'. At least one mother dealt with this by sitting up late to do sewing after her husband had gone to bed. She only went up herself when she was sure he was asleep.[84]

The issue of contraception received a major boost through the publicity given to it by Dr Marie Stopes, both in her books – which few working-class families were likely to read – and by a notorious libel case with which she was involved in 1923–4. The case arose because of a comment by a Roman Catholic doctor opposed to contraception that Marie was 'experimenting' with the poor through her birth control methods.[85] The lengthy airing which the subject received in the Press at the time of the court proceedings brought family limitation into the public arena in a way that had not occurred before. Significantly, when Dr Stopes and her husband opened the first birth control clinic in Britain in 1921, the number of those attending was at first relatively small, with only 518 women given help, of whom 471 wanted contraceptive guidance and 47 were looking for help in becoming pregnant. By 1922, after the clinic's first full year of operation, the total had risen to just over a thousand. But in 1923, the year of the trial, the figure of attendances reached 2,368.[86] By 1925 the number of those helped at the clinic had reached five thousand, with a further thirty thousand coming to receive information at the clinic's outer office. In addition, thousands of letters, seeking help, were sent to Dr Stopes from women of all classes.[87] Many were from working-class wives and they revealed the difficulties such women had in obtaining information. Mrs E., for example, was aged 40 and had had twelve children, of whom nine had survived. She lived 'in dread of having any more which for the sake of the others I can't afford to keep, my health has been taxed to the utmost . . . I dread my husband touching me'.[88] In another case a midwife from Barrow-in-Furness, who was in private practice, described some of the distressing cases with which she had to deal. They included a mother aged 38 who had had eighteen children born but only two had survived. She, too, asked for contraceptive information which she could pass on to her patients.[89]

Marie Stopes set the birth control issue in a broad eugenist setting. She saw contraception 'as the keystone in the arch of progress towards racial health and happiness'. She sought to associate family limitation with respectability and responsibility, and as a means of ensuring that healthier babies were born. This was the basis of advice given in her clinic.[90]

Marie's initiative was followed by others. In November 1921, eight months after her clinic had opened in Holloway, the Malthusian League opened one in Walworth. Later the Workers' Birth Control Group extended the gospel of family limitation to Wales and Durham. Despite initial anxiety they found most audiences keen to set up permanent clinics.[91] By 1930 thirteen contraception clinics were open throughout Britain but this was still inadequate to meet the demand for information and guidance. It was in these circumstances that Dr Stopes and her Society for Constructive Birth Control provided the first travelling birth control caravan in 1927. At first it operated in the London area, with the midwife in charge distributing leaflets, addressing public meetings and instructing women in the use of the cervical cap which was Dr Stopes's preferred method of contraception. Later a second caravan was acquired and the two operated in Wales and the north of England.[92]

Nevertheless, despite all these efforts, Elizabeth Roberts in her survey of working women in Lancashire, found no respondent who had had any contact

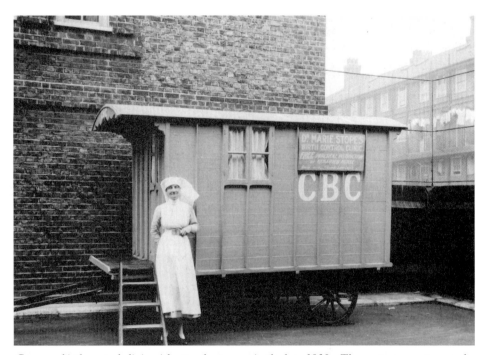

Caravan birth control clinic with attendant nurse in the late 1920s. The venture was sponsored by Dr Marie Stopes and her Constructive Birth Control Society and was designed to spread the message of planned parenthood over a wide area. (Wellcome Institute Library, London)

with a Stopes clinic or had read any of Marie's numerous publications.[93] Furthermore, many working-class families were reluctant to use contraceptive devices of any kind, partly on grounds of cost and partly because they were still considered not quite 'decent', being associated with prostitution in the public mind. Alice Onions, who learnt about family limitation by attending a lecture on the subject in her native Wolverhampton, later helped to establish a small clinic in a railwayman's cottage. Two rooms were rented and a woman doctor was in charge. Alice herself helped with secretarial work and in sterilizing the instruments, but she later admitted that her involvement in the scheme lost her friends among her working-class neighbours. Sometimes she would hear one whisper, '"She's just going off to *that* place!" I thought I ought to go around with a big A on my chest: the Scarlet woman!'[94]

In the case of Roman Catholic families birth control was strictly forbidden anyway.[95] Anglicans also had reservations on the subject, even when the Lambeth Conference in 1930 gave guarded acceptance to the principle of family limitation.

The governments of the decade, anxious about the falling birth rate and fearful of offending public opinion, refused to allow contraceptive information to be given through local authority maternal and child welfare clinics. In July 1924 John Wheatley, the then Minister of Health and himself a Roman Catholic, expressed the official view when he declared that institutions provided 'at the cost of public funds should not be used for purposes . . . which are the subject of controversy, without an express direction from Parliament'.[96] Not until 1930, following changes brought about by the 1929 Local Government Act, did the Minister of Health at last issue a memorandum permitting (but not requiring) welfare centres to give birth control advice to married women on medical grounds. Even then the process of change was slow; by 1937 only 95 out of 423 local authorities had explicitly authorized birth control advice to be given in their clinics.

Where family limitation was practised, therefore, it was likely to be in the traditional forms of sexual abstinence or of withdrawal (*coitus interruptus*). When this failed, women might resort to abortion or self-induced miscarriage. In this period the British Medical Association suggested that as many as 16 to 20 per cent of all pregnancies ended in abortion, and although that was perhaps an exaggeration, over the period 1926–33 figures suggest that 13.5 per cent of all puerperal deaths were due to abortions.[97] In many other cases self-induced miscarriages probably evaded detection, or medical staff preferred to turn a blind eye.

The methods adopted to achieve a miscarriage varied from taking vigorous exercise or strong purgatives to using such devices as a crochet hook. Some women, indeed, regarded abortion as a legitimate form of contraception, not understanding that it had been illegal for more than a century. *Nursing Notes*, the midwifery journal, drew attention to this in January 1928, when it warned midwives and nurses that many 'uneducated persons' had difficulty in distinguishing between contraception and 'procuring abortion. Midwives know very well how common the latter has become since the economic and housing difficulty has been so acute.'[98]

A London mother, Edie M., learned from her sister how to induce a miscarriage by using a soap and water injection. She found herself driven to do this repeatedly because of family poverty. She married in 1920 and had her first baby soon after. She and her husband lived in the East End, and for much of the inter-war period he was unemployed. She had various catering jobs, including washing up and working as a waitress, and so could not afford to be pregnant. 'I worked half of my young life with haemorrhages,' she confessed. 'Now I know that it could have been ever so dangerous, but then you just got up and went to work . . . I never knew anything else and I'm sure all the people I knew never did.' On two occasions the miscarriages were so serious that she had to go to hospital, where the staff were not sympathetic: 'They don't like abortions. "Did you do anything?" You tell a lie up to your teeth. "No, I've never done anything".'[99]

Even women less determined than Edie M. made efforts to abort their babies from time to time. One reluctant mother was Mrs Daisy Hewitt from Knutsford, Cheshire. Her first child was born in 1924 and during the latter stages of the pregnancy she was so embarrassed by her large size and the fact that she had no proper maternity clothes that she refused to go out. She was attended at the birth by a midwife, for whom she had paid by having a 'nurse box' in which she put 1d. a week. 'Every six months someone came from the nursing association to collect 2s. 6d.' Her second child was born in 1928 and by 1938 she had had six children. She never received any proper antenatal care and knew nothing about birth control. When she found out she was pregnant she took 'salts and all sorts to get rid of it', though without success. Her attitude may have been influenced by the fact that her sister had died in childbirth.[100]

So while some women accepted repeated pregnancies in a fatalistic spirit and did their best to feed and clothe the children as they came along, others began to take steps to restrict their fertility.[101] Yet when birth control methods were practised, they were often regarded as something to be ashamed of. Some women, as at a birth control clinic in Cambridge, came secretly, anxious to conceal their visit from their in-laws and neighbours, who were likely to disapprove and would certainly gossip.[102] Indeed, many mothers of small families were the subject of malicious comments. A Preston wife who, on medical advice, had only one child, remembered bitterly that she was 'insulted like a lot that only had one. It was, "What have you been doing?"' It was thought she had procured an abortion. 'You would cry your eyes out. They wouldn't believe you that the doctor had said, no more. It was, "They know how it's done."'[103] Slowly those prejudices died away as small families became the norm.

During births at home – where 85 per cent of all births were still taking place – few poorer women had access to the means of pain relief.[104] It was to remedy this that the National Birthday Trust Fund, a charitable body, was set up in 1928. It had the backing of a number of influential figures, including Mrs Baldwin, the wife of the Prime Minister. In a speech at the Fund's inauguration she described as barbarous a system which allowed women to suffer 'in the way they do, when there are anaesthetics at hand . . . I want to see anaesthetics given in every maternity case that occurs, not as a concession, but as a matter of course.' However, the work of the Fund in providing analgesics and extra nutrition to needy mothers had little effect before the 1930s.[105] More effective in the latter respect were the welfare clinics set up by local authorities and voluntary organizations to provide food for mothers and babies. Cicely Hale, who worked as a Health Visitor for St Marylebone Borough Council between 1918 and 1934, remembered mothers bringing their babies for weighing and for advice from the doctor: 'We could get them free or cheap milk and cod liver oil if they attended the clinic.'[106] In Stepney, the Dame Colet Maternity and Child Welfare Centre, a voluntary organization, fulfilled a similar role, buying food and then retailing it at low cost to the mothers. However, in 1925 it was reprimanded by the Stepney Maternity and Child Welfare Committee for its refusal to treat some Jewish mothers. Its excuse was that a number of Jewish women attending its clinics 'lived in the less poor streets and were therefore in a better position to purchase food at retail prices'. But, as Lara Marks points out, no such distinction was made about the social standing of non-Jewish patients. The following year Jewish mothers were refused treatment by Stepney School for Mothers.[107] Even in such a sensitive area as maternity and child welfare, therefore, racial prejudice could raise its head and barriers could be erected between mothers of different ethnic origins.[108]

CHAPTER 6

Professionalism, Politics and Power

It was a long and painful business clearing away the barrier of disfranchisement and securing for women an equal voice and an established position in the counsels of the great political parties which determine the trend of legislation and the character of administration. And it is a job which is not finished yet. . . . It will doubtless be a still longer and more painful job to convince those parties that women are not satisfied with the standard of human values which they find . . . that the kind of work which is amenable to factory legislation and eight-hour days is not the only kind of work that is being done in the world.

The Woman's Leader, 17 July 1925.

In the aftermath of the war the criticisms levelled at working-class women who sought to retain 'men's jobs' once hostilities had ended were also extended to their middle-class counterparts, including those in the professions. Career women were reminded that they were depriving men of their own class of the salaries due to them and the MP George Barnes was not alone when in August 1920 he declared firmly that if he were an employer he would 'have every enquiry made as to the condition in life of . . . women workers, and . . . would weed out all those not dependent on their own work for means of living'.[1]

The short shrift accorded to some was made clear in a letter sent to the *Western Mail* in January 1919 by an anonymous married teacher from Wales. She protested that not only had she been given notice to leave but she had been informed that if the man for whom she was substituting had not returned to the school by the end of February, she would have to carry on as a supply teacher on a day-to-day basis. 'This means that any . . . married women who are retained will not receive . . . payments for holidays . . . Thus have the services of the married women teachers been "recognized." . . .'[2]

With the passage of the 1919 Sex Disqualification (Removal) Act many feminists hoped that the discrimination and restrictiveness of the pre-war years would end and fresh fields of employment would be opened up in previously male-dominated professions. Under the Act no person was to be disqualified on grounds of sex or marital status from exercising any public function, holding any civil or judicial office, entering any civil profession or vocation, or being admitted to any incorporated society. Only the Civil Service was explicitly exempted from these provisions, and there the argument was soon being advanced that although the legislation ensured that a woman was not under 'an inherent disability from holding certain posts because she [was] a woman or because she [was] married', that did not mean that she was *entitled* to be appointed on the same terms as a man.[3] Consequently not only were female civil servants excluded from overseas postings but they were disqualified from positions in home departments which dealt with overseas affairs.[4] In addition, despite promises that females would be able to enter the prestigious administrative class of the Service in open competition with men, it was not until 1925 that the first open examination was actually arranged, because of the need to provide for ex-servicemen before they could be considered. In that year eighty men and twenty-seven women took part, of whom nineteen men and three women were appointed. The latter took up duty as assistant principals in the Ministry of Health, the Public Record Office, and the Board of Trade. Thereafter the number of female candidates fell, and in the period 1927 to 1935 only eighty-eight women competed, of whom just eight were successful.[5] Throughout the Civil Service a marriage bar also continued to be applied, and efforts by women's leaders to secure equal pay for equal work were repeatedly thwarted.

Inevitably the Civil Service example encouraged similar policies among other public authorities. The London County Council also operated a marriage bar, despite efforts by the Labour councillor Susan Lawrence to have it rescinded. For the local authority the arrangement had the advantage of ensuring that women in their mid- to late twenties, who had moved up the salary scale, were regularly replaced when they left to marry by younger colleagues receiving lower pay. This helped to ensure that females continued to be a source of cheap labour. At the same time most of the women accepted the arrangement without complaint because – as in the Civil Service – when they left to marry they received a lump sum, or dowry, providing they had served a specified period. In the London County Council this was a minimum of six years.[6]

Yet the 1919 legislation did at least ensure that women were able to enter the legal profession for the first time and to become members of engineering, accountancy and other chartered bodies. The first females admitted by the Chartered Accountants and the Chemical Society entered during 1920, and the Law Society and the Institutes of Public Administration and Structural Engineering had their first female members two years later. But welcome though these developments were, experience showed that the process of change was to be painfully slow, as many professional bodies – and employers – conformed grudgingly to the letter rather than the spirit of the law. In 1922 a contributor to the feminist journal *Time and Tide* lamented that married women teachers, nurses and others were still being dismissed on marital grounds, despite the provision in the Sex Disqualification Act that no person was to be 'disqualified by sex or marriage'; 'we have been hoaxed' was the bitter conclusion.[7]

A survey produced a few years later by the anti-feminist writer Charlotte Haldane confirmed this sense of disillusion. Mrs Haldane contacted about thirty professional organizations and among the twenty-two which replied she discovered a total membership in the mid-1920s of 107,705. Only 3,622 were female and they included 2,580 women doctors.[8] Part of the explanation for this poor showing lay in the experimental character of the first admissions. There was a need to find out whether women were able to qualify for a profession and whether, having qualified, they were likely to prove competent.[9] But more significant was the continuing anti-female bias which existed in many male-dominated organizations. Thus in 1928 the senior physician to Westminster Hospital justified the hospital's reversion to its pre-war practice of excluding female students by claiming that it was embarrassing to teach coeducational classes. Furthermore, when they had qualified, about half the women doctors, 'and those the most brilliant', abandoned their profession upon marriage. No such wastage occurred among the males. He failed to mention that as a result of the marriage bar a number of female doctors were given notice to leave by the public authorities which had recruited them.[10]

Nor was the Westminster the only hospital in the capital to refuse clinical places to women. In 1922 the London Hospital had adopted a similar policy, and it was followed in 1924 by St Mary's, and in 1928 by King's and Charing Cross. Although provincial medical schools continued to pursue a coeducational approach, in many respects women's medical education marked time during the decade. Even in 1930, when Josephine Barnes went up to Oxford to study medicine she found herself one of only five females out of a total intake of forty-three students. After gaining a first-class degree she entered University College Hospital, London, where she was one of twelve females, compared with about sixty men: 'We had to be better [than the men], because unless you were good you didn't get in at all.'[11] Like many leading women doctors she subsequently specialized in obstetrics and gynaecology, benefiting from the new interest in maternal health and welfare during the inter-war years. Particularly important in this regard was the appointment of Dr Janet Campbell to head the Maternity and Child Welfare Department of the Ministry of Health. She had six women doctors under her as inspectors.[12]

In the banking world a similar gender bias applied. In 1922 branch managers of the Westminster Bank were asked whether they wished to continue to employ female clerks now that the manpower shortages of the war years were over and most opposed the idea. The view of the manager of the Aldersgate Street branch in London was typical: 'I prefer a male staff for efficiency, drive and discipline.' His colleague at Romford considered that if females were to be employed it should be only in the larger London offices, 'where they need not come into contact with the public', rather than in 'smaller Country Branches where they cannot be hidden'.[13] It was felt that customers would not have faith in advice given by female staff. In such circumstances it is not surprising that the Bank's permanent women employees fell from 1,327 in 1921 to 1,174 in 1930, while the number of permanent males rose from 5,961 to 7,695 over the same period.[14] A marriage bar was also applied, and the parents of female entrants had to promise to supplement their salary, should they be appointed to a branch which involved their living away from home.[15]

It was, however, in the police force that some of the strongest prejudice against females was displayed. Women police had been recruited on a temporary basis during the war to work at munitions factories, around army camps, and in a few towns, including London. One of their main functions was to check female prostitution and to prevent girls 'getting into trouble'. To do this they patrolled streets, alley-ways and parks, but they also did valuable work by being present with female prisoners in Court, and by carrying out social work in connection with women and children.[16] Despite a Home Office report in 1919 in favour of their retention, there was a marked lack of enthusiasm for them in male police ranks. Chief Constables argued that there was insufficient work to justify their continued employment, and in 1924 the Police Federation of England and Wales claimed that policing was 'a man's job alone', and that women were useless. In 1922 expenditure on women police was identified as a target for economy by the Geddes Committee, and their disappearance seemed imminent. The Home Secretary, Sir Edward Shortt, proposed their complete abolition in the Metropolitan force, claiming that their role had been 'welfare work . . . not police work proper', and that they only kept down crime 'with the sense in which the schoolmaster keeps down crime'.[17] Feminist organizations responded by lobbying fiercely for their retention and vigorous support was given to the cause by the two women MPs, Lady Astor and Mrs Wintringham. In 1923, in a report to her constituency, Lady Astor referred to 'the fine work' the women had done 'in dealing with girls in critical and dangerous positions, and in helping to prevent and detect horrible crimes against little girls'. Child molestation was seemingly on the increase and more information was needed on its incidence and scale.[18]

As a result of this campaign, the Home Secretary retreated, leaving local police authorities to decide for themselves whether to keep female staff.[19] In practice, about half of them did terminate the women's contracts, but they continued to a limited extent elsewhere. Only in the Metropolitan force and in Lancashire did they survive in any numbers.

Among those working for the Met. was Ann Campbell, who eventually became a Chief Inspector. In 1922 she gave the lie to any assertion that women's policing was merely social work when she headed a team of female officers sent to Ireland during the disturbances which accompanied partition. Their role was to help the local constabulary and the army by searching women suspected of harbouring firearms or documents relating to terrorist activities. In June 1922 Ann admitted to a friend that although she had become used to shooting in the streets, 'when the gunmen snipe from the roofs one feels it is an especially fearsome thing'.[20] Later she was despatched to Cologne as part of a Military Police contingent to patrol the streets and to train German women for police work.

By 1928 the Metropolitan force had forty-eight women officers, while the Lancashire constabulary had eighteen; Gloucestershire came third with eight. But in the country as a whole in that year there were fewer than 150 policewomen at work, including those in London and Lancashire. The Chief Constable of Cardiff undoubtedly expressed a common view when he declared that policing was not a woman's job because there were 'so many things a woman police officer cannot do and so few that she can do'.[21] In 1928 no police force in the principality employed women officers.

Anti-feminine bias on the part of male practitioners was, however, not the only reason why women failed to enter the newer occupations in the numbers anticipated. Many girls were themselves reluctant to move outside traditional 'female' spheres to become engineers, architects, accountants, policewomen and the like. In the mid-1920s the Institute of Mechanical Engineers had just one female member, and the equivalent bodies for Civil and Structural Engineering had two apiece. The growing effects of economic depression and of sharply rising male unemployment added to the difficulties, and made it harder for girls to get a foothold in such occupations. Also significant was the fact that at centres of engineering excellence like Loughborough College, where instruction had been given to women during the war under the aegis of the Ministry of Munitions, this was withdrawn in the early 1920s.[22] At the same time expert female staff members like Miss E.J. Linford, who had been a demonstrator in the Department of Automobile Engineering from at least 1919, and who was one of the first women graduates admitted by the Institution of Automobile Engineers, left their post in the early years of the decade.[23] Even the Women's Engineering Society, formed in 1919 and with the redoubtable Caroline Haslett as its secretary, had difficulty in holding its ground during the mid-1920s, as its journal, the *Woman Engineer*, makes clear.[24] Greater success attended its offshoot, the Electrical Association for Women, which Miss Haslett helped to set up in 1924, with the aim of promoting 'the wider use of Electricity in the service of women'. Through its various activities it stimulated domestic demand for electricity.[25]

Another factor inhibiting female recruitment to professions like medicine, engineering and architecture was the reluctance of parents to invest in the lengthy and expensive training these required, especially when prospects of employment afterwards were uncertain. The schooling most girls received likewise hampered their efforts to enter occupations requiring knowledge of mathematics and science. Consequently, as Charlotte Haldane drily observed, despite the 'notorious inadequacy of the average home with regard to heating, lighting and water facilities', and the fact that the majority of women were destined to spend much time at home, there was a virtual absence of female professionals working in the housing field. The Royal Institute of British Architects claimed just twenty-one female members in the mid-1920s out of a total membership of almost six thousand, and the Institute of Plumbers had not a single woman member.[26]

So while the career of a female pioneer like Miss Victoria Drummond, who in 1926 became the first certificated woman marine engineer, aroused considerable press attention, the true position was more sombre.[27] In most of the newer fields of female employment, the number of women entrants to formerly all-male professions remained minute.

Even in the law, where a modest degree of success was apparent, the advance was limited. Within hours of the 1919 Act being passed, the first aspiring woman barrister, the feminist Helena Normanton, was accepted by the Middle Temple. She was called to the Bar three years later.[28] Others followed and a number of women were also articled as solicitors. According to Helena Normanton, in an article in *Good Housekeeping* in 1922, those wishing to pursue a career as town clerk, company secretary or director of education were well advised to qualify as a solicitor first.[29] By 1931 there were almost two hundred female barristers and solicitors, compared with thirty-seven so recorded in 1921, and none at all before 1919.

Part of the reason for the relatively untroubled entry of females into the previously closed world of the law lay in the melancholy fact that out of the five or six thousand barristers, solicitors and articled clerks who had joined up during the war many had either been killed or had returned from the front too badly scarred, physically or mentally, to continue with their profession. Hence lawyers anxious to keep their practice in the family and having daughters competent to take over, decided to give them a chance.[30] Nevertheless the cost of training could be a deterrent. In the case of solicitors, the premium alone might amount to over £500. 'Training for the legal profession is neither cheap nor rapid,' concluded Vera Brittain in her 1928 survey of women's work in England, 'though it is both shorter and less expensive than a medical training. A legal career has also the advantage that, unlike medicine, it can be adopted comparatively late in life, and even after many years' practice of some other occupation.'[31]

Further, less costly, areas of professional work where women made progress included journalism (especially on weekly papers and magazines or in the provincial press), librarianship and social work. This latter benefited from the opening up of positions in child care, juvenile employment supervision, probation, and hospital almonry. With regard to librarianship, the big expansion was due to four main factors. The first was the creation of the county library service from 1920, to serve rural areas which had been unable to support their own facilities. A second influence was the government's decision to offer grants to municipal authorities to enable them to improve their libraries. Much of this was spent in making provision for children and for schools – both areas where female staff were likely to be recruited. Thirdly there was the relaxation in 1919 of the limit on the amount of rate revenue earmarked for libraries. Instead this was left to the discretion – and the resources – of individual councils. Finally, both industry and trade began to realize the importance of good information and research provision, and this, too, meant more libraries. The work particularly attracted girls who had left secondary school at sixteen or seventeen with matriculation or school certificate and who were able to gain immediate employment as a library assistant. They were then encouraged to study in the evening for a qualifying diploma, which might take up to five years to complete. Most female librarians in the 1920s were young and single (almost 96 per cent of them were unmarried in 1931), and their numbers increased from just under a thousand at the beginning of the decade to almost three and a half thousand in 1931. By that time they outnumbered male colleagues by more than a quarter although, significantly, the most senior posts in the profession still went to men.[32]

At the top of most other professions a similar gender bias existed. Only in nursing and midwifery did that not apply. Women quickly discovered that entry to their chosen career was only a first step. Many other barriers had to be surmounted, particularly as regards promotion or the securing of equal pay for equal work, while the growing application of the marriage bar forced large numbers to abandon their profession at an early stage. This acted as a deterrent to parents contemplating the financial sacrifices needed to see daughters through a long training period and also to employers, who were often dubious about the merits of recruiting females anyway. Firms could plausibly argue that it was uneconomic to train women for senior posts when they would probably leave within a few years. As Eleanor Rathbone sadly observed, that meant 'women were, with few exceptions, not at all anxious to call attention to themselves by demands for equal pay, provided they could stay in employment on any terms'.[33]

So during the 1920s, as in the pre-war period, it was teaching and nursing, the traditional female 'caring' professions, which offered most opportunities to career women. According to the 1921 Census, 90 per cent of *all* female professionals worked as teachers, nurses, midwives, or mental nurses, and a decade later that figure had fallen only a little, to around 87 per cent. The change was largely attributable to a fall in the number of women teachers, which itself arose from the government's economy drive, the falling birth rate and an increasing application of the marriage bar in the profession. By 1927 a Board of Education Survey indicated that 153 out of 194 local education authorities operated a bar of some kind. This included 61 authorities which employed married women teachers on a temporary basis only.[34] The motives behind that were expressed bluntly by the director of education for County Durham when he declared in 1921 that at a time when newly qualified teachers were unable to obtain posts, 'a policy of continuing to employ married women . . . whose husbands were in a position to maintain them' was indefensible.[35] In Wales, where unemployment among young teachers was severe in the early 1920s, married women were only kept on when there were no men or single women available.[36] Such circumstances gave rise to stories of married couples in South Wales living and teaching as single people in different valleys, so that the wife could keep her job.[37]

Elsewhere married teachers with children were criticized on the ground that it was impossible for them to do two jobs properly at one time. In Norfolk, Archdeacon Buckland bluntly told the Education Committee that a woman's first duty was to her husband and children, 'and she could only carry out her duties as a teacher by neglecting them'.[38] In vain feminists like Helena Normanton pointed to the value of married women in instructing girls on sexual matters and mothercraft. In addition they acted as a 'constant shield and preventive against the dangerous atmosphere of spinsterism becoming too dominant' in a school. But, in Normanton's opinion, there was also another reason for 'public policy' to 'ban the dismissal of the married teacher':

> It is to the national interest that the healthy and intelligent woman should undertake the sacred trust of motherhood. Teachers . . . should be encouraged to become wives and mothers, to produce healthy offspring for the State. . . . Everything fostering the reverent conception of wifehood and motherhood should be instilled into the minds of girls. Dismissal for marriage is likely to promote notions contemptuous of marriage as an institution.[39]

But not even this reference to the emotive 'wives and mothers' question persuaded the advocates of the marriage bar to change their policy.

For the women themselves, the experience of being dismissed in this way was embittering. Freda Corbet, who had to give up teaching when she married in 1925, subsequently described it as 'a very incautious thing to do. . . . For ten years I have eaten my heart out because I have not been able to do the thing I liked and loved.'[40] Another London teacher, Miss Cox, remembered her mother telling her that she would be a fool to give up teaching, with its security and pension, merely to marry.[41] She took the advice.

Nevertheless there were differences in the way that the marriage bar was applied by local authorities. Often, as in London and Manchester, Conservative councillors were in favour of it while Labour members opposed it. But there were loopholes, too. One woman remembered that when she joined the staff of a London school in 1926 she was required to sign an official declaration that she would resign on marriage. Two years later when she did marry she duly resigned, but, like many other married teachers in the capital, she was then offered supply work. Eventually she was approached by an official from the local education office. He suggested she should apply for a permanent post at a village school in Sussex. This she did and although there were ninety-six other applicants, including single girls with college training, she got the job. Later two of the unsuccessful spinster applicants wrote to complain about her selection on the grounds that she was married, but the managers ignored them.[42]

Similarly at Wingrave in Buckinghamshire, the wife of the headmaster of the village school taught there even after the birth of three children. She employed a day servant to carry out the household chores and a child-minder to look after her small daughter. A washerwoman came in each Monday to do the laundry, and in this way family life ran smoothly.[43]

Inevitably the structure of the teaching profession was affected by this approach. In 1921 out of 203,802 female teachers (including music teachers) recorded in the Census, 11.5 per cent were married. But in 1931, when the total had fallen to 199,560, that percentage had dropped to only 9.1. Yet teachers still comprised more than half of *all* professional women workers, compared to nursing, midwifery and mental nursing, which together contributed almost a third.

Part of the attraction of teaching and nursing lay in the fact that both were seen as suitable preparations for women's future role as 'wife and mother', even if, ironically, the marriage bar in each of them might discourage that step. But many practitioners also felt a genuine sense of vocation. Ida Rex, the daughter of a Methodist minister, worked in Hackney schools between 1916 and 1923. She described teaching in the East End at that time as 'a type of social work':

> It wasn't the money that you got, it was helping children. And we used to take our children out – they had never been to the zoo, or to the Tower of London or St Pauls. I used to go with my friends Ethel and Elsie who were also teachers and we would take two children who had never had the chance or had been poorly out for Saturday. We'd go on the bus and take sandwiches. . . . We had

The village teacher. Miss Stream, infants' mistress at Ivinghoe School, Buckinghamshire, with her pupils in 1927. She was so short that she rode a child's bicycle but she was nonetheless a firm disciplinarian! (C.A. Horn)

very few resources in schools. We bought a lot of stuff ourselves. . . . We had sixty children in our classes . . . It was [hard] work to teach the children, to fit them for adulthood and to interest them in whatever one could in the basic subjects . . . [44]

Elementary school teaching had a long history as a role model for any ambitious girl from an upper working-class or lower middle-class background wishing to improve her position in the world. With the establishment of a national salary scale in 1919–20, along lines recommended by the post-war Burnham Committee, it became still more attractive. Although the Burnham salary scale did not offer equal pay to men and women as feminists (particularly the members of the National Union of Women Teachers) demanded, it did award females 80 per cent of the male rate. Earnings varied according to the position held and the kind of school in which a teacher was employed, but whereas in 1918 the average annual salary of a female certificated elementary teacher had been £128 a year, under the Burnham scheme it rose to £200 per annum in 1920, and to £261 by 1922. It remained at, or a little below, that level for the rest of the decade.[45] Less advantageous for the women was their failure to hold on to their pre-war share of headships and the fact that the more prestigious posts in the schools continued to be held by men.

As regards nursing, the other major female profession, that was given a boost in 1919 when a Registration Act for the first time established a national standard of qualification for practitioners. Because of rivalry between the two principal nursing bodies – the Royal British Nurses' Association and the Royal College of Nursing – it was left to the Ministry of Health to draw up the scheme. In 1920 the General Nursing Council came into existence to begin the registration process and to oversee future qualifying examinations. Three broad categories of nurses were to be covered. They were existing nurses, who had been engaged in '*bona fide* practice' before the Act was passed; nurses who completed their training after the Act, but before the new entrance scheme was properly instituted; and future trainees who would qualify by passing the appropriate professional examinations.[46] The general part of the Register was confined to females, but there were special categories for male nurses and for those working with children or in fever hospitals and mental care. This division hampered the mobility of staff who wished to transfer to another field of work. Thus if a registered children's nurse wished to take up general nursing she had to train for two further years.[47]

At the time the Registration Act was passed the Marquess of Dufferin and Ava had expressed concern that the new arrangement would mean the ending of cheap labour in hospitals. He need not have worried. As Ruth Adam points out, even in 1930 the average pay of a probationer in a voluntary hospital ranged from £20 a year for the first year to £30 a year in the third:

> that is to say . . . at the end of a gruelling apprenticeship, the girl was getting as much as the 'lady help' required for housework in the vicarage . . . The bitter truth was that in the only profession run by women almost entirely for women, the girl beginners were exploited in a way which would have provided wonderful ammunition for the Women's Movement if only it had been arranged by men. Probationers were the underpaid, overworked, unskilled labourers of the hospitals – scrubbing, cleaning brass, serving meals – in return for their training. Without them, the 'voluntary' hospitals [i.e. the non-local authority ones] could not have balanced their budgets.[48]

Discipline was strict. In 1920 Dr Comyns Berkeley described the prospects of a girl who took up nursing as three or four years' arduous labour in an atmosphere of sickness and suffering: 'a perpetual sense of unnecessary restrictions, an exile from the world of art and letters and human progress and the narrowing effect of institutional life. And all the time there lurks around the spectre of *fear*. For if she thinks for herself and speaks out fearlessly and independently . . . she will incur the displeasure of the authorities . . . and forfeit the help of her training school when she launches out as a fully trained nurse.'[49] None of this appealed to the secondary school pupils whom the hospitals were hoping to attract as trainees.

A decade later a report in the medical journal the *Lancet* revealed that 84 per cent of hospitals surveyed did not allow nurses out after 10 p.m. unless they had a late pass, and they often had to be in bed by that time. Attendance at meals was compulsory at 58 per cent of the hospitals, and a probationer was regarded as 'pushing herself forward' if she sought acquaintance with a nurse outside her own year.[50] Many nurses, especially trainees, resented being treated like servants, and this implied linkage with domestic service was further underlined by the

The hierarchical nature of nursing, a profession dominated by women, is indicated in this photograph, with the matron seated in the middle of the front row and the lady almoner standing behind her, with assorted sisters, staff nurses and probationers around them. (The author)

uniforms both groups of workers had to wear while on duty. The limited amount of free time allowed to nurses restricted opportunities for a normal social life, especially as much of the time off had to be taken in the afternoon when other people were at work.[51] Like domestic service, therefore, nursing in the 1920s had a high staff turnover and a large drop-out rate. Its practitioners were increasingly young and single, so that in 1921, 85.5 per cent of general nurses were unmarried. By 1931 this had increased to 89.5 per cent and in that year nearly a third were under the age of twenty-five.[52]

Meanwhile the demand for nurses was rising, following the growth in the number of nursing homes, convalescent homes, and general hospitals during the period, as well as the increased provision for maternity and child welfare. No longer were hospitals regarded as appropriate only for the sick poor, as had been the case in Victorian times. And although the total of nurses, midwives and mental attendants rose from 111,501 in 1921 to 138,670 a decade later, it failed to keep pace with the demand.

Symptomatic of the problems experienced was the way in which a small specialist institution like St Mark's Hospital in London had to look more and more outside the capital for its recruits. In 1922 the hospital had a staff of five sisters and sixteen nurses, but between 1919 and 1930, 184 nurses (including 111 probationers) worked there. Of these, 17 per cent were from London, 17 per cent from the Home Counties, 20 per cent from Wales, 13 per cent from Ireland, and 33 per cent from the rest of the British Isles.[53] Nursing, like domestic service,

Even nursing had its lighter moments. Staff Nurses' Troupe outside the Nurses' Home at the Royal Sussex County Hospital, Brighton, Christmas 1927. (The author)

came to rely increasingly upon girls from the depressed areas, especially Wales, and from Ireland.

Overall, then, by 1930 women's restricted role within the professions and their general lowly status, except in nursing management, had changed far less than feminists had hoped when the Sex Disqualification (Removal) Act reached the statute book. Much the same could be said of the political sphere. In 1918 women had accepted that while they were to be eligible to vote only if they were aged 30 or more and had a property qualification (or were married to a man with one), *men* were to be enfranchised at the age of 21 without any such strings attached. They realized that any attempt to wreck the franchise bill, including the sections relating to male suffrage, in the interests of female equality, would have caused an outcry. As the veteran suffragist leader, Mrs Fawcett, declared when counselling acceptance:

> There had to be give and take on both sides: the suffragists got the abolition of the sex disqualification, but had to yield on the question of equality . . . [I]t might be fatal for us to come in from the outside and say we won't have this and we won't have that. Such a course might very well bring the whole delicately balanced structure about our ears.[54]

Dr Marion Phillips, the Labour Party's chief woman officer, was more enthusiastic, maintaining that the measure was

> the great charter of liberties, a promise of further reform and yet in itself having the possibilities of change of the most far-reaching kind . . . Women step

at one stride into the very centre of political interests. . . . No candidate and no party can in the future completely ignore their wishes. . . . It would be mere foolishness to pretend that the position of women in the Labour Party was the same when they were voteless as now when they may sway the result of an election.[55]

Many women realized that an equality bill would have meant that females became a majority of the electorate and that this was unlikely to be accepted in the immediate aftermath of the war. They were also assured repeatedly that the inequality was to be only temporary, with 1918 merely a first step towards universal adult suffrage. Even in 1919 the election manifesto of the coalition government declared: 'It will be the duty of the new government to remove all existing inequalities of the law as between men and women.'[56] In the election campaign five years later which led to the return of a Conservative government, the Tory leader Stanley Baldwin promised to rectify the anomaly, and during the interim there were unsuccessful backbench bills designed to give women the vote at 21. But the months passed without the promise being redeemed, and in 1926 Lady Rhondda founded the Equal Rights Campaign Committee to press for reform. She considered it important for women to take an *active* part in seeking the wider franchise rather than relying on discreet backstage lobbying.[57] On 8 March 1927, at a time when the Cabinet was turning its attention to the issue, she and Eleanor Rathbone led a delegation to the Prime Minister to ask him to ensure that the next general election would be fought with an equal franchise. Eleanor Rathbone also pointed to the injustice of a system under which Parliament enacted bills concerned with the conditions of women's employment and yet allowed most working women no means of influencing those deliberations, in the way their male counterparts had:

> There is rivalry between men and women workers in many occupations. It cannot be said that in this matter the already enfranchised women adequately represent the unenfranchised. The majority of the enfranchised are wives and mothers, who may look at these questions of sex competition from the point of view of their husbands and sons, rather than their unenfranchised sisters.[58]

Within the Cabinet itself, the majority accepted the need for change, both on account of the promise already made for franchise extension, which needed to be redeemed, and because the initial enfranchisement of women had led to no 'very fearful results'. Indeed Lord Robert Cecil argued that the move was likely to increase support for the Conservatives: 'generally speaking a woman is more conservative than a man because she is less adventurous and more religious, both of which characteristics make against revolution and Bolshevism'. Furthermore, if the Labour Party won the next election, they would introduce the reform, and this would doubtless strengthen their position among the younger women voters.[59] However, some leading figures, including Austen Chamberlain and Winston Churchill, remained hostile, although in the end they accepted a Speaker's Conference to consider the matter.[60] In April 1927 Baldwin announced, therefore, that the government had decided to introduce a Bill during the next session to extend the vote to women aged 21 and above, on the same terms as men.

The women, meanwhile, kept up the pressure. In November 1927 they paraded outside the House of Commons carrying umbrellas with the legend 'votes at 21' and sandwich-boards bearing the words 'On the same terms as men', in a mood reminiscent of pre-war suffragist demonstrations.[61] At last in the spring of 1928 the Equal Franchise Bill received its Second Reading in the Commons. In opening the debate the Home Secretary listed three reasons for its enactment. The first was that while in 1918 it had been desirable to treat the large influx of female voters as experimental, now they had voted in four general elections this was no longer necessary. Secondly, although there would be more than five million extra women over 21 who would be entitled to vote under the new measure, about two million of them were women *over 30*. They included daughters living at home, domestic servants, and others who had been excluded under the 1918 provisions. Almost a third more were married women between 21 and 30, who had taken on the responsibilities of running a home and bringing up a family, and were surely mature enough to vote. Of the remainder, the vast majority were women in occupations. 'Can anyone . . . say that . . . women who are capable of earning their living are not justified in asking for the same right to vote as the men who work by their side in the shop or the factory?' he asked rhetorically.[62]

The final factor was that under the 1918 Parliamentary Qualification of Women Act, women were entitled to become Members of Parliament at the age of 21, even though they could not vote for themselves or any other candidate at that age. To continue such an arrangement was clearly absurd.[63]

Critics quickly pointed out that if equality were granted women would become a majority of the electorate. One MP, Brigadier-General Sir George Cockerill, bluntly declared that if either sex were to predominate it should be the men. 'Outside this House I do not believe there are very many people who want to see men put in a permanent minority in every constituency.' Such attitudes ignored the fact that on the evidence of the elections held so far, women were no more likely to vote *en bloc* for a particular party than were their male counterparts. His colleague Colonel Applin also claimed that since the wealth of the country was 'produced by men on the scale of 10 to 1' that meant that with female majority rule women would have control of the 'taxable wealth of the country, to which they have contributed only one-tenth'.[64] Mr Samuel, MP for Putney, even felt that the Empire would be endangered if the vote were given to people who knew 'absolutely nothing beyond the village pump'.[65]

But despite these arguments and those put forward by the anti-Baldwin *Daily Mail* that 'Votes for Flappers' would give the Labour Party an opportunity to manipulate 'thousands of impressionable young females' in the interests of socialism, the Bill comfortably passed its Second Reading by 387 votes to 10. It became law on 2 July 1928. Henceforth women were to have equal franchise rights with men, and by 1929 they comprised almost 53 per cent of the electorate, compared with around 40 per cent in 1918.[66]

March by members of Faversham Constituency Labour Party, Kent, in favour of the equalization of the franchise in the mid-1920s. Some of the women had brought their children with them. (National Museum of Labour History, Manchester)

But at a deeper level, genuine equality was as far away as ever. Even in 1929, when fourteen women Members were elected, they comprised just 2.3 per cent of all MPs. And in the matter of candidatures, they fared little better. In 1918 the seventeen women who contested seats were 1 per cent of the total candidates. In 1929, when there were sixty-nine of them, they formed 4 per cent of the total.[67] More significantly, prior to the 1929 general election only thirteen women had managed to reach Westminster during the decade which had elapsed since Lady Astor became the first woman to take her seat.[68] Eight of these were married or widowed, and seven of them had inherited their husband's seat, or had entered Parliament in his stead. Sometimes, as with Mrs Wintringham in 1921, they had succeeded to a deceased husband's seat. Of the thirteen, six first came to the Commons through a by-election, and most were middle-aged and relatively affluent.

It may be asked why so few women participated in the Parliamentary process which their Victorian and Edwardian predecessors had struggled so hard to reach. For this there seem to be three main explanations. The first was the difficulty they experienced in gaining selection to contest a seat. As the Countess of Iveagh commented bitterly in 1928, although women were 'politically better organized than men, are politically much more active than men, it is extremely difficult to get a woman candidate adopted in a constituency'.[69] She had been elected for her husband's safe Conservative seat of Southend at a by-election the previous year, when he had succeeded to his title. Similarly, in 1924 the newly elected Labour Member for Middlesbrough East, Ellen Wilkinson, acidly quoted a senior party organizer's view concerning women and seats: 'There is about a hundred-to-one chance in that division, but it might be won. It is just the sort of seat a woman ought to fight.'[70]

Especially frustrating was the experience of Leah Manning in 1930. With the backing of her Union, the National Union of Teachers, she was put forward at a by-election to contest the safe Labour seat of Bristol East, only to be advised by the leadership of her Party to step down to allow Stafford Cripps, then an unknown lawyer, to take her place. Reluctantly she agreed. The following year she successfully contested the much less safe seat of East Islington, only to lose it at the general election held shortly afterwards. Forty years later the incident still rankled.[71]

An examination of women's candidatures at general elections between 1922 and 1935 confirms that even when they were selected women usually had to contest hopeless seats. Out of 196 female candidates of all parties over the period 83.6 per cent stood in seats held safely by another party, while only 6.6 per cent were able to contest those held by their own party; the balance were held by an opponent with a narrow majority.[72]

The women's own lack of experience, which made activists reluctant to choose them in constituencies where there was a chance of winning, was partly to blame for this situation. Only if there were some other influence at work, such as a husband's backing (as with Lady Astor and the Countess of Iveagh) or strong trade union support, as with Ellen Wilkinson at Middlesbrough in 1924, could this be overcome.[73]

The second factor was straightforward prejudice. In 1922 Sir George Younger, the Conservative Party chairman, told its women's conference that constituency parties were usually shocked if they were asked to consider a female candidate. But three years earlier he himself had been notably lukewarm over Lady Astor's adoption: 'the worst of it is the woman is sure to get in'.[74] Rural seats were considered particularly unfavourable for women, and of those who did succeed in country districts in the 1920s one – Mrs Wintringham – was able to build upon her late husband's reputation at Louth, as well as her own wartime involvement in agriculture; the other – the Duchess of Atholl – succeeded at the general election of 1923 in an area where her husband was a major landowner and in a seat he himself had represented between 1910 and 1917.

But while prejudice partially accounted for the small number of women's candidatures, it was not the only reason. Also important was their own reluctance to come forward, perhaps through feelings of insecurity or because of family commitments, or on account of financial considerations. A women in Parliament had fewer opportunities than male colleagues to boost her income by following a professional career or taking up lucrative directorships in the City or in business. Younger married women also had special problems, as witness Lady Cynthia

*Lady Astor (1879–1964)
electioneering in Plymouth
during her first campaign in
1919. (University of Reading
Archives)*

Mosley's miscarriage four days after her successful campaign as a Labour candidate in 1929.[75] Significantly, the first three women to take their seats in the Commons – namely Lady Astor, Mrs Wintringham and Mrs Hilton Philipson, who won her husband's seat at Berwick-on-Tweed when he was unseated through the fraudulent practices of his agent – did so largely through their husbands' influence. Not until the first three Labour women entered in 1923 was there an inflow of unmarried women who took their places on the basis of their own ability and experience. All three had been involved professionally in the female trade union movement and had much personal expertise in the area of labour relations and kindred matters. One of them, Susan Lawrence, had been a member of the London County Council and of Poplar Borough Council. She was highly intelligent and deeply committed, so that in 1921 she joined twenty-seven other Poplar councillors when they were imprisoned for five weeks for refusing to collect the borough's poor rate. According to a niece she was 'deliberately frugal, not from meanness but from a self-denial which enabled her to give generously to the causes she had at heart'.[76]

Margaret Bondfield, another new Labour Member, won her Northampton seat in 1923 at the third attempt. She was chief woman officer of the women's section of the National Union of General and Municipal Workers at the time of her election and was also chairman of the General Council of the Trades Union

*Margaret Bondfield, the first woman
Cabinet Minister. She became
Minister of Labour in the 1929–31
minority Labour government.
(National Museum of Labour
History, Manchester)*

Congress. Margaret became the first woman to hold ministerial office, when in 1924 she was appointed under-secretary of state at the Ministry of Labour in the minority Labour government. Five years later, when the second minority Labour government took office, she became the first female Cabinet minister, as Minister of Labour. Her selection owed much to her own trade union background and her ability to work with male colleagues on their terms; they accepted her as almost an 'honorary man'. But it owed something, too, to the desire of the Prime Minister, Ramsay MacDonald, and the Labour Party leadership to advance the female cause and thereby please potential women voters. In 1929 Margaret herself noted the huge pile of congratulatory messages she had received, especially from women's organizations: 'it is with a quiet jumble of pride and humility that I turn them over'.[77]

A final difficulty for women MPs was that because of their small numbers their work-load was relatively heavy since they were seen as representing their sex as well as their constituency. They were also expected to speak on 'women's issues', and in 1922 when Lady Astor reported to the President of the Plymouth Conservative and Unionist Association about the topics on which she had spoken in Parliament, she listed housing, 'the provision of milk for necessitous children and . . . the need for a better milk supply; . . . the care of the unmarried mother and her child; . . . pensions for civilian widows with children', and the training of unemployed women and girls, as among the principal items. Also covered had been the 'protection of children from criminal assault and . . . women police'.[78] Similarly, when Susan Lawrence made her maiden speech in 1924 she chose school feeding as her subject. This, she declared, was 'one of the many things for which we felt women to be especially needed in the House'.[79] Four years later Ellen Wilkinson ruefully commented that she sometimes felt that she was 'the Member for widows rather than the Member for Middlesbrough' because of the pressures exerted on her during a debate on widows' pensions.[80]

This situation helped to create a sense of solidarity among the early women MPs, even though they often held widely different political views. Lady Astor, for example, formed a close friendship not only with the first Liberal woman MP, Mrs Wintringham, but with the fiery Labour Member, Ellen Wilkinson. 'Since our talk together I have slept better than I had done for weeks,' wrote Ellen on one occasion. 'I felt that something was helping me. It has made such a difference for I was very near the end of my strength when I spoke in the House.'[81] On another occasion she referred to Lady Astor's 'own nobility of soul' which had enabled her to give assistance.[82]

However, if the Parties were slow to select women to contest parliamentary seats, they showed more zeal in seeking to recruit them to membership. All three major Parties rapidly made arrangements to cater for females. In the case of the Conservatives this meant converting the pre-war Women's Unionist and Tariff Reform Association into the Women's Unionist Association, with headquarters at Central Office. A network of area committees was set up to coordinate action at local level. By 1928 the Women's Department had a staff of twenty-nine and was training many female organizers. Yet, despite this, the women's role remained advisory rather than one of initiating policy.[83]

At local level the Area Committees engaged in house-to-house canvassing and the holding of cottage meetings to cater for those unable to reach large gatherings. Annual women's conferences were held, and issues of particular interest to females were pinpointed. For example at the annual meeting of the Eastern Area Committee in June 1921, one member brought forward the issue of women JPs, pointing out the number of Labour women who were being made magistrates and pressing for something to be done to appoint Conservatives, too. A few months later another member drew attention to the 'seditious teaching given in Socialist Sunday Schools' and pressed for Women's Unionist Associations to accept the need 'for organization amongst children and young people'.[84]

By 1925 the Association's national leaders were praising the growing sophistication of the members. Whereas in the early days speakers had been asked to lecture on topics like 'How to Vote' or 'Why Women should Vote', half a decade later there were demands for talks on 'German Reparations', 'Taxation', and 'Social Reforms affecting Women'.[85] As a result of these efforts, by the late 1920s about a million women belonged to the Conservative Party and evidence suggests that, on balance, females were more likely to support the Tories than their political rivals at election time.[86]

The Labour Party, too, reacted speedily, with the pre-war Women's Labour League absorbed into the mainstream party in 1918 and its branches becoming the women's sections of the constituency parties. Under the 1918 constitution females had the option of joining the women's sections only, or the mainstream Party, or both. In addition, a number chose also to belong to the Women's Cooperative Guild, which combined social and educational activities with political work. 'In the decade following the first female suffrage grant of 1918,' writes Pamela Graves, 'working-class women surged into the Labour Party and the Cooperative Movement as if they had been waiting for the doors to open.' By 1922, after four years' recruitment, one hundred thousand women had joined the women's sections of the constituency parties, and the Women's Cooperative Guild had a membership of thirty-five thousand.[87] By the end of the decade the Labour Party's female membership had reached about a quarter of a million and at least half of its individual membership was female. In some branches it was more, so that in Cardiff 75 per cent of the individual members were women.[88]

In Gorton, Manchester, Stella Davies responded to the desperate poverty of her neighbours by organizing the first women's section of the local Labour Party from her home:

> I saw the struggle these women had to keep their children decently clad and with shoes fit enough to wear to school. . . . I saw them line up outside Gorton Town Hall on Friday afternoon when parcels of grocery were distributed, the result of the Lord Mayor's Fund, raised by public subscription.[89]

Lily Watson of North Shields spoke for many other activists when she gave as her reason for joining in 1920 her belief that: 'The Labour Party . . . stands for the comradeship of the sexes.'[90] But that was to prove over-optimistic. As in the Conservative Party, although women became enthusiastic members, with their own special Conferences, they played little part in the policy-making area:

> They had only token representation on the national executive committees. No more than a handful were elected as delegates to annual conferences where male trade unionists and cooperators continued to decide on matters of policy.[91]

This lack of influence was demonstrated clearly over the controversial issue of birth control. The Women's Labour Conference was one of the first female organizations to press for advice on contraception to be given at the new maternity and child welfare centres which were being set up. Each year from 1924 to 1927 they passed resolutions demanding that the ban on this be lifted, and each year the Labour Party Conference did its best to ignore the issue. In June 1927 a deputation from the women's organization even attended one of the Party's National Executive Committee meetings to ask that this should form part of the policy of a future Labour government. But in the end the Committee fell back on a decision reached at the 1925 Conference that such a subject, by its very nature, was not one which should be made a Party issue. It should 'remain a matter upon which members of the Party should be free to hold and promote their individual convictions'.[92]

This reluctance to get involved was due partly to a feeling among many male members that so personal a matter as family planning was inappropriate for political debate. Partly it arose from an anxiety not to offend Roman Catholic supporters, who were opposed to birth control and were also influential in certain constituencies. But there was a fear, too, that such a debate might provoke conflict between the sexes within the Party itself. Dora Russell, a Labour activist in the birth control campaign and a member of the 1927 deputation, reported an interview with Dr Marion Phillips, the party's chief woman officer, three years earlier. This had seemed to indicate that Dr Phillips regarded her job as less to help Labour women organize 'than to keep them in order from the men's view point'.[93] That conclusion was underlined in 1928 when a Labour delegation led by Marion Phillips and Susan Lawrence attended a conference of European women socialists in Brussels. They were disturbed to find the other delegations were not only enthusiastic supporters of birth control but insisted on debating it. The British women sought to get the question dropped, with Susan Lawrence apparently saying: 'If our men had known that birth control was to be discussed, *they would not have let us come.*' That incident, concludes David Doughan, indicated 'the predicament sincere Labour feminists found themselves in and is . . . another illustration of the fact that whenever there was conflict of loyalties between feminism and something else, it was usually feminism which lost out'.[94] In the event, although the birth control issue disappeared from party deliberations at the end of the 1920s, in 1930 the minority Labour government relaxed the ban, with the then Minister of Health announcing that he had no powers to prevent local authorities supplying information. This left the matter to individual initiative, but many authorities were slow to take advantage of the change.[95] (See also Chapter 5.)

The Liberal Party, too, had its women's associations, but at a time when the Party itself was under severe financial and electoral pressure, their role was confined primarily to personal visiting, the distribution of party literature, and the holding of public meetings. Younger women became involved in the activities of the League of Young Liberals.[96]

However, while the parties sought to cater for newly enfranchised women members through these various organizations, they also emphasized their 'domestic' credentials in appeals to female voters. 'I firmly believe that the progress of a nation depends upon a contented fireside,' stated the Conservative candidate for Huddersfield in 1922.[97] A year later Labour's candidate for Wellington sounded a similar note: '*Motherhood is the pivot of our National Life.* The Labour Party comes and sits at their firesides and their tables and deals with things of real importance.'[98] Among suffrage campaigners, too, there were those like Mrs Fawcett, who felt at the end of the 1920s that politicians' attitudes towards women had been changed by the granting of the vote.[99] In support of this view she, and those who thought like her, could point to the mass of legislation relating to women which had been passed in the aftermath of franchise extension in 1918. This included the 1919 Sex Disqualification (Removal) Act, the 1922 Married Women (Maintenance) Act, which allowed a woman up to 40s. a week for herself and 10s. for each child under a separation order, the 1923 Matrimonial Causes Act, which allowed a wife equal grounds for divorce with a husband, and the 1925 legislation to introduce Widows' Pensions.[100] But critics could mention

Dr Marion Phillips (1881–1932), chief woman officer of the Labour Party from 1918. She was elected Labour MP for Sunderland in 1929 but lost her seat in 1931. (National Museum of Labour History, Manchester)

the weakness in the operation of the 1919 Sex Disqualification Act and the failure to tackle controversial issues like birth control and equal pay, as well as the tardiness to equalize the franchise itself, as evidence of the restricted nature of the reforms. For them it was clear that much of the pro-female legislation of the period was concerned with improving women's position as 'wives and mothers' rather than with granting them equal political power or professional parity.

It was on these grounds that *Time and Tide* railed bitterly against the half-hearted, 'door-mat attitude' adopted by some women's organizations in advocating reforms they believed would save the lives and protect the well-being of thousands of children each year, or would give justice where no justice as yet existed: 'They say . . . "these things do not *really* matter, for they are only what *we* want".'[101]

Part of the reason for this tentative approach was the feminists' own lack of unity, once they had achieved the initial granting of the franchise. Some, like Lady Rhondda's Six Point Group, continued to press for equality between the sexes at all levels of economic and political life. This was exemplified by Lady Rhondda's own repeated, though unsuccessful, efforts to take her place in the House of Lords as a peeress in her own right. In 1926 the Group emphasized that its two main priorities were 'Equal Political Rights', and 'Equal Occupational Rights', and that its guiding maxim was 'Equality First'.[102] Other activists followed the example of the National Union of Societies for Equal Citizenship (NUSEC) and while favouring equality, were concerned to tackle the special problems experienced by women as wives and mothers. This led to pressure for the payment of family allowances and for the retention of legislation designed to protect females in the workplace. Family allowances were particularly dear to the heart of NUSEC's president, Eleanor Rathbone. In 1925 she attacked those (such as the Six Point Group) who were preoccupied with such 'elusive and difficult' subjects as equal employment opportunities and equal pay, and with removing from the statute book 'the remaining traces of legal inequality'.

> . . . we have done with the boring business of measuring everything that women want, or that is offered them, by men's standards, to see if it is exactly up to sample. At last we can stop looking at all our problems through men's eyes and discussing them in men's phraseology. We can demand what we want for women not because it is what men have got, but because it is what women need to fulfil the potentialities of their own lives.[103]

But Lady Rhondda and her supporters saw this approach as an admission of weakness and of pandering to the anti-feminist sentiments of those who subscribed to the 'separate spheres' ideology in regard to men and women.

Other former suffragettes, like Mary Richardson, joined the Fascist Party which had first been established in 1923 by Rotha Lintorn-Orman, 'a forthright spinster of 37 with a taste for mannish clothes'. She was the granddaughter of a field-marshal and was reacting to fears about the rise of socialism. The election of a minority Labour government in 1923–4 seemed to some alarmists to presage the arrival of a 'Red Terror'. Members wore no uniform but they were encouraged to carry a black

Faversham Constituency Labour Party demonstration, c. 1925, indicating women's commitment to the peace movement. (National Museum of Labour History, Manchester)

handkerchief and to wear a badge on which the words 'For King and Country' and the initials 'B.F.' were inscribed.[104] Not until the 1930s, however, under the leadership of Sir Oswald Mosley, did British Fascism become a major movement. Meanwhile, another former suffragette, Flora Drummond, in 1928 set up the Women's Guild of Empire, which was also opposed to Communism and to strikes.[105]

A number of left-wing feminists participated in various campaigns to promote peace, disarmament, and the League of Nations. Many joined the League of Nations Union and the No More War Movement, formed in 1921. There were also exclusively female demonstrations against war, such as the Peacemakers' Pilgrimages held in the summer of 1926, when about ten thousand women from a variety of organizations gathered in Hyde Park. This flurry of activity arose partly from the signing of the Locarno Pact and the decision by the League of Nations to set up a Disarmament Commission.

But 'the most typical and responsible form which women's participation took' in the anti-war movement was through their support for the League of Nations Union. Its membership grew from about a quarter of a million in 1925 to over four hundred thousand six years later.[106] Among the Union's regular speakers in the 1920s were Vera Brittain and Winifred Holtby, whose pacifist zeal had grown out of their bitter experiences in the First World War. Winifred, according to her friend, joined the League immediately she went down from Oxford 'in the belief that she was working with a group of genuine pacifists who were prepared to sacrifice national pride and imperial privileges in the cause of world peace'.[107] There is evidence that some Conservative women's leaders were anxious for more Tories to support the movement, to prevent its overwhelming domination by Liberal and Labour Party members.[108]

But in the narrower sphere of party politics the failure of feminists to impose their ideas could be attributed primarily to male determination to keep them on the fringes of the decision-making process. Then, too, in their anxiety to live down the pre-war suffragette image of violent protest, most were concerned to look as sober and responsible as they could.[109] For younger activists, solidarity with their chosen political party and its ideals was more important than involvement in non-party feminist issues. By the late 1920s, membership of all feminist organizations was falling at a time when female members of the mainstream parties were increasing rapidly.

It was, indeed, in the sphere of local politics that women were to be most effective. The number of female councillors rose from 754 in 1923 to 1,174 in 1930.[110] But as in Parliament itself, so on the councils women were rarely involved in planning, finance, or transport issues. They concentrated on 'domestic' questions, such as education, housing, public amenities and maternal and child welfare. Hannah Mitchell, elected to Manchester City Council as a Labour/Independent Labour Party member in 1924, was particularly active in promoting the building of public wash-houses by the Corporation in the more congested areas of the city. Housewives could take their laundry there, and the family wash could be completed in a couple of hours, while the home was kept free of wet clothes and steam.[111]

Yet despite Mrs Mitchell's resolute character, she admitted that one of the first things she sensed in public life 'was the strong under-current of anti-feminism which [pervaded] most public bodies'. Similarly, Mrs Yearn of Oldham, who sought election to the town council there in 1925, remembered having 'many a rough word' when she went out canvassing. On one outlying farm the owner threatened to lay a stick across her back if she did not leave. 'I cannot believe my own e'en,' he declared. 'If that's edication, no barn of mine 'ill come to that pitch I'll tell thee.'[112] Although Mrs Yearn failed to get on the council she was appointed to a number of public offices and in 1928 became a magistrate.

Even at local level the family commitments of these women hampered their political activities. Mrs Yearn paid tribute to her husband who had 'allowed' her to leave home 'without a grumble. He is a great believer in women.' But her use of the word 'allowed' was revealing, for it suggested her underlying belief that he had the *right* to demand that she stay at home to fulfil her domestic responsibilities. Much the same was true of Mrs Mitchell. She had bluntly refused to join the women's sections of the Labour Party because she 'was not prepared to be a camp follower . . . or official cake-maker'. Yet once she was elected to the council she found 'the tyranny of meals' manifesting itself, 'for strange to say, even when men are willing for their wives to take on public work, they never seem to understand that this cannot always be done between mealtimes'.[113] In the end a cooperative neighbour agreed to cook the dinner for her husband on the days when she was out. She also provided lunch or tea for some of Hannah's friends if they called while she was out. In their small way, these incidents illustrate the difficulties politically minded women had to overcome if they were to work in the public sphere.

Despite individual successes, therefore, at the end of the 1920s women were still seen as intellectually inferior to men and as lacking the experience and knowledge required to exercise power effectively. This was made clear in the patronizing tones with which some of the newspapers reported the 'Flapper' election of 1929, when younger women voted for the first time. The *Oxford Mail* was typical in its story of Hampstead electors who were so 'overcome by stage fright' that they 'hung back when they reached the polling booth until the opportunity came for them to slip in unseen'. Then there was the Oxford girl who changed her dress before she went to vote so that she would appear in non-partisan colours. The *Western Mail* adopted a similar approach in its reporter's account of one young elector who toured the polling booths looking for her chosen candidate. She carried a horseshoe decorated with blue ribbons and clusters of blue cornflowers, and announced her intention of using it to bring good luck to the candidate:

'I'm going to throw it at him,' she explained. I could not help thinking that if she hit him with it he would be a dead man! If he is alive today he owes his life to the fact that women cannot aim straight. . . . Some of the women voters gave curious reasons for exercising their newly conferred privileges. One in the Epping Division said, 'I am voting for Mr Churchill because his dog belongs to the Wagtail club and my dog is a member too.' . . . But the general view was expressed aptly by a pretty shingled girl only just old enough to vote who told a reporter that she would not have missed her vote for anything. . . . 'Whatever party gets in it will do so largely on our votes. It's a great opportunity and I would not have missed it for worlds.'[114]

CHAPTER 7

Life in the Countryside

There are big differences . . . between the lot of a woman labouring in the fields of Northumberland and that of a woman poultry-farmer in Cheshire, or between that of a smallholder's wife in the south-west and the wife of an agricultural worker in the arable farming regions. . . . Similarly, the worker who is in charge of cattle or poultry, or who is engaged in the dairy or labouring in gardens or fields (weeding, spreading manure, singling turnips, planting and lifting potatoes), generally finds herself faced (unlike the corresponding man) at the beginning and end of her wage-earning day, with a greater or lesser amount of domestic work.

The Practical Education of Women for Rural Life: Report of a Sub-Committee of the Inter-Departmental Committee of the Ministry of Agriculture and Fisheries and the Board of Education

(HMSO, 1928), p. 9.

Women living in rural areas formed very much the minority of their sex during the 1920s. At the 1921 Census about 20 per cent of the total population of England and Wales resided in country districts and that proportion dwindled further during the succeeding decade.[1] Part of the reason lay in the continuing migration of people from villages to towns – and even overseas – in search of employment; that included the movement of younger women to urban posts as maids. But much was attributable to the growth of suburbia, as former agricultural land on the fringes of towns was covered with bricks and mortar. The greater use of motor vehicles also undermined some of the former isolation of country living. In Suffolk, the young farmer Adrian Bell noted how village wives chose to travel by bus into the next town to do their shopping for the sake of the outing, even though the fare added to their housekeeping expenses. As a consequence the trade of the local shopkeeper was reduced.[2] Similarly a woman from Hill Farm near Stokenchurch in Buckinghamshire remembered that when in 1920 a bus began to take people from her small community to High Wycombe four times a day, a 'new world' was opened up.[3]

Not all country people welcomed the changes. The retired Surrey wheelwright George Sturt and his sisters were not alone in resenting the intrusion of motor cars, black-tarred roads and new villas into their hamlet near Farnham. Sturt particularly disliked the way in which a speculative builder had replaced the once

Village shop run by two spinster sisters, Alice and Kate Carter, at Badwell Ash, Suffolk, c. 1926. There was one other female-run business in the village – that of Mrs Pratt, beer retailer. (Suffolk Record Office: Suffolk Photographic Survey)

beautiful tree-rimmed, gorse-covered acclivity 'atop of Vicarage Hill' with large numbers of 'tasteless' dwellings.[4]

Only in the more remote areas, as in parts of Wales, did much of the old way of life survive, with wives travelling to market on donkeys or in pony carts, as their Edwardian predecessors had done. Indeed, in some areas this gave rise to such a strong sense of community that local young men resented suitors from other neighbourhoods coming to court the girls in their district. Such intruders might have to put up with a good deal of rough horseplay, including having the tyres of their bicycles deflated or torn. For the girls, acceptance of the advances of a stranger could lead to loss of status and might prejudice their prospects of subsequently marrying within their home locality.[5] However, as the countryside was increasingly opened up, such outside contacts became more common and, as such, more readily accepted.

But while certain aspects of rural life were affected by these developments, the daily round of most village women remained very different from that of their urban counterparts. This applied to the domestic amenities they enjoyed, as well as to the closeness of their ties with neighbours, and the kind of work they carried out. On the surface, the countryside was male dominated. Men not only owned most of the land but also farmed it, so that the 19,440 female farmers recorded in 1921 (59 per cent of them middle-aged or elderly widows) were outnumbered more than twelve to one by the 244,653 male farmers and graziers. But this apparent economic subordination could be misleading. The contribution of wives and daughters was often crucial to the success of a rural enterprise in a way which rarely applied in the towns. That was especially true of the families of farmers and smallholders, but it applied to tradespeople, too. A large number of village shops were owned by women like Mrs Ward of Tur Langton, Leicestershire; she combined the running of a sweetshop and post office with that of a smallholding. The latter she looked after with the aid of a handicapped son.[6] Public houses, cottage laundries and dressmaking establishments were other small businesses in female hands in many villages, while some wives went out as charwomen to better-off neighbours.

Even for agricultural labourers, a wife or daughter's assistance in cultivating the garden, looking after poultry or working on the land, perhaps for the farmer who was employing her husband or father, was essential for the well-being of the household. Sometimes it was a condition of employment of a male labourer that his wife or daughter lent a hand when needed.[7] 'The women in the country homes are partners in a very special sense,' declared an official report in 1928. 'The intimate association of these women with their menfolk . . . is not normally found in industries other than agriculture, of which it is an essential and characteristic feature.'[8]

On these grounds, therefore, at least one writer has argued that in areas like much of Wales or Cumbria, where holdings were small, the success of a family farm largely depended on the resourcefulness of the farmer's wife:

> In addition to her household duties, she looks after the poultry, collects the eggs, makes the butter and sells all these products. . . . From the sale of her domestic products . . . the wife derives the housekeeping money with which she buys groceries, clothes herself and the younger children and replenishes the stock of household equipment. The wife's budget is thus largely independent of that of her husband.[9]

Mrs Pattie Lewis, who was born on Knap Farm, Llangwm in Wales, remembered the importance of butter churning day on the family farm. Afterwards people came from the village to buy the finished product, and her grandmother would take some in panniers on her donkey to sell at Pembroke Dock. The family also sold rhubarb and cut flowers in season.[10]

Farmers' daughters worked for their keep and received small sums of pocket money at irregular intervals. But not all of them relished that arrangement. One Suffolk farmer's daughter remembered that her elder sister ran the family milk round in the early 1920s without receiving any pay. It involved carrying large 17-gallon churns on the back of the milk float, and using a small can to go from door to door, with a pint measure to ladle the milk out into the jug that the householder provided. However, she grew tired of giving her services free and left home in order to earn a proper wage. The younger sister then took over. 'I used to keep a few chickens down the meadow in an old hut and I used to have a few eggs and that was the only way I got my pocket-money.' After two years, when she was 17, she, too, left home, taking a job on a neighbouring farm, where she was paid

Retail delivery of milk from a churn, Manor Farm, Notgrove, Bourton-on-the-Water, Gloucestershire. The farm comprised about 1,000 acres and had four enterprises: dairying, fat lamb production, bacon pigs, and poultry for eggs. (Webster Cory Collection, Rural History Centre, University of Reading)

15s. a week – later increased to 17s. 6d. – for milking, looking after the poultry, and making butter. She remained there until 1929, when she married a fellow worker on the farm. They were both aged 20 and, greatly daring, they moved to Norfolk to take a county council smallholding.

> We spent £20 on . . . second-hand furniture . . . We only furnished one room, the front room was always empty . . . And outside we saved up and got three or four cows. We went to the bank manager and opened up an account with him and we got three or four cows. We had a very kind farmer lend us a horse for £5 . . . And with . . . five cows we used to make butter.[11]

Often, as in Cumbria, a wife would keep the accounts and be referred to jocularly by her husband as 't' Chancellor of the Exchequer'.[12] On the smaller holdings there and in Wales, farmers also worked together to shear the sheep or to harvest and thresh the grain, and it was the wife's responsibility to provide generous hospitality to those who were giving their services free of charge. Elaborate meals were prepared, the best cutlery and china were brought out, and every effort was made to give the guests a warm welcome. At Gosforth in Cumbria, wives saved up the finest hams for these occasions, and it was not unusual for them to remark after such a communal gathering that they would

Haymaking at Raglan, Monmouthshire in 1927. (Farmers' Weekly *Collection, Rural History Centre, University of Reading)*

'have to scrat along' as best they could for many a week in order to compensate for the outlay.[13] However, any display of niggardliness would have reflected badly on the whole household. 'There was a real competition between the various farmers to see that you were up to the standard of the other farmers,' remembered Mrs Pattie Lewis at Llangwm. 'You gave the best you had for the haymaking people.'[14]

Even when paid employees were at work, it was common to provide meals at harvest time. At Neatishead, Norfolk, a farmer's granddaughter remembered carrying baskets containing hot rabbit pies or steak and kidney puddings, basins of hot potatoes, and jam puffs or apple pie, all carefully covered with white cloths, to the workers in the harvest field. They were prepared by her grandmother, who also sent along copious quantities of tea or, for those who preferred it, 'something stronger out of stone jars kept in the shade of the hedge'.[15] In parts of Wales it was also customary to reward helpers by allowing them to set a drill of potatoes in a field, and, as with Mrs Lewis's mother, there might be gifts of ham, or eggs, or milk in lieu of cash.[16]

In the West Country and East Anglia, which were attracting growing numbers of cyclists, walkers, and holidaymakers, farmers' wives catered for their needs by offering teas and bed and breakfast accommodation. The returns from these became a useful part of many a holding's income. Indeed, Mrs Hicks, whose husband farmed 100 acres near the north Norfolk coast, even moved her sons from their bedrooms and sent them to sleep over the barn during the summer so that she might take in visitors. And in Devon, which was especially popular with holidaymakers, the women's efforts in selling dairy produce and catering for paying guests saved some small farms from bankruptcy during the difficult years in the middle and late 1920s.[17]

For those living near the coast the sale of produce to holiday resorts was a further possibility. A disabled ex-serviceman on a 3-acre holding in Dorset was able to build up a business, with the help of his wife, selling milk and garden produce in and around Bournemouth. This couple also kept pigs, poultry, and rabbits, and within five years were able to afford to rent another $3\frac{1}{4}$ acres of land.[18]

In yet another case, Mrs Cramp, the wife of a yeoman grazier in Leicestershire, was the dominant figure in her household. From the time she rose in the morning she issued a stream of orders:

> Domestic daily helpers and the family must be thrust into orbits that fitted her master plan for the day. From the kitchen command centre, messages would flow to the limits of house and farmyard. . . . Even salesmen whose call broke into [the] morning routine were likely to receive a sharp reproof. But knowing [her] and keen to take orders for cattle food, they suffered in silence. They knew too that her temper alternated with startling generosity and likely as not, they finished by the kitchen fire, taking tea and rock cakes and nursing the cat.[19]

Mrs Cramp took great interest in the poultry, not merely for commercial reasons, but because whenever there were minor debts to settle with her neighbours she would give them the option of cash or eggs. Eggs were thus used to pay for knitting socks and scarves, for making and altering dresses, for sweeping the chimneys, and for beating the carpets. They were bestowed as gifts on the aged and the sick, and were donated as prizes at local whist drives.[20]

Alongside these individual female contributions to farming and community life, there were important regional differences in the work and responsibilities women took on. These varied according to the agricultural character of the locality. On the arable holdings of Northumberland, where female work on the land was traditional, women in 1921 still formed over 25 per cent of the county's agricultural labourers and farm servants. They performed heavy jobs like loading and spreading dung, and ploughing, as well as more customary female tasks like singling turnips, cutting thistles, working with the livestock, and helping out at haytime and harvest.[21] By contrast, in Cardiganshire, where female labour was also widespread, the chief concern of farmers was breeding and rearing stock. Hence most of the women's work involved animals. It included milking, butter- and cheese-making, feeding calves, pigs and poultry, and cleaning pens and cow-houses. Girls were trained to the work from an early age, with children as young as ten learning to milk and to operate the separator used in the making of butter.[22] Because of the county's poor soil and the consequent difficulty in earning a livelihood, farmers had always kept down expenses by using the labour of wives, daughters and maids rather than of more highly paid men. As a consequence, a visitor to the area at the end of the First World War considered that female labour

Feeding the poultry. (The author)

was used more extensively there than in any other county in England and Wales. The women also worked harder than those in any other county in South Wales.[23]

In East Anglia, the development of sugar beet as a field crop during the 1920s, as a response to a government subsidy in 1925, created extra demands for female labour. At the end of the decade Mrs Rosamund Noy from Suffolk was one of many who went out hoeing the beet and, later on, pulling and carting it, as well as stooking the sheaves of corn at harvest. During the months she was at work she went out for about six hours a day for five days a week. This meant rising early to do her household chores before she set off, 'and then you'd got to do a lot of things in the evening, you'd got to prepare things for the next day'. She also kept a pig and poultry, and earned a little by selling cockerels to the butcher.[24]

Women in the Holland division of Lincolnshire began their seasonal tasks between March and May by setting potatoes. They hoed and weeded crops from April, picked soft fruit and cut cabbages from May, and continued with various horticultural and farming tasks until potato picking in the autumn. Sometimes the younger children would go with their mother and would play in the fields while the mother worked.[25] The wives of foremen and waggoners in this part of Lincolnshire often had charge of a farm's poultry, and were paid so much a couple for rearing the birds and so much a score for the eggs.

In Kent there was much seasonal labour associated with the large acreage of orchards and hop gardens. Some women went out for a few weeks picking cherries in June and July, while others worked in the hop gardens in the autumn, and then spent the rest of the year on household duties. They were paid on a piecework basis, according to the quantity of fruit or hops they gathered. So great was the pressure at 'hopping' to bring in the crop that a farmer's wife laughingly confessed that when she married she had to promise never to leave her husband in September, should their marriage founder.[26]

But the county also had many permanent workers, with nearly one in ten of Kent's agricultural labourers and farm servants female, according to the 1921 Census. They included women like Mrs Daisy Record, who was born at Hunton in 1904. After a brief but unhappy career in domestic service she went on the farm full time. She and her husband worked at Ulcombe, where much fruit was grown and where she and a female colleague always worked for the same farmer, although

> we din't agree on a wage like the men. There was never anything official said about us women. . . . We 'ad to work from eight 'til four o'clock, an' 'e paid us fivepence ha'penny an hour . . . But we 'ad to make the most of it, and take the good with the bad.[27]

It was this use of women as cheap labour which aroused the hostility of the agricultural trade unions towards females on the land, even though their leaders recognized the importance of a wife's contribution to family income. One activist argued that efforts should be made to organize the women so that they would receive equal pay with the men, thereby removing the cheap labour label. At the same time pressure should be exerted to raise male wages so that it was not necessary for a wife or daughter to go out.[28] Another man pointed to the adverse effect a wife's labour had on family comfort, with the husband returning home after a day's work to find 'no nice fire to greet him, no tea ready, and the house . . . in all probability untidy, as the woman cannot be working in the fields and in the house at the same time'.[29] These comments encouraged female unionists to join in the debate, and to argue bitterly that while a few wives liked the work, most were forced to go out because of financial necessity. One wrote angrily that during the war when women had taken the men's places, 'they were called saviours of the Empire, but in peacetime they [were] termed invaders and superfluous'.[30] A second wife added acidly, 'just as the woman helps the man to augment the income, let the man put his shoulder to the wheel in the home. Let him help make the fire, help clean the house, help put the children to bed. The home is his as well as hers.'[31] But few male farm workers accepted such feminist arguments. It was shortage of cash rather than conviction which led most of them to accept the need for female land work, at least on a seasonal basis.

Meanwhile, there were some like Mrs Record who enjoyed being out in the fields. 'I'd whistle me teeth out,' she confessed. She also described her routine once fruit picking had ended. In the winter she and her female fellow worker would

> goo up the wood with the men that was doin' the spiles and palings [for fencing] and . . . shave all them. Then you'd be turnin' out yards, . . . and you'd

goo spreadin' the manure on the fields . . . Then it'd be hoein' strawberries all up, and puttin' the straw underneath the fruit. Then we'd git the potaters in, and the swedes and wurzels. An arter that come hayin' – we 'ad five or six weeks o' that . . . First I used to goo out with a hay-rake, and rake that all in; then, when that was nice and dry, you'd cock it up into lumps. Then the time came you'd gotta pitch that up onto the hay-cart: or, if they was pitchin' too high for me, they used to say, 'You come up and load, an' we'll pitch up to you.' . . . Then, between haytime and harvest, there was the 'wild white' clover to git in: and arter that was harvest – wheat and barley and oats. Then you're pickin' up your mangels and swedes. . . . And up there they used to 'ave . . . Kentish cobnuts, and we 'ad to go pickin' them; and then it was potatoing time. Arter *that*, you come round to winter again, and that was threshin' time. . . . I either 'ad to stand on the stack and push sheaves down to the thresher, or I 'ad to stand in the thresher and cut the bonds round the sheaves; or else I 'ad to build the straw stacks, and thatch 'em.[32]

Despite her formidable skills, Mrs Record ruefully admitted that although she 'could do everything a man could do . . . they never give me no man's money!'

Mrs Phyllis Tibbetts in Buckinghamshire was more fortunate. She was a bailiff's daughter but often helped out on other farms at haytime and harvest. The casual labour rate for men was 1s. an hour and for women 6d., but as she was experienced in all aspects of farm work she refused to work for 6d. 'I . . . said if I was doing a man's work I expected a man's pay, and I got it too. The men also got a beer allowance, which the farmer brought to the fields . . . As I was teetotal I got 3s. 6d. a week in lieu of the beer.'[33] The fact that her father was bailiff on a private estate, rather than an ordinary farm worker, may have had something to do with her more favourable treatment, as well as her own obvious skills.

In parts of Somerset, Nottinghamshire and the Warwickshire/Worcestershire border area a large number of women were employed on osier stripping, preparing the raw materials for basket making. In the Trent Valley some worked through the winter, spring and early summer, but in most districts they were needed for a few weeks only in the spring and early summer. The work was undertaken as 'a sort of annual outing, combining pleasure and profit', rather as hop-picking and fruit gathering were in Kent. It attracted only hardy workers because they had to stay out in all weathers, and there was heavy wear and tear on their clothing. Married women welcomed the work not merely because of the income it generated but because of its flexible hours. They brought their youngest children with them, even babies in prams, and those who were old enough assisted in the work. A grower with 30 acres of osiers would need, on average, thirty-five women to peel the rods during April, May and June.[34]

Around Wensleydale, cottage wives sometimes kept a few geese and a gander to help pay their rent. The sitting geese were housed in the kitchen, perhaps under the table or in a corner, with a few stones around and a little bedding, or under the shelves in the dairy. As many as five or six geese might be sitting at any one time. Each bird knew its own nest and would walk in and out as it pleased. When the goslings had hatched and were about a month old, they were sold to dealers.[35]

Peeling osiers at Bidford-on-Avon on the Warwickshire/Worcestershire border. (Miss Wight Collection, Rural History Centre, University of Reading)

Finally there were formidable matriarchs like Grannie Beeforth, who lived on a small farm at Fryup on the north-east Yorkshire moors until her death in the early 1950s at the age of 95. On Saturdays she took butter, eggs, chickens, honey and beeswax to Whitby market, and she also broke in horses. At the end of the First World War, when a neighbouring family was struck down by the influenza epidemic, she fed their stock and milked fourteen cows. She laid out people when they died, free of charge, and prepared mead, wines and herbal remedies. She herself inhaled an infusion of wild sage to treat the quinsy from which she was a perennial sufferer.[36] And at a time when trained midwives were still relatively rare in rural districts, she rode round to deliver babies. In this connection it is significant that maternal mortality was higher in many rural districts than it was in towns, and as late as 1925 almost 20 per cent of the population of West Suffolk – to quote but one example – had no district nurse available to them.[37] In country areas like these the services of a Grannie Beeforth, with all her imperfections, was much valued by wives.

These, then, were some of the regional influences which affected women's daily round in the countryside during the 1920s. Equally sharp differences applied to basic amenities like housing, water and electricity, both between town and country and between one rural area and another. Although special encouragement was given by the government to local authorities to promote council house building in country areas, particularly from 1924, the process of change was slow. Sub-standard accommodation was widespread and families often lived in two-, three-, or four-roomed cottages which were low ceilinged, damp and dark, and which possessed only rudimentary cooking facilities. As late as 1939 it was estimated that an additional quarter of a million dwellings were needed to provide adequate homes for people employed on the land.[38] At the beginning of the 1920s, two-thirds of the cottages in rural Wales were considered unfit, and in 1926 a critic claimed that tied houses in Cardiganshire and Pembroke were 'a disgrace to a Christian land'.[39]

The 'tied cottage' issue was itself a cause of dissension, for while farmers declared they needed their workers to live close at hand if the holding were to run efficiently, the men themselves were well aware that if they lost their job or annoyed their employer, they could find themselves deprived of both work and home. One wife claimed that half the men in her village were not receiving their proper rate of pay because they lived in tied housing and were afraid to complain.[40] At Sealand, Flint, when the labourers went on strike in the summer of 1920, one of those involved, his wife and their five children were evicted from their tied cottage with just a week's notice. The farmer dumped all their furniture in the road and it was left to the local board of poor law guardians to give them shelter in the workhouse until alternative accommodation could be found.[41] Fortunately such actions were not typical, but they reinforced the anxieties which wives felt if their menfolk became involved in industrial disputes. Even ill-health, and a consequent inability to carry out the work required, could lead to eviction. In 1931, a typical year, the National Union of Agricultural Workers defended fifty-nine members in court proceedings for eviction from their homes and a further 236 were helped without their cases reaching the courts.[42] The abolition of tied housing was something for which the Union campaigned tirelessly in the 1920s, albeit without success.[43] It was also an aspect of family life which was peculiar to the countryside (and to mining villages), since in towns few workers lived in tied accommodation, and, if they did, they could usually rent another home without too much difficulty. That was rarely the case in villages.

In the provision of basic public utilities like piped water and electricity, rural areas also fared badly prior to the Second World War. Partly this was because of the heavy capital outlay involved in installing a national network of pipes and cables, and partly because of the sparse population in some districts, which made provision uneconomic. At the end of the 1930s less than half the farmhouses in England and Wales had a piped water supply, and in Anglesey that proportion dwindled to about one farmhouse in twenty, and in Suffolk to about one in six. Instead water had to be brought in from wells, rivers and streams. Mrs Thomas of Llangennech, Dyfed, recalled that in her family everyone used to take a pitcher to the pump night and morning, to make sure there was plenty of water in the

Mary Jane Lewis, aged 16, fetching water for the home at Llangennith, Gower, 1924. In many country areas carrying water for household use was a laborious daily chore. (National Museum of Wales: Welsh Folk Museum)

house. A special effort was made on Saturdays, to ensure there was enough to last for the Sabbath. 'You'd never fetch water on a Sunday.'[44]

For lighting, families relied on oil lamps and candles, which added to the difficulty of caring for livestock during long winter nights. Just over a quarter of farms in England and Wales had electricity at the end of the 1930s, although in Hertfordshire, with its close links to London, the proportion was over half. On the other hand, in Radnor about one holding in a hundred had electric power at that date and in Anglesey around one in thirty-three.[45] A decade earlier the position was far worse. Furthermore, where connections were made there were often restrictions on the supply. An East Anglian woman whose home was linked up to electricity in 1930 remembered that she and her husband were allowed to have just three lights and one power point installed.[46]

Only the well-to-do, such as the larger farmers, the parson and other middle- or upper-class householders, could afford new labour-saving devices, such as an oil cooker to supplement the kitchen range, or an inside flush toilet, for which a septic tank had to be constructed.[47]

A farmer's daughter from the Chilterns remembered that on their holding the water supply was a perennial problem during the summer months. There was a pond on the farm but as they had about twenty milking cows, each of which drank ten gallons of water, the pond soon dried up. There were also three underground fresh water tanks to collect water from the roofs of the house and buildings, but they often ran dry too. During the drought of 1921, all the ponds dried up and the water for the livestock had to be brought in by water barrel from five miles away. 'This meant continuous shifts of water-cart day and night. The water was "bucketed" out of a small lake.'[48] To collect drinking water for the house her mother had to drive about four miles to a spring.

But cottagers, too, suffered, not only from water shortage but from the threat of contamination and of outbreaks of typhoid. One such occurred at Ivinghoe, Buckinghamshire in 1921 when a well became polluted by night soil from nearby gardens.[49]

In the Forest of Dean Winifred Foley remembered that water for her home had to be carried from a well a quarter of a mile away. The only local source was rainwater collected off the roof. For lighting, there were paraffin lamps and candles, but sometimes cash was too short in the Foley household to pay for these. 'Many's the time I've been sent around trying to borrow "a stump o' candle". Come to that, I was often sent for "a pinch o' tay", "a lick o' marge", "a screw o' sugar", "a sliver o' soap", or "a snowl o' bread".'[50] Even food for the pig was obtained in this way, with Winifred's mother pledging part of the animal for potato peelings from neighbours and one of the hocks for bran from the grocer.[51] However, she added drily that nobody was 'ever optimistic enough to try to borrow money'.

The lack of water added to the burdens of wash-day. In Winifred Foley's village, when the women had carried the water home, or had persuaded their husband to bring it in for them, they had to heat it in a copper. Then it would be poured into a wooden tub over the dirty washing. The 'clothes and our mams were brought to a lather by the use of the unwieldy heavy wooden "dolly"'.[52] After being rinsed and put through the mangle, the clothes were hung out to dry. But in some working-class households, wardrobes were too limited to permit of a long drying period. If the weather was bad, everything had to be dried round the fire and in long wet spells, wrote Winifred, 'you might hear a woman call across the garden to her neighbour, "I'll 'a to turn me britches an' shimmy this wik for we can't get near our vire for tryin' to dry the pit clothes out"', her husband being one of the many in the Forest who worked in the mines.[53]

Shopping, too, presented difficulties for those living on the more remote farms and in isolated hamlets. Mrs Hayhoe, whose husband was a blacksmith on one of the big fenland farms at Gislea in Cambridgeshire, remembered having to bicycle along a muddy track on the top of a fen bank when she went to the village to collect supplies. On her return she had to carry the paraffin for the lamps on her handlebars.[54] At Llangwm in Dyfed, women went into Haverfordwest once a week riding donkeys with panniers to carry the goods. They themselves rode side-saddle and carried a large market basket in which to stow any produce they had for sale. When the donkeys were not in use they were left to graze on the beach. According to a local woman, each donkey knew the way into town and the stopping-places en route where garden produce was sold to regular customers. While the women did their marketing the donkeys would be put up at an inn or left to graze on the Green.[55]

In other cases, particularly on farms where the wife made butter and cheese or sold eggs, these might be disposed of to a mobile shopkeeper, on a barter system. The shopkeeper supplied items which the family could not make or grow for themselves, or those which were regarded as special treats for Sunday tea – such as tinned pineapple and tinned salmon. In return he took the farm's produce. Mrs Green, wife of a Norfolk smallholder, made butter to sell under these arrangements. She also kept poultry and used an old broody hen to hatch turkey eggs. 'I used to sell the hen and eight turkeys for 25 shillings.' Similar arrangements applied with regard to supplies obtained by her husband from the corn merchants. They would say of a debt, '"Let it stand till harvest", and they'd take the corn . . . and square up and then give us the balance of the money'.[56] Like all barter systems, these transactions placed the small farmers and cottagers very much at the mercy of the shopkeeper or merchant involved, especially when they were in debt.

So far, in looking at women's lives during these years it is the static, unchanging aspects which have been stressed. This has applied not merely to their way of life but to their efforts to balance an uncertain family budget. In practice, however, their daily round was very far from static in the 1920s.

The First World War itself initiated developments which proved of major significance for rural women. The first was the encouragement given, particularly from 1916, to wives and daughters living in villages to take up land work, in order to make good the loss of the men who had joined the armed services or moved into other occupations. This reversed a trend of declining female involvement in agricultural labour which dated back half a century. As a consequence of the campaign, by February 1916 at least 140,000 women had come forward and even in July 1918 nearly 91,000 females were at work under the scheme, with many more working on an unofficial basis.[57] In addition, also in 1916, a Women's National Land Service Corps was set up to cater for middle-class volunteers, and within a year about two thousand girls had been accepted and had undergone training.[58] Finally, in 1917 the Women's Land Army (WLA) was formed to attract recruits from all sectors of society, including many from urban areas, and to provide them with necessary instruction. The WLA achieved a peak membership of about sixteen thousand in September 1918, and although after the war most of its recruits – like the village women – returned to their normal duties, some stayed on. Despite the initial reservations of farmers concerning their efficiency, the majority of Land girls were effective workers. They were particularly useful in the traditional areas of women's employment, such as milking and dairy work, and in market gardening.[59]

Not until late November 1919 was the WLA finally disbanded. Then some of the remaining members who wished to continue in farming were offered free passages to the dominions. Training schemes for 'colonial work' were offered by many of the agricultural colleges which catered for women, and in 1927 the

Women's Farm and Garden Association published a report on *The Training and Employment of Educated Women in Horticulture and Agriculture*. This suggested that for those with some capital and technical expertise South Africa offered a

profitable future . . . In Canada and Australia there is a large unsatisfied demand for the girl who will also do household work, and no doubt anyone going out in this capacity could eventually obtain outdoor employment by watching her opportunity.[60]

A few women were settled on land in this country, including some under the provisions of the 1919 Land Settlement (Facilities) Act, designed to provide local authority small holdings for ex-servicemen. But the female share in this initiative was tiny. In late 1923, a mere 228 women had been certified as suitable and had been settled on a holding. By contrast, a year later, around 22,000 males had been allocated one of these properties.[61]

In other cases, middle-class women attended one of the female agricultural colleges to receive instruction in poultry keeping, dairying, market gardening and the like. At the Midland Agricultural and Dairy College at Sutton Bonington, near Loughborough, catering for fifty female students, short courses, lasting a few weeks, were offered in poultry keeping, dairying, and horticulture. Longer certificate and diploma courses, for one or two years, were also available. A similar

Butter-making class in Wales, c. 1920. These classes were designed to raise the standard of farm-produced butter. (National Museum of Wales: Welsh Folk Museum)

provision was made at the Agricultural and Horticultural College at Studley Castle, Warwickshire, where the objects of training were defined as equipping women to run their own farms or market gardens and enabling them to take posts as forewomen and head gardeners.[62] Frances Perry, who was to become one of the most knowledgeable female gardeners of the century, was among those attending the leading horticultural college for women at Swanley, Kent. After graduating in 1925 she returned to her home area of Enfield and began working for Perry's Nurseries. Five years later she married the son of the owner, but continued to work part-time for the firm.[63]

Elsewhere dairying courses were offered on a part-time basis to improve the butter- and cheese-making skills of farmers' families. One such was an evening class at Tonyrefail primary school in Wales during 1927. It was arranged by a local farmer and instruction was given in butter-making. Other classes covered cheese-making and poultry trussing.[64] However, at the Chadacre Agricultural Institute in West Suffolk girls were only accepted 'during such portions of the year as accommodation . . . may not be required for the primary purpose of training boys'.[65]

Competitions to improve skills were organized by county agricultural committees. In 1928 the Cheshire committee considered that its milking tests had done much to raise standards of performance within the county. The winner in the section for farm workers and weekly wage-earners in that year was a woman, although the competitions were open to both sexes.[66]

It was doubtless with operatives of this calibre in mind that an advertiser in the *Farmer and Stockbreeder* in 1929 appealed for a 'Dairy and Poultrymaid':

> must be thoroughly experienced in all branches of dairy and poultry work, and able to keep official milk and other detailed records; commencing wage £2 5s. per week, with living quarters, light and coal; board by arrangement.

In the same issue a Mr Anderson of Ruthin wished to recruit an

> Energetic Girl . . . for Grade A herd, take charge dairy, sterilization utensils, assist feeding young stock, pigs; good milker . . . butter-maker; able pack dairy produce; cottage available; place suitable girl with mother or widowed sister, for whom light work offered.[67]

Yet while there were a few such openings for 'professional' female land workers, the vast bulk of those remaining on farms after the war did so either as members of the family or as ordinary labourers and farm servants. As such, they merged into the general female work force. By 1921 32,265 females classed themselves as agricultural labourers and farm servants in the Census. Even the agricultural returns submitted by farmers in that year showed that the number of women employed on either a regular or casual basis had fallen sharply from its wartime peak. According to the returns there were 73,000 'regular' female workers and 53,000 female 'casuals' in that year. The discrepancy with the Census figure arose partly from the fact that many of the 'regulars' were probably relatives of the farmer or of his labourers and, as such, did not regard themselves as farm employees, even though they carried out daily tasks like milking or looking after poultry. Others may have been domestic servants who worked in the farmhouse but were expected to lend a hand at the busy seasons of the year by working in the hay and harvest fields or in the dairy. The casual category included those recruited to weed crops, pick fruit and potatoes, gather hops and carry out similar short-term tasks.[68] Clearly, the wartime initiatives to increase the number of female landworkers had had only a brief impact.

The government's role in boosting the supply of women's labour was, however, only a minor part of its involvement in agriculture during the war. Of far greater significance was the decision to establish a scheme of guaranteed prices for wheat and oats under the 1917 Corn Production Act, and to draw up separate arrangements to provide a guaranteed price for potatoes. The aim was to encourage farmers to concentrate on producing the food crops urgently needed by humans and horses. At this stage the guarantees were little more than gestures to engender confidence, since throughout the war the market price of the commodities covered was always higher than the guarantees. The 1917 Act was also important for workers because it established a Central Wages Board, supplemented by district committees, to set minimum rates of pay for farm workers throughout the country. Almost immediately a national minimum of 25s. a week was fixed, which meant a modest rise for workers in the worst paid counties. By 1920 that minimum had climbed to 46s. a week and although prices had also risen sharply, workers and their wives in most areas were enjoying an advance in living standards.[69] Support for the agricultural trade unions was increased, with the National Union of Agricultural Workers claiming 170,000 members in 1919–20 and the agricultural section of the Workers' Union over 100,000 members.[70]

Meanwhile, as demand for food grew, farmers prospered during the final months of the war and its immediate aftermath. Some took advantage of the break-up of landed estates between 1918 and 1921, when a quarter or more of the agricultural land of England and Wales changed hands, to purchase their holdings. Often they bought with borrowed money or incurred heavy mortgages which hung like a millstone around their neck when the good times came to an end in 1921. Soon some were going bankrupt, with 3,569 failures reported between 1920 and 1929 alone. Mrs Doreen Rash, whose husband farmed near Diss, remembered that one of their friends hanged himself because he could not bear the disgrace of bankruptcy.[71] Even well-established farmers like the Cramps in Tur Langton were consumed with anxiety. One of the sons recalled being much affected, as a schoolboy, by overhearing crisis talks between his parents, and these worries were intensified when he learned that a farmer they knew had shot himself.[72]

As late as 1920, under the terms of a new Agriculture Act, the government had reaffirmed its policy of price guarantees and workers' wages machinery. But within months, following a revival in world agriculture and the consequent slump in prices of farm produce, it hastily enacted the 1921 Corn Production Act to end all guarantees and minimum wages. As a result, between 1920 and 1922 the price of barley and oats approximately halved and that of wheat dropped by over a third.[73] Although the situation briefly stabilized in the mid-1920s, with the onset of world depression in 1929 the downward pressures were intensified. Farmers responded by cutting back on their arable acreage and switching to more profitable livestock production and market gardening, or they allowed their land merely to tumble down to rough grazing.[74] By 1925 milk and dairy products alone accounted for more than a quarter of the total value of agricultural and horticultural produce sold off farms, while fruit, vegetables, flowers and other horiticultural products contributed over a tenth – more than the total contribution of corn.[75]

For farmers' wives, these changes meant they had to economize in their housekeeping. On most holdings eggs were kept for sale rather than for home consumption, and there was a sharp drop in the amount of cream used by the family. At the same time, increasing imports of dairy produce were beginning to erode the price of farm-made butter and cheese, so that much of the milk was sold for liquid consumption.

Poultry keeping and dairying, which had once been regarded as the wife's pin-money, now became an important part of a farm's total income. Higher standards

Grading eggs at Manor Farm, Notgrove, Bourton-on-the-Water, Gloucestershire, c. 1930. (Webster Cory Collection, Rural History Centre, University of Reading)

of hygiene were also demanded and if there was some reduction in women's work as a result of the decline in butter-making, this was counterbalanced by the increasing regulations for clean milk production. These primarily affected the farm's womenfolk.[76] Those small producers who were unable to meet the new standards were forced out of business. Among them was Mrs Edith Plumb of Hawkedon, Suffolk. When she first married in 1928 she and her husband supplied the village with milk, carrying round two small churns on the carrier at the front of a three-wheeled trade bicycle. But eventually the 'restrictions got very bad, both with the cow-house and the dairy and I gave it up'.[77]

The economic decline which so blighted the fortunes of farmers affected their workers, too. Faced with a collapse in produce prices, they reacted by cutting their labour force and reducing wages. Although the government had established voluntary Conciliation Committees, on a county basis, to replace the former statutory wages machinery, these proved of little value to workers.[78] From late 1921 wage cuts were widespread, so that by March 1922 the minimum rate in Norfolk had fallen to 30s. per week, compared to the 46s. payable the previous August. That dropped to 25s. a week by the beginning of 1923, a cut far sharper than any fall in the cost of living. As a correspondent for the Conservative newspaper the *Morning Post* noted: 'With wages at twenty-five shillings a week, the labourer is worse off than he has been in the memory of living man. . . . Pleasure and harmless amusements have been utterly banished from his life.'[79] Sometimes the men sought to resist the downward pressure by striking. Disputes lasting for several months occurred in both Norfolk and Northamptonshire from late 1921 to the spring of 1922, but in the end the wage reductions had to be accepted.

Matters finally came to a head in Norfolk in the spring of 1923 when farmers' representatives on the county Conciliation Committee offered a wage of 22s. 6d. (or 5d. an hour) for a week of fifty-four hours. This represented a cut of 2s. 6d. a week in pay for four extra hours' work. Although the offer was subsequently modified to 24s. 9d. for fifty-four hours, the workers' representatives rejected that too.[80] Early in March a strike began and within a week about ten thousand men had stopped work. For wives, the strain was immense, for not only had they to feed their family on an inadequate strike benefit but for those living in tied cottages there was the constant fear that if their husband were dismissed they would be evicted from their home. To add to the pressures, certain employers, who were members of the Farmers' Federation, recruited strike-breakers from other areas. One man brought in from Cambridgeshire in that way was Hory Rushmer from Gislea. He was a 'catch-worker', picking up a living where he could and combining this with poaching, which sometimes meant he was sent to gaol. Hory's wife remembered how he and his friends went as 'black labour' into Norfolk:

the big farmers . . . used to pay our men, whether they went or not, so that they would always be ready if they wanted them. And they used to go in a block . . . and sometimes us women used to go too, to cook for the men. There were scores of them used to go down there. They'd stand in, for more money, for the harvest. . . . But it was a rough old job. They wouldn't let them walk through, in Norfolk, our men had to go in numbers, in tumbrils . . . They would have done them harm. Women used to come out with long brooms. . . . They were paying our men . . . more to go up there than they were paying their own men, just to make their own men suffer.[81]

The Norfolk dispute of 1923 dragged on until 18 April, when a compromise was reached. The employers agreed to pay their workers 25s. for a guaranteed fifty-hour week, with overtime up to four hours a week paid for at the ordinary rate of 6d. per hour. Beyond that, higher overtime rates were to apply.[82] After further negotiations it was also agreed that there would be no victimization of the strikers. That soon proved an empty promise. Union officials later claimed that over a thousand of their members were never re-engaged. Many were forced to leave their cottages and were unable to obtain employment elsewhere in the county.[83] Meanwhile, membership of the unions slumped. By 1924 the agricultural membership of the Workers' Union was only about 20 per cent of its post-war peak and two years later National Union membership was at a similar level.

In 1924, with the return of a minority Labour government, a new statutory system of wage regulation was set up, with County Committees having powers to set a minimum rate for their area, and a Central Wages Board appointed to oversee the scheme but with no authority to amend the conditions fixed by the counties. Inevitably this led to great variations in wages and hours of work, but overall, minimum pay moved upwards. Thus in Buckinghamshire, where the pre-Board wage had been 27s. a week, this rose to 30s. at the end of 1924 and to 31s. by 1929. Similar advances were registered elsewhere.[84] (See Appendix 3.) Yet problems persisted, for not only was pay still very low, but many farmers failed to observe the legal minimum. In 1926 fifteen inspectors were appointed to check on the position and they discovered that of more than nine hundred workers investigated over 20 per cent were underpaid; similar findings occurred in later years. Sometimes this may have been due to ignorance but often it was clearly intentional on the part of the employers.[85]

For the wives and mothers of farm workers, budgeting became a nightmare, particularly where there were young children. In 1924 household surveys revealed that out of a sample of forty budgets of families with more than three children, 70 per cent of expenditure went on food and a further 14.7 per cent on fuel and light. There was little left over for anything else. Furthermore, although individual outlays varied, the average level could not be met from the prevailing weekly wage of an adult male worker. Extra earnings were needed to meet the deficit, either from overtime or from the contributions of the wife and children.[86] (See also budgets in Appendix 3.) It was in such circumstances that Mrs Uzzell, a union activist from Berkshire, wrote of mothers half-starving themselves in order to care for their family: 'It is deplorable to realize that in 1925, and in Christian England, many of our women are going to bed hungry to enable them to give their children breakfast.'[87]

In an attempt to boost family income a number of wives undertook the farm tasks discussed earlier in this chapter. Efforts were also made to take advantage of the food that was 'for free'. A Norfolk girl remembered her family would collect 'watercress from running streams, rabbits, pigeons, wild raspberries, wild plums and blackberries, crab apples, hazel nuts, chestnuts, walnuts. No squirrels hoarded these more carefully than we did.' Other women turned to traditional domestic crafts like lacemaking, gloving, netmaking for the fishing industry, and similar tasks in order to earn extra cash. But here changing fashions, mass production methods, and the effects of foreign competition combined to undermine prices and profits. In the case of domestic lacemaking, even at the end of the nineteenth century difficulties had been experienced, with pressure from machine-made lace and the effects of fashion changes. As a result, a number of philanthropic Lace Associations had been set up by well-to-do ladies to try to preserve the craft and to find worthwhile outlets for the finished products. These continued after 1918, but with diminishing success. Many workers were old, since younger women were reluctant to devote time to learning

Sarah Jane Cook of Ivinghoe, Buckinghamshire, one of the last of the straw plaiters. She made plait for the hat industry in nearby Luton. Under her arm she held a bundle of split straws, ready for incorporation into the plait. (The author)

an intricate craft which brought such poor returns. Mrs Clara Webb, whose mother worked at Paulerspury, Northamptonshire, remembered that on one hot day she and her mother walked 15 miles to the other side of Towcester to deliver lace that had been previously ordered. On reaching the customer's house they were turned away by the servants, 'the mistress . . . having left word to say that the lace was no longer wanted, fringes being all the rage now!'[88] By the late 1920s the Lace Associations had faded away and with their demise, pillow lacemaking as a commercial proposition virtually ended.[89]

A similar decline occurred in the straw plait trade around the hat-making centre of Luton. Here cheap imports of foreign plaits largely destroyed the industry. In the 1920s a few women continued at work, for example at the village of Offley. At Ivinghoe in Buckinghamshire, too, Kate Dollimore and Sarah Jane Cook are remembered busily working away as they gossiped to neighbours. Sarah Jane was also keeper at the local Wesleyan Reform chapel and pupils at the Sunday School can recall that she continued to plait even when they were having their lessons.[90]

Outworkers employed in the leather glove industry in Worcestershire, the West Country and Oxfordshire were more successful in preserving their craft. In the latter county the three main centres were the small market towns of Woodstock, Chipping Norton and Charlbury, with eight glove factories in Woodstock alone at the beginning of the 1920s. The gloves were cut out at the factories and some were also made up on the premises by girl machinists. But the bulk were sent to skilled workers in nearby 'gloving' villages. On fine days the hand sewers would sit outside to work, and to talk to friends who were probably similarly engaged. One noted centre was Leafield, and Mrs Wright, who was born in the area in 1905, recalled the gloves coming to the village in bags, each with the name of the worker attached to it. Her mother, Mrs Faulkner, acted as 'bagwoman' for the firm of Atherton & Clothier of Woodstock and she would wheel the finished gloves in a perambulator to a neighbouring village where she met the firm's representative. She then returned with a fresh consignment of raw materials and the payments due for earlier work. Any gloves which had failed to reach the required standard would be returned for rectification and some makers bitterly recalled that if trade were bad the manufacturers would try to find fault, in order to delay paying them.

The Faulkner cottage was used as a depot, with the workers taking their completed gloves there. Both mother and daughter were skilled makers on their own account, and with the money they earned they were able eventually to buy their own cottages. One of Mrs Wright's aunts, who lost her husband in the First World War, also supported herself by working at the trade, although in her case she used a machine which she had bought and installed in her own cottage.[91] Despite foreign competition, gloving continued to occupy hundreds of outworkers in the counties where it was concentrated throughout the 1920s.

Around Bridport in Dorset and Lowestoft in Suffolk 'braiding' fishing nets was the major domestic industry. The twine was despatched by delivery van or village carrier once a fortnight by the firms involved, and the finished nets were collected in a similar fashion. However, after the establishment of a Trade Board

Hand stitcher sewing gloves at Tibberton, Worcestershire in 1920. She was using a pedal-operated 'donkey' to hold the leather in position while she worked. (Miss Wight Collection, Rural History Centre, University of Reading)

A joint commercial venture in the early days of motoring. Thomas Girling, haulage contractor and garage owner, with his wife Eva, standing beside their wayside petrol pump at Brandeston, Suffolk, c. 1930. (Suffolk Record Office: Suffolk Photographic Survey)

for the industry in 1919, minimum rates of pay were set and this, combined with a downturn in the fishing industry, led to a number of workers losing their job.[92] Some fishermen's wives in Bridport responded to this by offering holiday accommodation to summer visitors.

Employers recruited these domestic workers because they were cheap and their labour could be used flexibly, according to demand, in a way that was difficult with full-time factory-based staff. From the women's point of view, although the pay was meagre, the work offered an opportunity to earn a small wage while they carried out their domestic chores and looked after their children. It particularly appealed to those living in isolated communities, where alternative employment was difficult to find, and to the aged and infirm who were unable to work away from home and for whom it represented a small supplement to a pension. The Women's Institute movement, which first grew up in the war years, and enjoyed some backing from the Board of Agriculture until 1919, also did much to promote crafts such as basketmaking in the 1920s, alongside its broader social activities. (See Chapter 8.)

In coastal communities such as Llangwm in Dyfed, women gathered cockles and mussels for sale, or went shrimping during the summer. The cockles were boiled and then removed from their shells, before being pickled and sold in jars at markets or from door to door. On the Gower peninsula and at Marloes in Dyfed other women gathered laver, a special edible seaweed, which was used to produce a greeny-black gelatinous purée known as laverbread. This was prepared as a commercial product by a number of Glamorgan families and was sold along with cockles on market stalls. It was prepared by being shaped into small flat cakes, tossed in oatmeal and then fried in bacon fat. It was usually served with bacon.[93]

At Marloes, Mrs Jenkins, a fisherman's daughter, remembered that she and fifteen or so fellow pickers would start work three hours after high water. The tide allowed them about six hours of 'picking' time and they would take their food – bread and cheese, with bottles of tea - with them, to eat on the beach while they worked. The weed was gathered in sacks and then carried home in a donkey or pony cart. There it was sorted in a shed before being despatched by train weekly to the merchants in Swansea. Mrs Jenkins went to the beach every day throughout the year, whatever the weather, and she continued to do this until 1934. Despite the hardness of the work, however, it could be rewarding. In a good week a picker might earn as much as £3.[94]

Finally, some females still migrated in search of seasonal employment. That was true of the many families who came from East and South London to work in the hop fields and orchards of Kent during the later summer and autumn, or who went from the Black Country to carry out similar tasks in Worcestershire and Herefordshire. The high unemployment among unskilled male workers during the 1920s encouraged their wives to seek this seasonal work. In 1921 it was reported that in parts of Kent about a quarter of the women were starting work at

Scots fisher girls, c. 1920, gutting and cleaning herrings at Great Yarmouth. (Great Yarmouth Public Libary and Norfolk County Council)

5 a.m. instead of the customary 7 a.m. so as to maximize their picking time. A decade later thirty thousand of them were still coming to the Kentish hop gardens from London, travelling on special 'hop-pickers' trains' or by lorry.[95] Although they lived in bare huts and, often enough, slept on straw mattresses, they and their children welcomed the opportunity to enjoy the fresh air on the farms. In the evening suppers were cooked around camp fires, with potatoes sizzling in their jackets and meals often shared.[96] On Sundays local wives might earn a few pence by cooking joints or cakes for the hut dwellers. At the end of the picking season there were major celebrations, with the 'Queen of the Hops' crowned and everyone wearing flowers in their hats. There would be a 'hopping supper' held in the oast-house, with sausages, bread, cheese and cider from the barrel. The women returned home the next day, carrying pillow cases of garden vegetables, and fat cockerels hanging by the legs, to add to the luggage, as well as much needed cash in their purse.

In Great Yarmouth and Lowestoft there was a large-scale migration of fish girls from Scotland to gut and pack herrings. They arrived in September and returned home about the end of November. In the boarding houses where they lodged the rooms would be stripped down to the bare boards before they moved in. They had just a bed and wash-basin, with all non-essential furnishings taken out, to prevent them being impregnated with the smell of fish, for inevitably the girls and their clothes reeked of it. 'You could smell them before you got to 'em,' remembered Miss Rivett of Lowestoft.[97] They worked in rows, wearing scarves or shawls over their head and long skirts to protect them against the elements. They also wore bandages on their fingers to protect them against the sharp blade of the knife, but even so cuts were frequent. Among the townspeople the girls were welcome, not merely for the essential work they carried out but for the money they spent. Most came from remote parts of Scotland where there were few shopping facilities and the goods they purchased – including pianos and bedsteads – were often shipped north in the boats of the Scottish fishermen who came down for the herring season.[98]

The East Anglians paid tribute to the girls' toughness. 'Fancy standing back to the North Sea for ten hours or more handling cold fish!' declared one Yarmouth woman. 'There was really no limit to the day; . . . if the fish kept coming in they kept going. There was no official hours. It was incredible! They were strong, healthy and cheerful; and always knitting when not at work. Walking, talking, but always knitting!'[99]

Through the exercise of their ingenuity, therefore, many women in country districts were able to contribute to the well-being of their family not merely by carrying out domestic duties and caring for the children, but by taking on a variety of jobs. These ranged from land work and running small businesses, to herring packing and various cottage industries, although most of those were already in decline by the 1920s. The cash earned was often essential to the balancing of the family budget, even though many of the tasks the women performed eluded the eye of the population census enumerator.

CHAPTER 8

Leisure and Pleasure

There is a 'Smart Set' or its equivalent in every suburb and in every provincial town in England, a set which spends its time playing bridge in the afternoons, motoring round to see its friends, plays a little tennis, dances a good deal, keeps the most fashionable kind of dog it can afford, spends a large proportion of its time . . . at its dressmaker, spends all it can squeeze on jewellery. This public reads a large number of novels. It only glances at the papers; its interest in home politics is, for the most part, confined to thinking how wicked the working-man is to want the money and material comforts which it regards itself as all-important; its interest in foreign politics is non-existent . . . [Women] . . . trained in the leisured class, to idleness and irresponsibility [are] a focus of decay in the very centre of life.

Viscountess Rhondda, *Leisured Women* (1928), pp. 28–30, 54.

Hundreds of girl operatives and women from the adjacent cotton mills marching home to dinner arm in arm . . . A few still held to the picturesque clogs and shawls of yesterday, but the majority represented modernity: cheap artificial silk stockings, cheap short-skirted frocks, cheap coats, cheap shoes, crimped hair, powder and rouge; five and a half days weekly in a spinning mill or weaving shed, a threepenny seat in the picture theatre twice a week, a ninepenny or shilling dance of a Saturday night, a Sunday afternoon parade in the erstwhile aristocratic Eccles Old Road which incloses the public park, then work again, until they married when picture theatres became luxuries and Saturday dances, Sunday parades and cheap finery ceased altogether.

Walter Greenwood, *Love on the Dole* (1958 edn), pp. 29–30.

During the 1920s women of all classes enjoyed greater personal independence than they or their predecessors had had before the war. That included the freedom to smoke, to wear cosmetics, to raise hemlines, and to go out unchaperoned. However, the way they exercised those rights differed widely according to age, wealth, class and place of residence. Not only was there an immense difference between the leisure pursuits of affluent wives and daughters in fashionable Mayfair or in prosperous suburbia and their slum-dwelling counterparts in the centre of town, but between urban and rural areas. The increased availability of buses and bicycles had broken down some of the isolation

Tennis team at Ashton Bros., cotton manufacturers, Hyde, Cheshire in September 1921. (Tameside Local Studies Library, Stalybridge)

of country life, but for many villagers of both sexes amusements were still largely centred upon their home community and its immediate neighbourhood. Typical of many was Bowerchalke in Wiltshire, where a recreation hut was purchased at the end of the war and was used for games, dances, whist drives and dramatic performances.[1] In other cases a schoolroom served a similar purpose during the evenings.

Gender discrimination also applied in some spheres, so that females were unable to eat out after 10 p.m. in certain restaurants, cafés and other places of refreshment unless they had a male escort. This was ostensibly on grounds of public morality but it meant that respectable women, perhaps waiting for a late train, could be refused a cup of tea in a Station Hotel, as the writer Winifred Holtby discovered to her chagrin. Despite a protest by women against the practice in 1930, it continued to operate. Females were likewise excluded from entry to many clubs and even to community reading rooms in some areas. A wife from Resolven in Wales recalled that the womenfolk there were not allowed in the parish reading room until a wireless set was installed during the 1920s. Then, as a concession, they were invited in to listen to it. 'It was a very important evening!' she declared.[2]

Entry into public houses was discouraged, especially in Wales. If women did frequent such places they were ostracized by 'respectable' people and were excluded from membership of the chapel, which was, often enough, at the heart of social life in Welsh villages.[3] Elsewhere sanctions were less strict, although in Salford the appearance of a woman in a public house on Friday evening or Sunday dinner time caused resentment among male drinkers. On Friday nights, according to one Salford man, females were supposed to stay at home and shampoo their hair: 'if a woman came in, you'd see everyone look, "What's she doing out tonight?"'[4]

In Birmingham some wives combined business with pleasure on Saturday evenings by sitting in a public house to wait for the markets to close and the stallholders to sell off their remaining stocks of meat at reduced prices. Churchmen and members of the middle classes condemned late-night shopping for this reason, arguing that it encouraged female drinking. But for most women it was a welcome break in an otherwise drab routine, when they could gossip with friends and at the same time secure a bargain to feed to their families. Few wives who drank could afford to get drunk. They had too little spending money for that.[5]

Equally frowned upon by moralists was the growth in betting among women after 1918. Wives were accused of wagering some of their housekeeping money without their husband's knowledge, and of acting as illegal off-course betting agents. One who did was Ethel Kay of Harpurhey, who began by taking bets for her husband to the bookmakers. Later she collected bets as a favour for other relatives and neighbours of both sexes, until the bookmaker offered to 'put her on a fixed commission'. According to her son, Mrs Kay had been illiterate up to then, but 'taking the growing number of bets and dealing with the neighbours' winnings did . . . teach her to read and write.'[6]

One observer from Manchester in 1923 claimed to have seen women buying the *Sporting Chronicle* in large numbers: 'They are betting in sums as low as 3d.'[7] This female involvement, especially when combined with the use of children as messengers to carry betting slips to the agent, was condemned as a 'very great moral danger'.[8] Gambling by men was viewed in a far more relaxed fashion.

Gender distinction also applied to the leisure facilities provided by some firms. At Cadbury's there were separate libraries and swimming baths for men and women, and the female staff were given exclusive use of the 'Girls' Grounds'. These comprised about 14 acres of fields for cricket and hockey, tennis courts, athletic facilities and a pleasant, well-timbered garden. Mixed clubs existed, too, including dramatic and music societies and folk dancing and camera clubs, the company regarding these activities as a way of encouraging employee loyalty. As the *Works Magazine* commented approvingly after a wages office social in January 1922, such events were 'extremely valuable in creating that *esprit-de-corps* which is so essential'.[9] At both Cadbury's and Fry's charabanc excursions for workers were organized for similar reasons, as they were at other firms.[10]

But of the many factors influencing female leisure pursuits, wealth and social class were undoubtedly the most significant. Exotic pastimes such as learning to fly an aeroplane or taking a prolonged foreign tour, were outside the range of all but the comfortably off. Likewise an evening spent dancing to the latest jazz band at fashionable London venues like the Kit-Kat Club or Ciro's was very different from the weekly 'hop' in an austere church hall or factory canteen, which was the lot of those lower down the scale, with music provided by a gramophone or the uncertain notes of well-meaning amateurs.

The amount of time devoted to pleasure-seeking also differed widely. While society women, according to some critics, seemed to spend the greater part of their lives in enjoyment – so that it became almost a duty to move from one frivolous event to another – working-class mothers with a young family might have virtually no free hours at all.[11] In this respect, with their many domestic and child-care responsibilities, they fared worse than their menfolk. Not only did the cramped conditions of their home preclude the pursuit of hobbies, except perhaps reading a novel or magazine when their offspring had gone to bed, but they had a multiplicity of chores to perform, to say nothing of shopping. Often enough this meant they spent the evening sewing or ironing, although during the summer they might snatch a few moments to sit outside with a neighbour, exchanging confidences as they stitched busily away. Or a husband might read snippets from the daily newspaper to his wife as she worked.

Neighbourhood loyalties resulted in women lending a hand to help one another in time of distress, while gossip was a way not merely of passing on information but of maintaining local standards. 'You wouldn't tell them personal details,' remembered an Ordsall woman. 'You'd discuss your children, your work, what you were going to have for dinner or tea – sometimes your husbands.' Discussions about others would be constrained by a number of factors, not least of which was the difficulty of knowing 'who was related to whom in neighbourhoods where families rarely moved away.'[12] As Melanie Tebbutt notes, however, these communal influences could be restrictive. Women who held themselves aloof from street gossip were thought of as 'self-consciously rejecting the neighbourhood value system'.[13] Equally, those who were not fully accepted, perhaps on grounds of religion or ethnic origin, would be excluded from the community network. At Ordsall one woman recalled that two Irish Catholic wives were kept at arm's length in this way. 'They were never invited [to pay respects to a dead neighbour], never especially. They weren't allowed into anybody's house in fact. They were tolerated in our street. They were always drunk, rowing and they'd rather drink than spend money on the children. . . . They weren't outcasts because if they really needed help both Maria and Sarah Jane Wilkes would have gone in to them.'[14] For their part, the Irish Catholics maintained strong links with their own community. When they married they rarely crossed the sectarian divide, and two devout Catholic sisters who reached marrying age just after 1918 could not recall even one of their friends marrying a Protestant.[15]

Between the two extremes of the well-to-do socialite and the overburdened woman from a poor working-class neighbourhood there were, of course, large numbers of females who had periods every day which they could devote to their own interests, perhaps during the afternoon when they had finished their household chores and their children had not yet returned from school or, if they were working girls, after they had returned home in the evening from office, shop or factory. For these latter the amount of free time available depended on the kind

Group of women on holiday at Lowestoft, 1928. (The author)

of job they did and the distance they had to travel to and from work. Some might elect to go straight from the workplace to an evening class or sporting activity before they returned home. In London Mollie Stack, who founded the League of Health and Beauty in 1930, began by holding exercise classes for office workers and shop girls in her own studio and at their places of employment. Later she hired a large hall and three months after the League was formed it had a membership of a thousand. Each girl paid 2s. 6d. to join, plus a further 2s. for an entrance badge, which had to be worn at every class.[16]

Resident domestic servants fared badly in regard to leisure pursuits. Unlike mill girls, clerks or shop assistants, they were tied to the requirements of their employers, even in the evenings. At most they would be allowed time off once or twice a week. Nor were they permitted to entertain friends on their employer's premises, unless special permission were given. When a suggestion was made in 1923 that there should be more liberty in that regard, the Lady Mayoress of London, for one, was unenthusiastic. 'I always say I do not mind a few visitors,' she observed coolly, 'but . . . I cannot have a crowd.'[17]

In the matter of holidays class differences also applied. At the end of the 1920s the vast majority of manual workers of both sexes had no paid vacation. Any summer holiday they took had to be saved for during the rest of the year, perhaps by joining a club at their place of employment. In 1920 only about a million manual workers were entitled to a paid holiday. That had increased to one and a half million by 1922, and it remained at around that level for the rest of the decade.[18] Even where holidays with pay were allowed it was common for firms to discriminate between manual and non-manual employees, with the latter given more days off than the former. At Cadbury's female shop floor workers received six working days' holiday after a year's service. This was increased to seven days after three years' service and to eight days after five years, with an extra day for each additional five years with the company thereafter, up to a maximum of twelve days.[19] By contrast office workers commenced with ten days' summer holiday, and were awarded an additional day for every seven years they served with the firm.[20] Even this was meagre, however, compared with the minimum of fourteen days allowed to female bank clerks at the National Provincial Bank. After fifteen years' service that was raised to twenty-one days' holiday, and to the dizzy heights of twenty-four days after thirty years' service – though few can have enjoyed that particular privilege, since there was a retirement age of fifty as well as a marriage bar.[21]

School teachers fared best of all, with a month or so allowed in the summer and about two weeks at both Christmas and Easter. Perhaps not surprisingly, members of the profession were among the women most likely to take advantage of the Continental package holidays which were being offered by a few firms. They included organizations like Goodwill Holidays, which arranged trips for women and girls to France, Holland, Switzerland, Italy and Belgium at a cost of between £10 10s. and £17 for fourteen days, including excursions.[22] Then there were the Workers' Travel Association and the Regent Street Polytechnic, which provided opportunities for foreign travel for as little as £4 or £5 for a ten-day holiday.[23] The railway companies joined in, with the London and North Eastern Railway advertising 'Ideal Holidays in Belgium' and the Southern Railway concentrating on Cherbourg and Western Normandy.[24]

But for most women able to afford a holiday, that meant a week in an English seaside resort, with places like Blackpool or Clacton catering for the mass market and Torquay, Llandudno, the Cornish coast, and Bournemouth attracting those seeking quieter and more select destinations. In other cases, as at Hastings, socially 'shared' resorts were fairly clearly segregated, with the working classes patronizing one part and the middle classes another. At Hastings Ethel Mannin remembered that her family always chose a 'select beach', away from the pier, the band, the Punch and Judy shows, the ice-cream stalls, and the motor boat trips. On Sundays they avoided the beach altogether because only 'common' people and trippers sat on the sands on the Sabbath. Instead they strolled in the public gardens and listened to the band playing sacred music in the park, or walked along the promenade to the neighbouring genteel resort of St Leonards.[25]

In considering the broad influences which affected women's leisure activities it is also important to include the effect of technical change. Most significant in this regard was the development of mass broadcasting from 1922, following the formation of the British Broadcasting Company, and its conversion into a public corporation five years later. Already by 1923 manufacturers of wireless receivers, such as Marconi, were drawing attention to the new medium's importance in reducing the isolation of rural life. Even remotely situated dwellings could ring 'with the music, the speeches, and the latest news announcements transmitted from distant cities' by investing in the firm's Marconiphone two-valve wireless

Families on a charabanc excursion from Oxford. (The author)

receivers.[26] 'Wireless' picnics were recommended: 'You realize what an "enchanted forest" means when you stop the car at the fringe of a leafy glade, take out your Marconiphone Wireless Receiver, lightly sling an aerial across a convenient branch, and listen-in to music.'[27]

It was from the later 1920s, when the scope and quality of broadcasting had improved and cheap and efficient wireless sets were available, that listening to the radio became a mass entertainment. By 1931 44 per cent of households in the London region had wireless licences, and even in less favoured areas like Wales, Cumbria, Durham and Northumberland, it was between 20 and 24 per cent.[28] 'Throughout the period,' comments Mark Pegg, 'there was usually a wireless set on sale to suit almost any pocket.' That ranged from a few shillings for an early crystal set, often home assembled and of variable effectiveness, to £2 10s. for the Gecophone made in 1923 by General Electric, and £19 17s. 6d. for the Marconiphone, which came complete with headphones, valves and batteries. At the other end of the price scale as much as £73 was charged for a large valve set made by the Oxford Wireless Telephone Company.[29]

Women who spent much time at home were particular beneficiaries from the new medium, and their vision of the world was greatly broadened by the opportunity it gave to listen to music, talks, plays and other features. Although broadcasting hours were limited in the early years, some wives with a wireless would invite friends in to listen with them. Or they would plan the evening's listening for the family, taking advantage of the programme details published in the newspapers. Autumn normally saw the launching of a new listening season, not merely because of restricted outdoor pursuits but because the quality of signals was better during the winter.[30] Touring demonstrations were also arranged by wireless retailers. At one conducted at Henley, Oxfordshire, during 1923 the local newspaper claimed reception was so good

> that a large portion of the audience actually clapped and applauded . . . The dance music was so greatly appreciated and was so loud and distinct that many couples danced to it.[31]

Mass production techniques made available low cost wind-up gramophones, too. In the autumn of 1923 John Barker's of London were advertising portables for as little as £2 19s. 6d., while the Mead gramophone could be purchased for 39s. 6d. cash down or 2s. 6d. a week.[32] At around the same time Barker's were offering second-hand pianos on hire-purchase terms, while Drages of High Holborn advertised a 50 guinea piano for £5 deposit and £1 10s. a month thereafter, until the debt had been settled. Their advertisement showed a satisfied 'Mrs Everyman' confessing she had 'longed to have a really good piano all my life. This is indeed a very happy birthday for me.'[33] For the first time advertisers were targeting female consumers in a major way, recognizing their growing role as purchasers in their own right as well as managers of the household budget.

Some middle-class women were able to afford motor cars and motor cycles, or were able to share in the use of the family car. According to the *Evening Standard*, business girls were acquiring motor bikes so that they could go off to 'a country home for the weekend' or could take parents for a spin in their side-car. Many donned men's clothing to ride the bicycles and smeared their face with plenty of cold cream to protect it against the ravages of dust and wind. Hair was hidden under a cap, but 'if I want to show a curl or two under my cap, I wear the kind you pin on,' confessed one enthusiast.[34]

As regards cars, Ford's were offering their runabout in 1923 for £120, including a starter motor, which most lady drivers chose in preference to attempting to crank the vehicle manually. Lesley Lewis, who learned to drive when she was 17, regarded it as 'a liberation but there were many competing claims on the cars, and bicycles were essential for everyday purposes'. Only when an Austin Seven was added to the family fleet for the nominal use of its female members did she have ready access to a car.[35]

The hire-purchase system had penetrated the car market by 1923. Under the new 'Wolseley Scheme for Motoring Out of Income', a Wolseley Ten could be purchased for £50 down and twenty-four monthly instalments of between £10 3s. and £15 16s., depending on the model selected. A year later *Vogue* claimed that the 'only possessions . . . really necessary at present are a motor, a pocketful of money, and a few hundred cigarettes'.[36] By then cars had ceased to be the exclusive toys of the very rich, although at no time in the 1920s did they become objects for mass purchase, in the way that the gramophone and the wireless did. Nevertheless, Stella Davies, whose husband was an industrial chemist in Manchester, remembered that they bought a second-hand two-seater Rover with a dicky seat for a mere £15, trading in their motor-cycle and side-car to purchase

Female motor cyclist in Queens Head Lane, Brandeston, Suffolk in 1925. Ownership of a motor cycle could widen the scope of a woman's working and leisure activities. (Suffolk Record Office: Suffolk Photographic Survey)

it. They and their two small sons then used it to go camping and hiking for their summer holidays.[37]

Against this background of changing leisure opportunities, therefore, it is time to look in detail at the sort of activities in which women engaged. These can be divided into pursuits taken up outside the home, including holidays, and those followed within it.

Amongst the young of all classes, dancing was probably the most popular pastime, with around eleven thousand dance halls and night clubs opened between 1918 and 1925. Among the social élite this frenzy for dancing and associated night-club activity led Mrs Meyrick, who ran a string of clubs in London, to claim that her dance hostesses could earn as much as £80 a week in tips and presents. The girls were expected to dance with customers and to keep them company at their table. Some ended up by marrying wealthy clients.[38] 'To feed and dance, always to be moving, that is the thing,' wrote a participant in the London Season of 1928. 'We daren't risk more than an hour or two in sleep, in case something happens while we aren't there.'[39]

To cater for the sexual needs of the man-about-town there were the professional prostitutes, whose total was put at around three thousand in London by the early 1930s. They were supplemented by unknown numbers of 'casuals', including married women from the suburbs seeking 'sex, adventure and an augmented dress allowance'. They would solicit discreetly, particularly near

Victoria Station and afternoon cinemas, while the better-class 'professional' frequented the haunts of the wealthy and fashionable, taking good care to keep within the law.[40]

Among ordinary working-class girls, meanwhile, the dancing craze was satisfied by the opening of a national network of Palais, Mecca and Locarno dance halls, to say nothing of weekly hops held in drill halls, works canteens, church halls, and the increasingly numerous dance schools, many with roped-off enclosures for learners.[41] Youngsters whose days were spent stooping over a factory bench or office typewriter welcomed the opportunity to dress up in their finery and to exercise to music in the company of friends. There was also an aura of romance and a hope that boyfriends would be met and perhaps a permanent partner. A Bradford woman who got to know her husband at a dance in the canteen of the textile firm where she worked, remembered this as a regular Saturday night outing:

> My father was very, very strict but he always let me go to these dances at the mill because he knew where I was. It was New Year's Eve, 1925. I was 17 and me and my mate were dancing together, and for some reason she got a bit upset and just walked off and left me, and this boy must have seen . . . and he came straight up to me. And he turned out to be a brother of Doris who I worked with, and that's how I met him . . . and he had a motor bike and he used to come and meet me from work.[42]

Dances arranged in connection with churches often had firm rules and regulations, in order to maintain a proper moral standard. One girl who went to church dances in Barrow, Lancashire, recalled the vicar insisting that proceedings should begin with games. Only when he left were they able to have non-stop dancing.[43] But even at Barrow town hall couples were not allowed to dance cheek to cheek. If they got too close the master of ceremonies would intervene to separate them.[44] It was part of the widespread anxiety of parents and dance promoters to avoid conduct which might encourage sexual promiscuity and perhaps unwanted pregnancies. For the same reason many fathers insisted that daughters must be in by 10 p.m., even when they were engaged to be married. Sometimes, however, pregnancy would force a marriage and Mary Chamberlain has recorded how, even fifty years later, this could leave a lingering bitterness. '"You don't think I'd have married him if I didn't have to, do you?" was a not unusual private comment.'[45]

By the end of the 1920s the dancing craze was on the wane and in Liverpool, for example, a number of dance halls had to close down. In areas of high unemployment, young people could not afford to go dancing to the extent that they had once been able to do.[46]

The other great mass entertainment of these years was the cinema. By the middle of the decade there were about three and a half thousand picture palaces in Britain and the motion picture had moved from being 'the province of servant girls and children' to being 'the popular entertainment of the age'.[47] In the early 1920s newspapers like the *Pall Mall Gazette* included occasional reviews of newly

The customary 'white wedding'. Marriage of Stanley Orton, a metalworker employed by the London, Midland and Scottish Railway, and Florence Wagstaffe, a farmer's daughter from Egginton, Derbyshire, in 1929. The bridegroom's two sisters were the bridesmaids. (Mrs P. Knight)

released films, and royalty was beginning to bestow the accolade of social approval by attending charity performances. In July 1923 Princess Mary attended a special matinée in aid of St George's Hospital at the St James's Picture Theatre. 'An excellent programme was given, which included that magnificent film "Enemies of Women", together with the orchestra and effects from the Empire Theatre,' reported the *Pall Mall Gazette* enthusiastically.[48] With the appearance of Al Jolson in *The Singing Fool* in 1928 the era of the talking picture came into its own, and within a year nearly all the picture houses in the major towns had been wired for sound.[49] The silent film was on its way out.

Films offered glamour, excitement and romance. They were often set in exotic locations and for many women they provided a welcome break with the mundane realities of the daily round. One keen filmgoer remembered queuing with a crowd of other girls to see her screen idol, Rudolph Valentino, in *The Sheik*. This was based on a best-selling novel of the same name and was filled with 'melodrama, lust and violence'.[50] That particular fan bought every photo of Valentino she could get and displayed them around her bedroom. When he died prematurely in 1926 thousands of young women like her were devastated.

Another film enthusiast took a part-time job as an usherette so that she could see all the latest releases, while for a third, the screen gave a peep into another world. 'How I have longed to cast off the dulled shackles of today and step, free and proud and ecstatic, into that misty dream-world,' she wrote.[51]

For mothers with young children the cinema offered a welcome refuge where they could sit in the warmth on comfortable seats and forget their cares. According to Leonora Eyles, who worked for a time as an usherette, the 'Tower' picture house in Peckham was

> one of the most frequented rest cures I ever heard of. I have watched tired, dull women thronging in in the afternoon, always with one baby and several small children . . . The women certainly go to the picture palace to 'lose themselves' for an hour; if they only lose themselves in dozing it rests their nerves; if they are sufficiently interested to keep awake, the new train of thought roused by the picture rests their minds, or rather wakens them.[52]

The growth of the cinema weakened support for the music-hall in working-class areas, while the theatre appealed mainly to the better-off. During the 1920s light comedies and musicals were in vogue, particularly on the London stage. In 1927 Noel Coward had four shows running simultaneously in the West End, and his glamorous leading lady, Gertrude Lawrence, matched perfectly the flippant, brittle, cynical mood of such Coward plays as *Bitter Sweet* and *Private Lives*.[53] Miss Lawrence would arrive at the stage door in a luxurious Hispano-Suiza car, with orchids on her shoulder and an escort of attractive young men wearing top hats and white gardenias.[54]

Gladys Cooper combined a career in the theatre with her role as 'wife and mother'. She is shown with her youngest child, Sally, in the early 1930s. Mother and daughter were frequently photographed; they made the covers of both The Queen *and* The Lady's Companion *in a single week. (The author)*

Gladys Cooper was another major theatrical figure. Not only was she one of the leading actresses of her day and a popular pin-up, but, when she joined the management of the Playhouse near Charing Cross, she became the only woman (except for Lilian Baylis at the Old Vic) to run a London theatre before the Second World War. After an amicable divorce from her first husband in 1921, Miss Cooper spent most of the 1920s running the Playhouse, acting on stage and screen, bringing up her two children, and taking an active part in High Society.[55] She remarried towards the end of the decade.

A third glamorous figure was Sylvia Hawkes, reputedly the daughter of a London ostler. She began her career modelling clothes at Revilles and then progressed to the chorus at the Winter Garden in *Tonight's the Night*, before appearing in the first cabaret show to be put on in London. In 1927 she married Lord Ashley, son and heir of the Earl of Shaftesbury, in the face of bitter opposition from his family. Lady Ashley was featured regularly in society magazines but her marriage ended in divorce in 1933, with Lord Ashley proving to be the first of five husbands.[56]

In the cosmopolitan society of London's West End people from the theatre and the arts mixed easily with self-made men and the members of long-established aristocratic families. It was a time when 'Dukes' daughters married commoners, and actresses married peers,' commented one observer. Hence Beatrice Lillie became Lady Peel, the dancer June became Lady Inverclyde, although the marriage ended amid scandal, Rosie Boote was transformed into the Marchioness of Headfort, and the Edwardian stage star, Gertie Miller, became the Countess of Dudley. Other marriages between peers and players included that of Lord Robert Innes-Ker, son of the Dowager Duchess of Roxburghe, to the musical comedy actress, José Collins, in 1920. Three years later Lord Northesk succumbed to the charms of Jessica Brown, an attractive, high-kicking American dancer.[57]

On a more mundane level, sport became a major leisure pursuit for younger women. Tennis was particularly popular among middle- and upper-class girls, and in 1929 *Vogue* was able to reassure anxious mothers that they need not be afraid of their daughter 'contracting a "tennis face", with muscles set into a dreadful frown of concentration' because there were 'so many proofs that it is possible to play it marvellously and at the same time look pretty and be perfectly fit':

> One very noticeable thing about our girl champions at Wimbledon is their grace, distinctly the reverse of what some people have prophesied – that hard exercise and strain would thicken the ankles, coarsen the complexion, and lead to general ungainliness.[58]

Others took up swimming, cycling and walking, while team games like netball, rounders and hockey appealed to the more energetic. Golf and sailing were taken up by the affluent, with the former described by *Vogue* as '*the* weekend sport'. It offered admirable opportunities for pairing-off couples 'with matrimonial prospects in a discreetly casual manner; . . . most women look well in the kind of clothes that are suitable for golf; . . . the golf umbrellas in black and yellow check or red plaids are alone worth the game'.[59]

For the wives and daughters of country-house families, field sports were a regular feature of life, especially during the autumn and winter. Anne Messel, later the Countess of Rosse, frequently hunted on three days a week, and particularly favoured the Blackmore Vale, of which her cousin was the Master. Unlike most of her sex she was a skilled salmon-fisherwoman, and after Christmas took part in shooting parties, invited by her father.[60]

Lady Marjorie Stirling, a daughter of the 8th Earl of Dunmore, remembered country-house weekends during the summer and autumn when there would be tennis, swimming and golf, with very grand homes having their own golf course. At the appropriate seasons there would be fishing and shooting, too. She also recalled the vast quantity of luggage needed for these visits. 'Even for a shoot in Scotland – a seven-day shoot – you had to dress for every day of the week. And naturally that meant a different hat; and a hat box.'[61]

Lesley Lewis, who joined in shooting parties on her uncle's property in Scotland, remembered it as 'very much a man's world', where women were welcome if they made themselves 'as useful and inconspicuous as possible':

> You knew how to mark down birds and were rather like the dogs themselves – no bright colours, no loud voices or laughter, no lagging behind, no nonsense of any kind, but what sheer bliss it was. I wore a sober felt hat sometimes relieved by a jay's or pheasant's feather, or the highly prized pin-feathers of a woodcock. My tweed coat and skirt . . . would last for years, starting off when new for point-to-points and other country race-meetings, progressing from organized shoots with birds driven over butts, to rough days walking in line, until the chilliness made it apparent that they were well and truly worn out. With these was assumed an 'Aertex' shirt of cellular cotton, and at least one jersey which could be shed at need into the haversack in which I carried the indispensable Burberry and my lunch if it was not the sort of day when the picnic was sent up on a pony. On informal days I carried an ash walking stick to beat out the bracken or, for driving days, a shooting stick on which I perched in somebody's butt.[62]

All the female members of the party were expected to carry their own things, as the men were already loaded with their guns and cartridges. Sometimes 'you added to your burdens the care of a half-trained dog, still on a lead'.

Lesley thoroughly enjoyed these gatherings but not all women shared her enthusiasm. Shy girls like Lady Marjorie Stirling found the evening round of games, charades, and practical joking an embarrassment, while high-spirited intellectuals like Nancy Mitford had little in common with the hearty, sporting couples who were at the centre of most such parties, 'the husbands damning and blasting their way across the grouse-moors while their wives spent the day embroidering chair-covers and discussing the servant problem'.[63] Nancy disliked following the guns and having to sit in the butts for hours in total silence, frozen to the bone. When she could, she escaped to her room to read and to write long letters to her brother. 'Let's have an anti-sport league,' she suggested on one occasion. 'Let's go abroad for *two* years together, we could buy a small palace in

Venice by way of a pied-à-terre & a very tiny but luxurious flat in Paris.'[64] She recommended every female guest to equip herself with some embroidery as this acted as a 'barricade and a topic of conversation'. 'When you are asked to go for a walk, play bridge, or do anything else that you particularly dislike you can entrench yourself behind it.'[65]

Few women, even at this relatively late date, took an active part in shoots. Their role was primarily that of onlooker and admirer of the prowess of their menfolk.

More to Nancy Mitford's taste were country-house visits to her friend, the Countess of Seafield, who had succeeded to the title at the age of 9. Nina Seafield owned vast estates in Scotland and in 1928 when Nancy went to stay with her at the end of the London Season she described the juvenile pranks she and her fellow guests got up to, in a letter to her brother:

> this visit is being a perfect orgy . . . We haven't once been to bed before 2, pyjama parties every night in Nina's sitting-room which is like a gala night at the Florida. Last night we had a dress up dinner. Hamish & I draped our middles in calf-skin chiffon & wore vine leaves . . . Mark just came in a bathing dress & a wreath & Nina was a lady at the court of Herod. You should have seen the Troll [Hamish] & me standing in a bath together staining our bods with coffee!! In the afternoon we all olive-oiled each other & lay in the minimum of bathing dresses in a pretty scene. I'm literally black now! . . . Hamish, Nina & I wrote the gossip for the next *Vogue* & put in lovely things about ourselves of course . . . Oh the fun of it![66]

For more sober members of the prosperous middle classes, there were weekend visits to friends and relatives, or perhaps motor drives to a cottage they owned in the country or by the sea. Dinner parties were arranged as well as sessions of bridge and mah-jongg, two of the most popular games among the well-to-do during these years. As Rose Luttrell, wife of a Bath bank manager, remembered, she and her husband had 'a tremendous lot of friends in the neighbourhood and we used to go away for weekends. . . . You just moved among your own friends or your own contemporaries and they were all leading the same sort of life.'[67]

Alongside these private entertainments, there were collective organizations like the Women's Institute, the Cooperative Guild and the Townswomen's Guild, which offered women the opportunity to meet together to discuss common problems and perhaps press for reforms. The largest of these was the National Federation of Women's Institutes, which was concentrated in rural areas. By 1927 it had a membership of around a quarter of a million spread over about four thousand villages.

The movement had started in Anglesey during the autumn of 1915 when a Mrs Watt, who had been a member of its Canadian forerunner, opened the first Institute. By 1919 there were 1,405 Institutes and in that year the WI launched its own magazine, *Home and Country*.[68] Initially the movement had to overcome the prejudices of many husbands and fathers, who saw it as threatening their own status and domestic comfort. One man declared he would 'never let *my* women go gadding about the lanes in the evening', while in another village a member recalled that when the Institute started, although people gave in their names it was difficult to decide just who would attend:

> You didn't know how the Husband would take it, if he would let his wife go out at night. We didn't do as we liked then as we do today; the man was the Master of the House. But at the end of that first year the membership was ninety.[69]

Similar difficulties had to be overcome elsewhere. In Yorkshire husbands refused to let their wives join what they labelled 'that secret society', while in 1928 a letter was sent to *Home and Country* by a 'mere man', complaining 'about the amount of time spent on, and involvement with, the WI by wives'.[70]

In the end the WI succeeded, not by challenging the female domestic role but by emphasizing its importance within the family context. As one member wrote in 1930, while she accepted that household work was always the woman's responsibility, that did not imply 'subservience . . . "Not masculine tyranny, not wifely submission, but . . . equal comradeship and the happy atmosphere are the real essentials of a lasting happy home".'[71]

Another factor in the movement's success was its determination to remain non-party political and non-sectarian, thereby eliminating possible causes of conflict between members. It was also democratic. Lady Denman, who in 1917 became the first President of the National Federation of Women's Institutes, insisted that a secret ballot must be held for the election of all officers and committee members, so as to prevent petty squabbles and avoid the ordinary village members being dominated by the views of the squire's or parson's wife.[72] Apart from its role in encouraging jam-making, fruit bottling, vegetable growing, needlework guilds, and similar domestic pursuits, it soon widened its horizons. Drama groups were formed, trading stalls set up (thereby setting a value on the labour of the women who had made the items offered), and debates conducted on social issues and the international questions of the day. At Stoke by Nayland in Suffolk, for example, in 1920 there were two talks on first aid; after the second, on 'minor accidents and how to treat them', the secretary recorded the appreciation of the members, especially those 'who cannot easily obtain medical aid'. Again, at Stoke by Clare there was a lecture on 'Maternal Mortality' in February 1926, 'which we hope will prove useful advice to many of our members'. Earlier this Institute had debated the need for better footpaths and for 'small houses for the working class' in their village.[73] In other cases choirs from several villages joined together to go on tour and raise money for charity, while in 1922 *Home and Country* urged Institutes to promote maternity and child welfare schemes. Typical of many was the WI at Long Crendon, Buckinghamshire, which in the summer of 1925 reported that it had performed a two-act play and had also taken the lead in starting an Infant Welfare Centre in the village. At Longwick in the same county, an exhibition of needlework had been organized, and the Institute had managed to get a bus service started to connect the village with the railway station and market town. Its demonstrations of basket and soft toy making had enabled members to supply a stall at a fête in aid of the Village Hall fund.[74]

By encouraging women to run meetings, vote for officers, and relate the problems of their lives to wider issues in the community at large the WI broadened their perspective and gave them confidence to press for change. In 1918 the annual report of the National Federation noted that it had cooperated with the Rural Housing and Sanitation Association and the Women's Labour League to achieve improvements in housing. Later, feminists in Cambridgeshire sought to persuade members of local Institutes to stand for election to rural district councils.[75]

On a lighter note, the social events organized represented a clear assertion of women's *right* to have time off away from their domestic chores. One Somerset member was heard to say: 'I have always wanted to travel and now it is going to be possible through the WI.' She subsequently visited Cheddar Gorge on an outing and was impressed not so much by the stalagmites as by the electric lighting![76] Games and dancing were arranged during the 'social half-hour' which formed part of every meeting and refreshments were served. In this way companionship and light-heartedness were introduced into the lives of members. One early supporter claimed that women who had lived in the same village for years as total strangers were brought together through the Institute, while those who had never ventured out to church or chapel or village entertainment came eagerly to its meetings.[77]

Not until the late 1920s did the National Union of Townswomen's Guilds get under way to perform a similar role for those living in urban areas, and it was the 1930s before the movement became well established.[78] Some town dwellers, however, had already joined the Women's Cooperative Guild, which had been inaugurated in the 1880s. By 1930 it had a network of nearly 1,400 branches and a membership of about sixty-seven thousand.[79] Support was particularly strong in the North of England and in London. The Guild encouraged members to take an active part in the cooperative movement but it offered educational facilities, too, including lectures and debates. In Liverpool there were evening classes and concerts as well as dramatic and choral societies. Excursions and outings were arranged and there were whist drives and dances held at the cooperative halls.[80] Even small and less ambitious branches performed a valuable educational role. 'I would not miss going [to the Guild],' said one Welsh miner's wife, ' . . . as we have such very beautiful lectures from our different speakers that it seems to uplift us and help us to carry on from time to time'.[81]

For younger women and girls there were organizations like the Girl Guides and the Girls' Friendly Society to provide entertainment, education, companionship and moral guidance. In 1933–4 the Guides had a membership of 474,408 in England and Wales, and the Girls' Friendly Society 158,000.[82] This latter was popular among domestic servants, especially those living away from home, to whom it offered support and leisure facilities on their day off. Miss Goff, who first went into service in 1926, remembered that while she was working in Paignton she and her sister, who was also in service in the town, would spend the afternoon of their half-day off at the cinema and would then go to the Girls' Friendly Society meeting. There 'we met with our mates and always had a very pleasant evening, singing, folk-dancing, holding little competitions, and sometimes a social, or concert'. On Sunday afternoons, when they were also free,

A lady preacher addressing a Revivalist meeting at Brandeston, Suffolk, in 1919. Her listeners were also mostly female. (Suffolk Record Office: Suffolk Photographic Survey)

the local GFS secretary arranged for the library at one of the churches to be opened for girls who had no home in the locality. There for 6d. each they could meet and have a pot of tea prepared by the caretaker: 'we would pool all our food and have a nice tea'.[83] For youngsters like these the Girls' Friendly Society offered an important focus for their leisure hours.

Many women found inspiration and uplift through religion, and although support for both Church and Chapel weakened after the First World War, along with associated institutions like Mothers' Meetings, Sewing Guilds, Bands of Hope, and the like, in some communities they remained a potent force. 'All our social life was . . . with the chapel,' declared a woman from Llwynpia in Wales. 'Because there was something there every night of the week for us. Either little plays, or there'd be children's operettas. Or the big choir . . . And there'd be Young People's Society . . . Prayer meeting on a Monday night . . . Everybody went to chapel then. . . . Our social life was all around the church.'[84]

Mrs Clara Berry, who lived near Stalybridge, had similar memories. She rarely went 'to the pictures . . . 'cos we were always at Sunday School. You'd everything coming off at Sunday School . . . nearly every week.' She was a member of the Band of Hope, a temperance organization for young people, and took part in the ladies' sewing teas at the chapel, when about thirty attended to make night-

Ryecroft Independent Chapel Whit Walk at Audenshaw, Lancashire, in 1923. (Tameside Local Studies Library, Stalybridge)

dresses, chemises and pillow cases for the annual sale of work. Both Mrs Berry and her husband were Sunday School teachers and even before their marriage in 1922 they had attended the same chapel.[85]

In Lancashire and Cheshire there were special 'Whit Walks' associated with the various churches and chapels, when women and children paraded through the town, wearing their finery and headed by a brass band. At Stalybridge Mrs Ruth Bradley remembered groups marching in from nearby Mossley and Ashton, as well as from the town itself. Each group held aloft a banner with their particular place of worship upon it. They congregated in Stalybridge market place where, as she recalled, one blaring band would be still sounding loudly as the next approached 'playing a different tune'.[86] These events usually ended with a celebratory tea.

But for married women especially, family responsibilities and lack of cash meant that leisure pursuits were limited to the home, or to visits to close relatives. Links between mothers and married daughters were often strong in working-class areas. In Birmingham daughters in many of the city's poorest districts would try to live near to their mother, so that they could turn to her for help and advice.[87]

Even in more prosperous neighbourhoods, family gossip formed an integral part of life, giving a sense of cohesion, of 'belonging' to the kinship network and of sharing in its collective memories and experiences.[88]

When families were moved out of the inner cities to new council estates often these kinship links were destroyed and that contributed to the sense of isolation felt by some suburban wives. On the London County Council's massive Becontree estate, where households had migrated from the East End of London, many made great efforts to keep in touch with relatives still living near their old home. One wife, for example, went back to the East End each week to visit a grandmother and an aunt. Other aunts and uncles were visited about half a dozen times a year. Another family had an uncle out on a visit every other week, while in a third case a family who had migrated from Stockton returned there for their holidays.[89] During the summer, members of the family would come out to the estate on visits. But it was all very different from the time when they could meet a mother or aunt every day by merely walking along the street, or could obtain the services of a relative for child-minding, should the need arise.

Within the home itself, needlework and reading were probably the major leisure interests for women of all classes. However, there was a world of difference between the genteel embroidery taken up by the well-to-do and the basic sewing, darning, and 'making do' which were the lot of those lower down the scale.

The growing mass demand for reading material was met by a proliferation of magazines and newspapers to cater for all tastes, ranging from *Peg's Paper, Polly's Paper* and *Red Star* at the cheaper end of the working-class market to *Vogue, Good Housekeeping* and *The Tatler*, which were aimed at the fashion-conscious and affluent. There was also a wealth of novels, including detective stories and light romantic fiction. The latter appealed particularly to women, as the booming sales and borrowing figures demonstrated. Many novels, such as the works of Ethel M. Dell, Ruby M. Ayres and E.M. Hull, were purely escapist literature, enabling 'the weary and bored and depressed to transfer themselves temporarily to another sphere of life'. For some women they provided an erotic stimulation which was lacking in their own existence.[90] One of the biggest successes in this regard was *The Sheik*, written by Mrs E.M. Hull, the wife of a Derbyshire pig farmer, and published in 1919. It concerned the abduction of an aristocratic English girl by a handsome, cruel 'man of the desert'. After many trials and tribulations, love triumphed. The *Times Literary Supplement*, in reviewing the book in November 1919, commented, tongue in cheek, that, 'If there be a moral in this simple tale it is one of warning to young European ladies not to ride alone into the Sahara.'[91] Yet almost immediately the book enjoyed massive sales. By the summer of 1921 it was being described as 'the enthralling novel which all England is reading', and was already in its sixth impression.[92] Later it was made into a film which enjoyed an equally spectacular success.

For those unable to afford to buy books, membership of a public library or a branch of Boots Library could meet their needs. In the mid-1920s about twenty-five million volumes were exchanged annually by the various Boots branches, and a decade later, with over four hundred branches and half a million subscribers it was the largest circulating library of its kind in the country. In 1926 it cost 42s. a year to get books out from Boots 'on demand', but only 10s. 6d. for the ordinary service. This was cheaper than the small but exclusive London lending libraries, such as Day's, Mudie's and the Times Book Club, which tended to be favoured by the fashionable and the socially superior.[93]

Listening to the wireless became increasingly important as a home leisure pursuit. The young Jean Metcalfe remembered the excitement in her home when during the mid-1920s her father and uncle assembled a 'cat's whisker' crystal set. She was hauled out of bed and brought downstairs so that she might 'hear a man singing from a long way off'. She had to hold the headphones over her ears while her uncle adjusted the receiver.

> The sea-shell hissing and crackling stops, and there it is – a man's voice, deep and muffled, sounding like Father Christmas inside a chimney. 'Think of it,' says Mother, 'now you can say you've actually heard Peter Dawson.' I think they're disappointed because I'm not as excited as they are, but I like Mother's music better. We have a walnut piano with brass candle-holders on the front. She doesn't play very well but her voice is light and pretty when she sings my favourites.[94]

In other homes, attempts were made to produce 'do-it-yourself' loud-speakers. In one case this involved dropping the headphones into a large mixing bowl, so that the sound would reverberate. It seems to have been moderately successful.[95]

As wireless sets improved and owners became more adept at adjusting them, listening in became increasingly enjoyable. However, many women also continued to play the piano and family sing-songs were a regular part of life in countless middle-class households, especially on Sunday evenings, when there would be hymns and sacred music. Games, too, were a common feature in many families. Mrs Kathleen Abney remembered that in her Newmarket home these took the form of board games rather than cards. 'Being a racing town there was a lot of gambling and my father associated cards with that.'[96] Among the womenfolk there might be some clandestine 'telling of fortunes', using tea-leaves or cards.

Alongside these daily or weekly activities, there were the special events – birthdays, wedding anniversaries and annual holidays. More clearly than almost any other aspect of leisure, holidays underlined class differences. For those at the top of the social scale there were many opportunities to get away from home. The dreary period between Christmas and the springtime 'mimosa month' on the Riviera might be spent on the ski slopes of Switzerland or in the sunshine of Egypt or in some other exotic location. Later, after the London Season had ended in July, there was yachting at Cowes, followed perhaps by visits to Deauville and Le Touquet or, later in the decade, to Cap d'Antibes, where the Bright Young People swam and sunbathed. 'We practically live in bathing suits and coconut oil,' declared Méraud Guinness in 1927, and *Vogue's* diary for August in that year confirmed the impression:

> Bathing from rocks is a new-found pleasure. When one has seen the rocks at the Cap d'Antibes, terraced down to the sea, each with a little nook shaded by

umbrellas under which one has gin fizzes or tea while watching the diving; has seen the aquaplaning and the groups of people sunburned a deep mahogany, it is a scene to rival the Lido [at Venice]. In the way of pyjamas and bathing suits Miss Ina Claire takes the honours. Her Nowitsky pyjama suit has enormously full trousers. . . . No one wears beach robes to keep from being sunburned but only to change into from wet suits, or to lunch at the Casino.[97]

After lunch there would be a siesta, then cocktails, followed by a drive to Cannes or some other resort for the evening's entertainment or for gambling at the casino.

Later there might be a cruise in the Mediterranean on board someone's yacht, or on an ocean liner to more distant destinations. Small wonder that *Vogue* described the fashionable world as 'a nomad tribe', constantly travelling, 'like extravagant gypsies', from 'one colourful encampment to the next'. From Palm Beach and the Venice Lido to Tunisia and the French Riviera, 'the society gypsies were always on the move . . . Wherever they went, they took their own way of life with them.' Hence, along the French Riviera, small fishing villages were

Family picnic on the sands at Pendine, Dyfed, c. 1925. The kettle was boiled on a primus stove and the food was packed in the large basket to the right of the photograph. (National Museum of Wales: Welsh Folk Museum)

transformed into sophisticated resorts, with villas, tennis courts, smart restaurants, and gambling casinos.[98]

Some women began to travel by aeroplane, taking an Imperial Airways flight from Croydon airport. The planes were very small – eighteen passengers and a steward – and they were also noisy and bumpy. Ethel Mannin recalled that when she travelled by air to Frankfurt, Amsterdam and even Paris she was often the only woman on board. The discomfort experienced on many of the journeys doubtless accounted for this.[99]

Exotic vacations like these contrasted sharply with the week or fortnight at an English resort which was the height of ambition for most women. For poorer families even a day excursion could be beyond their means, despite the offering of special cut-price trips by the railway companies and bus proprietors, especially at Bank Holidays. In 1923 the Southern Railway alone advertised twenty-six day excursions from London over the August Bank holiday period and the General Omnibus Company offered forty-one different destinations. Bus trips from Charing Cross to Chislehurst cost 11d. and from Finsbury Park to St Albans 1s. 3d.[100] This company also suggested various 'Honeysuckle By-Ways' to cater for ramblers, with a sketch map to indicate possible routes to be followed.

For wives and daughters able to afford a week at the seaside, this normally meant staying at a boarding-house. Girls employed in textile mills often saved up for holidays through clubs at their firm. Mrs Clara Berry set aside 6d. a week so that she could take 25s. with her when she and friends from the mill went away. They spent 1s. a night each for their bed at the boarding-house. They provided their own food and the landlady cooked it. Full board would have cost 2s. 6d. a night, so Mrs Berry and her friends always chose the cheaper option. 'Some'd take a tin of salmon, some a tin of fruit, some tea and some sugar.' Other items would be purchased in the resort.[101]

Mr and Mrs Wood, who were both millworkers, went to Blackpool for their week's holiday, staying with a landlady who came from the Manchester area:

> sleeping money . . . were a shilling a night – two shillings if you slept together . . . and we'd arrange with her to buy any beef we wanted and she cooked it. We went and bought the other stuff, apart from the stuff we took with us. An' we'd a real good week for two pound ten! A weekly ticket at Central Pier . . . a shilling every night at the Tower or Winter Gardens and any spare cash we'd spend at South Shore. There's always been a fair ground there.[102]

Holidaymaking offered opportunities to eat out, which was not a normal part of working-class life at home. Fish and chips could be purchased for a few pence. At Blackpool there were the miles of promenade, the putting greens, the fun fairs and the piers:

> Palmists, ice-cream vendors, oyster carts, herbalists and contortionists livened up a walk in the balmy air of the promenade, and the Tower with its menagerie, slot machines, restaurants, bars, . . . and the ballroom was a haven on a wet day. At night there were theatres, where famous stars . . . performed. For young

Visiting the fortune-teller at a fair, probably at Marlborough, Wiltshire. (Long Collection,
Rural History Centre, University of Reading)

women above all there was the dancing in the Tower ballroom or elsewhere . . .
Picking up with different young men most nights of the week was all part of the
fun.[103]

Unlike the situation before 1914, these light-hearted flirtations were
encouraged by some of the women's magazines. In an article on 'Seaside
Romances', which appeared in *Violet* in July 1923, the anonymous author
described the summer holiday as a 'unique interruption' in most girls' humdrum
daily round:

> it would be sheer priggish nonsense to spend a week in any seaside boarding-
> house and refrain from getting on good terms with its inhabitants merely
> because you had not been 'introduced'. . . . I grant you that an awful lot of men
> *are* frauds. But a lot aren't. Moreover, the frauds are not an atom dangerous to
> the girl with gumption . . . I have no intention of preaching against flirtations.
> The only danger is that if you acquire a taste for flirtation you may never know
> what it is to understand the flavour of the real thing.[104]

For older women, especially the tired mothers of families, the chance to sit on
the beach and watch their children paddling and making sand castles was
something to look forward to. Most carried a large bag in which they stowed their
knitting or sewing, a pencil to write postcards, a magazine or two to read, and a
towel with which to dry the children's feet after paddling. As they stitched or
knitted in a desultory fashion they watched the 'goings-on' of other families or

Girls dressed in Dutch costume for Brighton Carnival in 1923. (The author)

the actions of the beach photographer. Sometimes, greatly daring, they took off their shoes and stockings and went paddling. Later they would sit on the crowded promenade and listen to a military band or spend the evening at a concert party on the pier, perhaps finishing up with a snack of whelks at one of the stalls, washed down with a Guinness.[105] At the end of the week there were souvenirs to buy and sticks of pink rock to take home as gifts for relatives at home.

For the large numbers of unemployed and the poorest families such breaks were out of the question, and even in 1937 only 33 per cent of the population had a holiday lasting a week or more.[106] Some families in the East End of London and parts of the Black Country might combine business with pleasure, by going to the countryside to pick fruit or hops. But most had no such opportunities. Their plight was summed up by an unemployed factory worker – a deserted wife, who had two children at school to support: 'I can always find enough to fill my time' she declared, 'there is plenty of sewing and mending, and I can sometimes borrow magazines to read on Sunday evenings, and I have a small garden that I like to do. But . . . however much I do I cannot earn the money for the children's clothes.'[107] As the world slipped into deeper recession at the end of the 1920s, her plight was shared by an increasing number of wives and mothers, even in families where the husband remained at home. In leisure, as in much else beside, Britain became increasingly divided into the 'haves', for whom living standards were rising and opportunities for pleasure and for travel were increasing, and the 'have-nots', whose economic situation was becoming ever more precarious.

APPENDIX 1

Working Women

(a) WOMEN'S MARITAL STATUS AND THEIR CONTRIBUTION TO THE
LABOUR FORCE: ENGLAND AND WALES: 1911–31

	Working women who are:			Men who are economically active	Women who are economically active	Women in total labour force
	single	married	widowed or divorced			
Year	%	%	%	%	%	%
1911	77	14	9	83.8*	32.5*	29.7
1921	78	14	8	87.1**	32.3**	29.5
1931	77	16	7	90.5***	34.2***	29.7

*   :   Relates to persons aged 10 and over, as shown in the Census.
**   :   Relates to persons aged 12 or over, as shown in the Census.
***   :   Relates to persons aged 14 or over, as shown in the Census.

Source: Catherine Hakim, *Occupational Segregation* (Department of Employment
Research Paper no. 9, November 1979), pp. 11, 25.

(b) AGE STRUCTURE OF THE FEMALE LABOUR FORCE: 1911–31

	Working women aged:			Total no. of working women (millions)
Year	under 35 %	35–59 %	60 and over %	
1911	71	24	5	4.8
1921	69	26	5	5.0
1931	69	26	5	5.6

Source: Catherine Hakim, *Occupational Segregation*, p. 10.

(c) MAIN CATEGORIES OF WOMEN WORKERS: 1921 AND 1931 (calculated from Census)

	1921	1931
Total no. of working women	5.0m.	5.6m.
Women employed:	%	%
Personal service	33.0	34.4
{ Domestic service	22.6 }	23.8 }
{ Charwomen	2.4 }	2.5 }
Textile workers	12.0	10.2
Makers of textile goods and dress	10.8	9.7
Shop assistants	6.8	7.0
Clerks, draughtswomen and typists	8.5	10.3
Total in above *five categories*	71.1	71.6

APPENDIX 2

Maternal Mortality

(a) PUERPERAL MORTALITY RATES FOR WALES, AND ENGLAND AND WALES 1924–30:

Year	Rates per 1,000 live births	
	Wales	England and Wales
1924	5.14	3.90
1925	4.97	4.08
1926	4.92	4.12
1927	5.78	4.11
	Rates per 1,000 total births	
1928	5.79	4.25
1929	5.58	4.16
1930	5.30	4.22

(b) COUNTY BOROUGHS RANKED IN ORDER OF THEIR PUERPERAL MORTALITY RATES PER 1,000 LIVE BIRTHS DURING THE PERIOD 1924–33:

Borough	Rate per 1,000 live births
Halifax	7.05
Oldham	6.88
Darlington	6.71
Bury	6.67
Rochdale	6.66
Wigan	6.44
Bolton	6.16
Barnsley	5.90
Merthyr Tydfil	5.84
Preston	5.82
Blackpool	5.78

(c) ADMINISTRATIVE COUNTIES RANKED IN ORDER OF THEIR PUERPERAL
MORTALITY RATES PER 1,000 LIVE BIRTHS DURING THE PERIOD 1924–33:

County	Rate per 1,000 live births
Anglesey	6.79
Denbigh	6.56
Cardigan	6.39
Carmarthen	6.34
Glamorgan	5.85
Pembroke	5.70
Flint	5.63
Lancashire	5.41
West Riding of Yorkshire	5.37
Cumberland	5.20
Monmouth	5.18
Durham	4.72

Sources: *Ministry of Health: Report on Maternal Mortality in Wales*,
Parliamentary Papers 1936–7, vol. XI; *Report on an Investigation into Maternal
Mortality*, Parliamentary Papers 1936–7, vol. XI.

APPENDIX 3

Income and Expenditure of Labouring Families

(a) AVERAGE WEEKLY WAGES OF ORDINARY AGRICULTURAL LABOURERS IN SPECIMEN COUNTIES: 1919 AND 1924:

	October 1919 (Wages Board)	October 1924 (Minimum Wages)	1924 Agricultural Wages Act, including hours per week	
	s. d.	s. d.	s. d.	Weekly hours
Eastern Division				
Bedford	36 6	27 0	29 0	48
Cambridge	36 6	25 0	30 0	48
Essex	38 6	27 0	30 0	50 in summer 48 in winter
Hertford	38 6	27 0	29 0	48
Norfolk	36 6	25 0	29 0 / 28 0	50 in summer 48 in winter
Suffolk	36 6	25 0	29 2 / 28 0	50 in summer 48 in winter
West Midlands and South Western Division				
Dorset	36 6	26 0	30 0	51
Hereford	36 6	27 0	31 0	52 in summer 48 in winter
Shropshire	37 0	30 0	31 6	54
Somerset	36 6	28 6	32 0	52
Worcester	36 6	27 0	30 0	53 in summer 48 in winter

South East and East Midlands Division

Berkshire	36	6	26	0	29	2	50
Buckinghamshire	36	6	27	0	30	0	50 in summer 48 in winter
Hampshire	37	6	27	0	30	0	50
Northamptonshire	36	6	28	0	30	0	50 in summer 48 in winter
Warwickshire	36	6	27	6	30	0	50 in summer 48 in winter

Northern Division

Durham	42	6	32	0	32	0	50
Yorkshire, West Riding	41	0	35	0	36	0	52 summer (no winter figure shown)

Source: Reg Groves, *Sharpen the Sickle! The History of the Farm Workers' Union* (1949), pp. 252–3.

(b) WEEKLY BUDGETS OF CAMBRIDGESHIRE LABOURERS' FAMILIES IN 1924–5:

Man, Wife and Six Children

Man, Wife and Three Children, none of the children working

Food – total 19s. 10d.	*s.*	*d.*
Bread	7	4
Half a stone of flour	1	5
4¼ lb margarine	2	3
Meat		1
Milk	1	0
½ lb tea	1	1
¼ lb cocoa		7
6 lb sugar	2	2
1 lb jam		9
½ lb lard		6
1 lb currants		8
¼ lb suet		4
Apples		3
Pepper, salt		2
Other Expenditure – total 4s. 9d.		
Coal, turf	2	8
Soap, soda		8
Oil, candles		9
Firelighters		3

Food – total 17s. 0½d.	*s.*	*d.*
Bread, flour	7	6
6 pints of milk	1	6
3 lb meat	2	0
1½lb margarine	1	6
3 lb sugar	1	1½
½ lb tea	1	4
½ lb cheese		4
½ lb bacon		10
½ lb currants		4
¼ lb cocoa		7
Other Expenditure – total 7s. 6½d.		
Soap, soda		8
Oil, candles, matches		9
Darning wool, papers		6
Blue for washing		1

Cotton	2	Coal	3 3½
Darning wool	2	Rent	2 3
Matches	1		
Total outlay	24 7	Total outlay	24 7

N.B. Rent is omitted from one of the lists and only one mentions the purchase of a newspaper. Neither budget includes any provision for clubs, insurance, boots, clothing and repairs to boots, nor is there mention of renewal of pans and brushes, any contribution to church or chapel, and recreational activity. Possible produce grown in garden and allotment is also excluded.

Source: J.W. Robertson Scott, *The Dying Peasant and the Future of his Sons* (1926), p. 92.

Notes

Chapter 1 From War to Peace: 1914–20

1. Susan Kingsley Kent, *Making Peace. The Reconstruction of Gender in Interwar Britain* (1993), p. 16.

2. C. Stella Davies, *North Country Bred. A Working-class Family Chronicle* (1963), p. 90.

3. Pamela Horn, *Rural Life in England in the First World War* (1984), p. 43.

4. Geoffrey Moorhouse, *Hell's Foundations. A Town, Its Myths and Gallipoli* (1992), pp. 50, 59, 71, 89, 111, 112.

5. Jennifer Ellis (ed.), *Thatched with Gold. The Memoirs of Mabell, Countess of Airlie* (1962), p. 133.

6. Anne de Courcy, *Circe. The Life of Edith, Marchioness of Londonderry* (1992), pp. 110, 130.

7. Ray Strachey, *'The Cause'. A Short History of the Women's Movement in Great Britain* (1928), p. 345.

8. Martin Pugh, *Women and the Women's Movement in Britain 1914–1959* (1992), p. 32.

9. Susan Kingsley Kent, *op. cit.*, p. 14.

10. Philip Ziegler, *Diana Cooper. The Biography of Lady Diana Cooper* (1983 edn), pp. 70–1, 73, 98.

11. Leah Manning, *A Life for Education* (1970), pp. 52, 54.

12. Quoted in Robert Dingwall, Anne Marie Rafferty and Charles Webster, *An Introduction to the Social History of Nursing* (1988), p. 74.

13. Gail Braybon, *Women Workers in the First World War* (1981), p. 44.

14. Martin Pugh, *op. cit.*, p. 9.

15. Martin Pugh, *op. cit.*, pp. 20–1; Barbara Drake, *Women in Trade Unions* (1920), Table III; *Report of the War Cabinet Committee on Women in Industry*, Parliamentary Papers, 1919, vol. XXXI, pp. 80–1.

16. Ray Strachey, *op. cit.*, p. 344.

17. *Report of the War Cabinet Committee on Women in Industry*, p. 96.

18. Sheila Lewenhak, *Women and Trade Unions. An Outline History of Women in the British Trade Union Movement* (1977), p. 156; Gail Braybon, *op. cit.*, p. 82.

19. Sheila Lewenhak, *op. cit.*, p. 157.

20. *Loughborough Technical College Prospectus 1918–19*, p. 121 in Loughborough University of Technology Archives, LC/PC10.

21. Gareth Griffiths, *Women's Factory Work in World War I* (1991), p. 21.

22. Gilbert Stone (ed.), *Women War Workers* (1917), pp. 35–6.

23. Gail Braybon, *op. cit.*, p. 79.

24. *Ibid.*, p. 90.

25. *Ibid.*, p. 169.

26. *Ibid.*, p. 149.

27. *Report of the War Cabinet Committee on Women in Industry*, p. 80.

28. *1911 Census of Population: Occupations*, Parliamentary Papers, 1913, vol. LXXVIII; Gail Braybon, *op. cit.*, p. 49.

29. Gail Braybon, *op. cit.*, pp. 49–50.

30. *Report of the War Cabinet Committee on Women in Industry*, pp. 89–90.

31. Stalybridge Oral History Transcripts, no. 004, at Stalybridge Local Studies Library.

32. Gail Braybon, *op. cit.*, pp. 48, 163.

33. Monica Cosens, *Lloyd George's Munition Girls* (n.d. [1916]), pp. 17, 108–9.

34. Gilbert Stone (ed.), *op. cit.*, p. 33.

35. Gail Braybon, *op. cit.*, p. 206.

36. C. Stella Davies, *op. cit.*, pp. 139–40.

37. Susan Kingsley Kent, *op. cit.*, p. 39.

38. *Ibid.*

39. *Report of the War Cabinet Committee on Women in Industry*, p. 80. This figure included nearly half a million women working on their own account or as employers.

40. Martin Pugh, *op. cit.*, pp. 13–14.

41.   *Western Mail*, 9 January 1919.
42.   *The Position of Women in Industry after the War*. Report of a conference convened by the Bristol Association for Industrial Reconstruction, 16–17 March 1918, at the Imperial War Museum, EMP 28/1, p. 5.
43.   Martin Pugh, *op. cit.*, pp. 16–17.
44.   Hilary Macaskill, *From the Workhouse to the Workplace. 75 years of one-parent family life 1918–1993* (1993), p. 9.
45.   *Ibid.*
46.   Martin Pugh, *op. cit.*, pp. 17–18; Hilary Macaskill, *op. cit.*, p. 11.
47.   Martin Pugh, *op. cit.*, p. 18.
48.   Lara Marks, 'Battling for the Health of Mothers in London, 1902–1936', in a History of Childbirth in the Twentieth Century Symposium held at the Wellcome Centre for Medical Science, 15 October 1993.
49.   Carl Chinn, *They Worked All Their Lives. Women of the Urban Poor in England, 1880–1939* (1988), p. 137.
50.   Anne de Courcy, *op. cit.*, p. 140.
51.   Manchester Transcripts, no. 819, at Stalybridge Local Studies Library.
52.   Manchester Transcripts, no. 28, at Stalybridge Local Studies Library.
53.   Geoffrey Moorhouse, *op. cit.*, pp. 105–6.
54.   *Western Mail*, 16 January 1919; Robert Graves and Alan Hodge, *The Long Weekend. A Social History of Britain 1918–1939* (1991 edn), pp. 17–18.
55.   Nicholas Mosley, *Rules of the Game. Sir Oswald and Lady Cynthia Mosley 1896–1933* (1982), pp. 19–20.
56.   *The Secretary*, September 1919, p. 217.
57.   *Ibid.*, p. 215.
58.   Irene Clephane, *Towards Sex Freedom* (1935), pp. 200–1.
59.   Ray Strachey, *op. cit.*, p. 371.
60.   Sheila Lewenhak, *op. cit.*, p. 165; Barbara Drake, *op. cit.*, Table III.
61.   Gail Braybon, *op. cit.*, p. 179.
62.   *Ibid.*, p. 208.
63.   Sheila Lewenhak, *op. cit.*, p. 165.
64.   *Weekly Reports by the Ministry of Labour: Department of Civil Demobilization and Resettlement* at the Imperial War Museum, EMP 80/25, Report for 26 July 1919, p. 8. See also report for 20 September 1919, which showed that over the twenty-nine weeks ending 18 September 1919, only 19.8 per cent of females who had appealed against their exclusion from benefit had been successful, compared to 80.2 per cent who were not; for male applicants the

respective figures were 29.1 per cent and 70.9 per cent; Gail Braybon, *op. cit.*, pp. 181, 182.
65.   Sheila Lewenhak, *op. cit.*, p. 161, 166.
66.   Gail Braybon, *op. cit.*, p. 183.
67.   *Weekly Reports by the Ministry of Labour: Department of Civil Demobilization and Resettlement*, Report for 11 January 1919, p. 14.
68.   *Report of the Ministry of Labour for 1923 and 1924*, Parliamentary Papers 1924–25, vol. XIV, p. 225; Sheila Lewenhak, *op. cit.*, p. 182.
69.   Calculated from *1921 Census of Population: Occupations* (HMSO, 1924).
70.   Ruth Adam, *A Woman's Place* (1975), p. 84.
71.   Paul Berry and Alan Bishop (eds), *Testament of a Generation. The Journalism of Vera Brittain and Winifred Holtby* (1983), p. 5.
72.   C. Willett Cunnington, *English Women's Clothing in the Present Century* (1952), pp. 146, 147; Robert Graves and Alan Hodge, *op. cit.*, pp. 43–4.
73.   *General Report of the 1931 Population Census* (HMSO, 1950), p. 100. See also Martin Pugh, *op. cit.*, pp. 222–3.
74.   Pamela Brookes, *Women at Westminster. An Account of Women in the British Parliament 1918–1966* (1967), p. 74. For the comment by Mrs Fawcett see Cardiff and District Women Citizens' Association D/D X 158/2/3 in Glamorgan Archives, Cardiff.
75.   Draft letter to F.F. Hawker, honorary secretary of Plymouth Conservative and Unionist Association, written by Lady Astor in March 1921 in 1416/1/1/621 of Astor mss at Reading University Library. The letter was finally sent in May 1921. Christopher Sykes, *Nancy. The Life of Lady Astor* (1979, paperback edn), pp. 219, 240, 250.
76.   Vera Brittain, *Women's Work in Modern England* (1928), p. 75; Ray Strachey, *op. cit.*, pp. 376–7.
77.   Ray Strachey, *op. cit.*, p. 377.
78.   *Woman Engineer*, March 1921, p. 61.
79.   Mrs Willson, 'The Entry of Women into the Newer Industries' in *Woman Engineer*, March 1921, p. 60.
80.   *Stalybridge Reporter*, 21 January 1944.
81.   *Western Mail*, 9 January 1920; Sheila Lewenhak, *op. cit.*, p. 168.
82.   Brian Harrison, *Prudent Revolutionaries. Portraits of British Feminists between the Wars* (1987), p. 303.
83.   *Western Mail*, 28 January 1921; *Oxford Chronicle*, 21 January 1921.
84.   *Western Mail*, 1 February 1921; Ray Strachey, *op. cit.*, p. 376.

85. Martin Pugh, *op. cit.*, p. 12.

86. Ray Strachey, *op. cit.*, p. 354.

87. Adelaide M. Anderson, *Women in the Factory. An Administrative Adventure 1893 to 1921* (1921), pp. 224–6, 236.

88. See, for example, *Annual Report of the Ministry of Labour for 1930*, Parliamentary Papers 1930–31, vol. XV, p. 129, which showed that in the final quarter of 1930, between 16.4 and 18.2 per cent of the insured female workforce was unemployed, compared with 19.3 per cent to 20.5 per cent of the insured male labour force unemployed at that time; Norbert C. Solden, *Women in British Trade Unions 1874–1976* (1978), p. 130.

Chapter 2   The Social Élite

1. Martin Pugh, *Women and the Women's Movement in Britain 1914–1959* (1992), p. 74.

2. *The Tatler*, 26 January 1921; Robert Graves and Alan Hodge, *The Long Week-end. A Social History of Great Britain 1918–1939* (1991 edn), p. 34. Georgina Howell, *In Vogue. Six decades of fashion* (1979 edn), p. 4.

3. Robert Graves and Alan Hodge, *op. cit.*, pp. 23–4.

4. *The Tatler*, 15 January 1919.

5. *The Tatler*, 1 January 1919.

6. Loelia, Duchess of Westminster, *Grace and Favour* (1961), p. 84.

7. Georgina Howell, *op. cit.*, pp. 50, 68.

8. Barbara Cartland, *We Danced All Night* (1970), p. 26.

9. *Ibid.*, pp. 46–7.

10. Janet Morgan, *Edwina Mountbatten. A Life of Her Own* (1992 edn), p. 84.

11. Raleigh Trevelyan, *Grand Dukes and Diamonds. The Wernhers of Luton Hoo* (1991), p. 311.

12. *Ibid.*, pp. 289–90.

13. *The Tatler*, 8 October 1919.

14. Barbara Cartland, *op. cit.*, p. 45.

15. Georgina Howell, *op. cit.*, p. 50.

16. *Ibid.*, p. 53.

17. Loelia, Duchess of Westminster, *op. cit.*, p. 146.

18. Evelyn Waugh, *Vile Bodies* (1938 edn), p. 123.

19. Georgina Howell, *op. cit.*, p. 66; Barbara Cartland, *op. cit.*, p. 193.

20. Georgina Howell, *op. cit.*, p. 66.

21. David Cannadine, *The Decline and Fall of the British Aristocracy* (1990), p. 352.

22. Loelia, Duchess of Westminster, *op. cit.*, p. 122.

23. *Ibid.*, pp. 119–22.

24. Anne de Courcy, *Circe. The Life of Edith, Marchioness of Londonderry* (1992), p. 198; Anne Chisholm, *Nancy Cunard* (1981 edn), pp. 212–14.

25. *The Tatler*, 3 December 1919.

26. [Kate Meyrick], *Secrets of the 43. Reminiscences of Mrs Meyrick* (1933), p. 268; Georgina Howell, *op. cit.*, pp. 65–6.

27. [Kate Meyrick], *op. cit.*, p. 271.

28. Robert Graves and Alan Hodge, *op. cit.*, p. 122.

29. Barbara Cartland, *op. cit.*, p. 150. Loelia, Duchess of Westminster, *op. cit.*, p. 93.

30. Selina Hastings, *Nancy Mitford* (1985), pp. 46–7.

31. Loelia, Duchess of Westminster, *op. cit.*, pp. 204, 213.

32. Barbara Cartland, *op. cit.*, p. 27.

33. Frances Donaldson, *Child of the Twenties* (1959), p. 98.

34. *Ibid.*

35. Georgina Howell, *op. cit.*, p. 53; Barbara Cartland, *op. cit.*, pp. 49, 256.

36. Selina Hastings, *op. cit.*, pp. 46, 69.

37. Diana Cooper, *Autobiography* (1979), p. 227.

38. Diana Cooper, *op. cit.*, pp. 227, 245; Philip Ziegler, *Diana Cooper. The Biography of Lady Diana Cooper* (1983 edn), pp. 143–72.

39. Margaret Blunden, *The Countess of Warwick* (1967), pp. 307–8.

40. Merlin Waterson (ed.), *The Country House Remembered. Recollections of Life between the Wars* (1985), p. 34.

41. Janet Morgan, *op. cit.*, pp. 190–2, 196.

42. Merlin Waterson (ed.), *op. cit.*, p. 111.

43. Loelia, Duchess of Westminster, *op. cit.*, pp. 182, 205, 232, 234.

44. Barbara Cartland, *op. cit.*, p. 14.

45. Georgina Howell, *op. cit.*, p. 55.

46. Frances Donaldson, *op. cit.*, p. 80.

47. Robert Graves and Alan Hodge, *op. cit.*, p. 39.

48. Barbara Cartland, *op. cit.*, p. 23.

49. [Josephine Ross], *Society in Vogue. The International Set between the Wars* (1992), p. 9.

50. Janet Morgan, *op. cit.*, p. 158; [Josephine Ross], *op. cit.*, p. 98.

51. Rosina Harrison, *Rose: My Life in Service* (1975), pp. 33–4.

52. *Good Housekeeping*, November 1928.

53. *The Woman Engineer*, March 1930; John,

Duke of Bedford, *A Silver-plated Spoon* (1959), pp. 30–1.

54. *Western Mail*, 14 May 1926; *The Tatler*, 12–19 May 1926; Barbara Cartland, *op. cit.*, p. 274; Loelia, Duchess of Westminster, *op. cit.*, pp. 123–4.

55. Janet Morgan, *op. cit.*, pp. 193–4.

56. Barbara Cartland, *op. cit.*, p. 276.

57. Loelia, Duchess of Westminster, *op. cit.*, p. 124.

58. Barbara Cartland, *op. cit.*, pp. 285, 289.

59. *The Tatler*, 26 May 1926.

60. *Western Mail*, 10 June 1926.

61. Lesley Lewis, *The Private Life of a Country House (1912–1939)* (1980), pp. 113–14.

62. Loelia, Duchess of Westminster, *op. cit.*, p. 106.

63. Lawrence Stone, *Road to Divorce: England 1530–1987* (1992 edn), p. 435.

64. Barbara Cartland, *op. cit.*, p. 68.

65. Anne Chisholm, *op. cit.*, pp. 60–1, 82.

66. Robert Graves and Alan Hodge, *op. cit.*, pp. 47–8.

67. *Eve*, 1 April 1920; Martin Pugh, *op. cit.*, pp. 216–17. In the 1920s 59 per cent of divorce petitions were sought by wives, compared with 55 per cent between 1911 and 1915 and 33 per cent between 1916 and 1920.

68. Maureen E. Montgomery, *Gilded Prostitution. Status, money, and transatlantic marriages 1870–1914* (1989), p. 173.

69. Rosina Harrison, *op. cit.*, p. 32; Loelia, Duchess of Westminster, *op. cit.*, p. 101.

70. Christopher Sykes, *Nancy. The Life of Lady Astor* (1979 edn), p. 283.

71. Stewart Perowne to Lady Astor, 1 January 1925 in MS 1416/1/2/36 in Astor mss at Reading University Library.

72. Running Expenses: 1 April to 30 June 1918 in MS 1416/1/6/132 in Astor mss.

73. Lady Astor to Miss Kindersley, 7 May 1929 in MS 1416/1/2/53 in Astor mss. The letter concerned Elizabeth Cowley and on the same date Lady Astor wrote to Elizabeth, emphasizing how much her work was appreciated and 'this little holiday' in Paris would do her good. See also John Grigg, *Nancy Astor. Portrait of a Pioneer* (1980), pp. 106–7.

74. Lady Astor to Elizabeth Vidler, 26 March 1929 in MS 1416/1/2/62. See also the letter from Mrs Vidler, dated 25 March 1929 and from Mr Vidler, dated 22 April 1929.

75. Rosina Harrison, *op. cit.*, pp. 60, 61, 64.

76. Lady Astor to the Westminster Bank, 12 November 1929 in MS 1416/1/2/62.

77. Diana Gittins, *Fair Sex. Family size and structure, 1900–39* (1982), pp. 157–80; Pamela Horn, *High Society – The English Social Elite 1880–1914* (1992), pp. 97–8.

78. [Josephine Ross], *op. cit.*, p. 123.

79. Rosina Harrison, *op. cit.*, p. 28.

80. Janet Morgan, *op. cit.*, pp. 167, 169.

81. Janet Morgan, *op. cit.*, pp. 201–2.

82. Nicholas Mosley, *Rules of the Game. Sir Oswald and Lady Cynthia Mosley 1896–1933* (1982), pp. 34, 45–6.

83. Ursula Wyndham, *Astride the Wall. A Memoir 1913–1945* (1988), p. 75; Alice Renton, *Tyrant or Victim? A History of the British Governess* (1991), p. 161.

84. Alice Renton, *op. cit.*, p. 162.

85. Correspondence between Lady Astor's secretary and Yvonne Grenant, for example on 15 and 22 November 1928. At other times Mlle Grenant was employed at Shedfield House, Botley; in MS 1416/1/2/44, at Reading University Library.

86. Selina Hastings, *op. cit.*, p. 40.

87. *The Tatler*, 6 April 1921.

88. David Cannadine, *op. cit.*, pp. 111, 115.

89. Heather A. Clemenson, *English Country Houses and Landed Estates* (1982), p. 136.

90. Katharine, Duchess of Atholl, *Working Partnership* (1958), p. 171.

91. Jennifer Ellis (ed.), *Thatched with Gold. The Memoirs of Mabell, Countess of Airlie* (1962), p. 175.

92. Emma Viner to Lady Astor, 30 December 1928 and 12 May 1929, in MS 1416/1/2/62, at Reading University Library.

93. Caroline Dakers, *The Countryside at War 1914–1918* (1987), pp. 189, 203.

94. David Cannadine, *op. cit.*, p. 415; *Dictionary of National Biography 1961–1970* (1981), p. 499; *Annual Register for 1929* (1930), p. 70; Michael Pearson, *The Millionaire Mentality* (1961), pp. 120–5.

95. Quoted in Barbara Cartland, *op. cit.*, p. 290.

96. Merlin Waterson (ed.), *op. cit.*, p. 34.

97. Merlin Waterson (ed.), *op. cit.*, p. 46–8.

98. Rosina Harrison, *op. cit.*, p. 64; Christopher Sykes, *op. cit.*, pp. 183–4.

99. Mrs Wintringham to Lady Astor, 14 November 1929, in MS 1416/1/2/62. See also Stewart Perowne to Lady Astor, 1 January 1925, in MS 1416/1/2/36.

100. Consuelo Vanderbilt Balsan, *The Glitter and the Gold* (1973 edn), pp. 179–81.

101. Martin Pugh, *op. cit.*, p. 175.

102. Nicholas Mosley, *op. cit.*, p. 118.

103. Harold Macmillan, *The Past Masters. Politics and Politicians 1906–1939* (1975), pp. 214–16.

Chapter 3 *Middle-class Wives and Daughters*

1. Raphael Samuel, 'The Middle Class between the Wars', Part I in *New Socialist*, January/February 1983, p. 30.
2. *Ibid.*
3. Irene Davison, *Etiquette for Women. A Book of Modern Manners and Customs* (1928), p. 31.
4. Gillian Avery, *The Best Type of Girl. A History of Girls' Independent Schools* (1991), p. 133.
5. *Ibid.*, pp. 133–4.
6. Penny Summerfield, 'Cultural Reproduction in the Education of Girls: A Study of Girls' Secondary Schooling in Two Lancashire Towns, 1900–50' in Felicity Hunt (ed.), *Lessons for Life. The Schooling of Girls and Women 1850–1950* (1987), pp. 159, 160.
7. Fernanda Helen Perrone, *University Teaching as a Profession for Women in Oxford, Cambridge and London: 1870–1930* (Oxford University D. Phil. thesis, 1991), p. 58.
8. Calculated from *Somerville College Register 1879–1971* (1976), pp. 100–39.
9. Fernanda Helen Perrone, *op. cit.*, pp. 277–9; Vera Brittain, *The Women at Oxford. A Fragment of History* (1960), p. 159.
10. This was the case in my paternal grandfather's family, where two sisters were kept at home.
11. The Viscountess Rhondda, *This Was My World* (1933), pp. 297–8.
12. *Ibid.*, p. 296; The Hon. Vicary Gibbs and H.A. Doubleday, *The Complete Peerage*, vol. V (1926), Appendix C, pp. 780–3.
13. Quoted in Sybil Oldfield (ed.), *This Working-day World. Women's Lives and Culture(s) in Britain 1914–1945* (1994), pp. 176–7.
14. *Good Housekeeping*, August 1922, p. 12.
15. *Eve*, 25 March 1920, p. 75.
16. Quoted in Sybil Oldfield (ed.), *op. cit.*, p. 178.
17. Fernanda Helen Perrone, *op. cit.*, p. 298.
18. Sybil Oldfield (ed.), *op. cit.*, p. 177.
19. Sheila Jeffreys, *The Spinster and her Enemies. Feminism and Sexuality 1880–1930* (1985), pp. 192–3.
20. Harold L. Smith (ed.), *British Feminism in the Twentieth Century* (1990), pp. 73–4.

21. Sybil Oldfield (ed.), *op. cit.*, p. 177.
22. Fernanda Helen Perrone, *op. cit.*, p. 299.
23. Charlotte Haldane, *Motherhood and Its Enemies* (1927), p. 149.
24. *Hansard*, 5th Series, vol. 145 (1921), cols 1799, 1804.
25. Ruth Adam, *A Woman's Place* (1975), pp. 95–6; Nerina Shute, *We Mixed Our Drinks. The Story of a Generation* (n.d. [1945]), p. 23.
26. Victoria Glendinning, *Vita. The Life of Vita Sackville-West* (1984 edn), pp. 199–200; Sybil Oldfield (ed.), *op. cit.*, p. 177.
27. Deirdre Beddoe, *Back to Home and Duty. Women between the Wars 1918–1939* (1989), p. 30.
28. Sybil Oldfield (ed.), *op. cit.*, p. 170.
29. *Women's Employment*, 5 December 1924.
30. *Women's Employment*, 1 January 1924.
31. *Girls' Friendly Society Magazine*, October/November 1926.
32. Angela Bull, *Noel Streatfeild* (1984), p. 74.
33. Rebecca Abrams (ed.), *Women in a Man's World. Pioneering Career Women of the Twentieth Century* (1993), pp. 1–6.
34. Pamela Horn, *The Rise and Fall of the Victorian Servant* (1990 edn), pp. 194–5.
35. *Nina Hamnett 1890–1956* (An anonymous pamphlet produced by Tenby Museum and not dated), p. 2; Nina Hamnett, *Laughing Torso* (1932), pp. 111, 118, 158–9, 162, 165.
36. *Nina Hamnett*, p. 3. Nina was born in Tenby and spent her childhood there.
37. Paul Berry and Alan Bishop (eds), *Testament of a Generation. The Journalism of Vera Brittain and Winifred Holtby* (1985), pp. 124–5.
38. *Hansard*, 5th Series, vol. 205 (1927), cols 1185, 1210.
39. Fernanda Helen Perrone, *op. cit.*, pp. 269–74; Vera Brittain, *op. cit.*, p. 172.
40. Susan J. Leonardi, *Dangerous by Degrees. Women at Oxford and the Somerville College Novelists* (1989), p. 21.
41. *Ibid.*, p. 22.
42. Fernanda Helen Perrone, *op. cit.*, p. 329. Perrone notes that in 1924 six women were of professorial standing. All were at London University.
43. Jane Lewis, *Women in England 1870–1950. Sexual Divisions and Social Change* (1984), p. 200.
44. Paul Berry and Alan Bishop (eds), *op. cit.*, p. 47; The Viscountess Rhondda, *op. cit.*, p. 299; Dale Spender, *Time and Tide Wait for No Man* (1984), p. 175.
45. Brian Harrison, *Prudent Revolutionaries. Portraits of British Feminists between the Wars*

(1987), pp. 102–3; Harold L. Smith (ed.), *op. cit.*, p. 107; Jane Lewis, 'Beyond Suffrage: English Feminism in the 1920s' in *Maryland Historian*, vol. VI (1975), pp. 2–3.
46.   Jane Lewis, *Women in England*, p. 102.
47.   *Ibid.*, p. 104.
48.   The Viscountess Rhondda, *op. cit.*, p. 299.
49.   Martin Pugh, *Women and the Women's Movement in Britain 1914–1959* (1992), p. 73.
50.   The Viscountess Rhondda, *Leisured Women* (1928), p. 43.
51.   Vera Brittain, *Testament of Friendship* (1980 edn), p. 115.
52.   The Countess of Oxford and Asquith (ed.), *Myself When Young. By Famous Women of Today* (1938), pp. 143–8.
53.   *Ibid.*, p. 153.
54.   *Good Housekeeping*, September 1923, p. 16.
55.   Vera Brittain, *Lady into Woman* (1953), pp. 116, 124.
56.   *Good Housekeeping*, January 1929, pp. 37, 102.
57.   Harold L. Smith (ed.), *op. cit.*, p. 55; Martin Pugh, *op. cit.*, p. 108.
58.   *Wife and Home*, October 1929, p. 10.
59.   See, for example, *Woman's Pictorial*, 4 December 1926, pp. 34–5. The magazine had first been established in 1919.
60.   Alice M. Head, *It Could Never Have Happened* (1939), pp. 60–1.
61.   *Ibid.*, p. 62; *Good Housekeeping*, September 1928, pp. 44–5; Cynthia L. White, *Women's Magazines 1693–1968* (1970), p. 103.
62.   *The Tatler*, 26 May 1926.
63.   Caroline Davidson, *A Woman's Work Is Never Done. A History of Housework in the British Isles 1650–1950* (1982), pp. 40–3.
64.   Letter from Mrs J. Etherton, Deputy Group Archivist, National Westminster Bank, to the author, 18 March 1994. Reminiscences of my late father.
65.   Letterbook of the Hanley Branch of the Manchester and Liverpool District Bank, ref. 20472, in the National Westminster Bank Group Archives; see, for example, letters dated 31 October 1919, 30 December 1925, 29 July 1926, 7 February 1929.
66.   Madeline McKenna, 'The suburbanization of the working-class population of Liverpool between the wars' in *Social History* (vol. 16, no. 2) (1991), pp. 181–2.
67.   Caroline Davidson, *op. cit.*, p. 38.
68.   Samuel Mullins and Gareth Griffiths, *Cap and Apron. An Oral History of Domestic Service in the Shires, 1880–1950* (Leicestershire

Museums, Art Galleries and Records Service, 1986), pp. 21, 23.
69.   *Good Housekeeping*, November 1923, p. 35; Diana Gittins, *Fair Sex: Family Size and Structure, 1900–39* (1992), p. 82, for statistics of middle-class fertility rates.
70.   *Good Housekeeping*, November 1923, p. 35.
71.   Mrs Ruth M. Quick to the author, 1 September 1974.
72.   Raphael Samuel, 'The Middle Class between the Wars', Part II in *New Socialist*, March/April 1983, p. 31.
73.   Steve Humphries and Pamela Gordon, *A Labour of Love. The Experience of Parenthood in Britain 1900–1950* (1993), pp. 95–6.
74.   Quoted in Raphael Samuel, 'The Middle Class between the Wars', Part III, 'Suburbs under siege' in *New Socialist*, May/June 1983, p. 30.
75.   Miss G.J. Goff of St Austell to the author, n.d. (*c.* 5 September 1974).
76.   Reminiscences of Mrs Ethel Cleary, born near Manchester in 1908, in Manchester Transcripts, no. 28, at Stalybridge Local Studies Library.
77.   *Ibid.*
78.   Steve Humphries and Pamela Gordon, *op. cit.*, pp. 91–3.
79.   Reminiscences of Mrs Ruth M. Bradley, Mrs Thompson's daughter, in Stalybridge Oral History Transcripts, no. 158, at Stalybridge Local Studies Library.
80.   Reminiscences of Mrs Ruth M. Bradley, *loc. cit.*
81.   Ken Arnold, Lesley Hall and Julia Sheppard, *Birth and Breeding; the politics of reproduction in modern Britain* (1993), p. 6.
82.   Ruth Hall, *Marie Stopes* (London, 1977), pp. 180–1; Diana Gittins, *op. cit.*, pp. 82–3 for details of fertility rates among professional families.
83.   Ruth Hall, *op. cit.*, p. 175; Ken Arnold, Lesley Hall and Julia Sheppard, *op. cit.*, p. 6.
84.   Steve Humphries and Pamela Gordon, *op. cit.*, p. 12.
85.   Vera Brittain, *Testament of Experience* (1979 edn), pp. 50–2; Jane Lewis, *Women in England*, p. 117.
86.   Steve Humphries and Pamela Gordon, *op. cit.*, p. 8.
87.   Jane Lewis, *The Politics of Motherhood. Child and Maternal Welfare in England, 1900–1939* (1980), p. 117.
88.   Steve Humphries and Pamela Gordon, *op. cit.*, pp. 29–30.

89.   *Ibid.*, pp. 93–4.

90.   *Ibid.*, p. 52; Cathy Urwin and Elaine Sharland, 'From Bodies to Minds in Childcare Literature. Advice to parents in inter-war Britain' in Roger Cooter (ed.), *In the Name of the Child. Health and Welfare, 1880–1940* (1992), p. 177.

91.   Victoria E.M. Bennett, *Health in the Nursery* (1930), p. 13.

92.   Steve Humphries and Pamela Gordon, *op. cit.*, pp. 51–2.

93.   C. Stella Davies, *North Country Bred. A Working-class Family Chronicle* (1963), pp. 173–7.

94.   Vera Brittain, *Testament of Experience*, p. 51; Harold L. Smith (ed.), *op. cit.*, p. 90.

95.   *Pall Mall Gazette*, 2 and 4 July 1923. The newspaper referred to 'King Baby' being to the fore during National Baby Week.

96.   Martin Pugh, *op. cit.*, p. 89.

97.   Jane Lewis, *Women in England*, p. 116.

98.   C. Stella Davies, *op. cit.*, p. 173.

99.   *Wife and Home*, October 1929, p. 21.

100.   Harry W. Richardson and Derek H. Aldcroft, *Building in the British Economy between the Wars* (1968), p. 74.

Chapter 4   Working Women

1.   *Western Mail*, 18 January 1921.

2.   Meta Zimmeck, 'Strategies and Stratagems for the Employment of Women in the British Civil Service, 1919–1939' in *Historical Journal*, vol. 27, no. 4 (1984), p. 910.

3.   *Ibid.*, p. 912.

4.   Quoted in Pamela Horn, 'Women Workers in the 1920s: Cadbury's of Bournville' in *Genealogists' Magazine*, vol. 24, no. 9 (1994), p. 399.

5.   *Ibid.*, p. 401.

6.   Calculated from *1931 Census for England and Wales: Occupations* (HMSO, 1934).

7.   Mark Savage, 'Trade unionism, sex segregation, and the state: women's employment in "new industries" in inter-war Britain' in *Social History*, vol. 13, no. 2 (1988), pp. 210, 226.

8.   Sheila Lewenhak, *Women and Trade Unions. An Outline History of Women in the British Trade Union Movement* (1977), p. 186.

9.   Teresa Davy, '"A Cissy Job for Men; a Nice Job for Girls"; Women Shorthand Typists in London, 1900–39' in Leonore Davidoff and Belinda Westover (ed.), *Our Work, Our Lives, Our Words. Women's History and Women's Work* (1986), p. 142.

10.   Jane Lewis, *Women in England 1870–1950. Sexual Divisions and Social Change* (1984), p. 192.

11.   Stalybridge Oral History Transcripts, no. 118, at Stalybridge Local Studies Library.

12.   Manchester Oral History Transcripts, no. 28, at Stalybridge Local Studies Library.

13.   Elizabeth Roberts, *A Woman's Place. An Oral History of Working-class Women 1890–1940* (1984), p. 64.

14.   Girls' Department: Rules and Regulations (Bournville: Cadbury Brothers Ltd, 1922), p. 28. A similar provision was included in the Rules issued in 1926. B. Seebohm Rowntree, *The Human Factor in Business* (3rd edn) (1938), pp. 136–7. The first edition was published in 1921.

15.   Miriam Glucksmann, 'In a Class of their Own? Women Workers in the New Industries in Inter-war Britain' in *Feminist Review*, no. 24 (1986), pp. 28–9.

16.   Meta Zimmeck, *op. cit.*, p. 917.

17.   Jane Lewis, *op. cit.*, p. 183.

18.   *Ibid.*, p. 169.

19.   Martin Pugh, *Women and the Women's Movement in Britain 1914–1959* (1992), p. 96.

20.   Vera Brittain, *Women's Work in Modern England* (1928), p. 192; Martin Pugh, *op. cit.*, p. 97, quotes figures that show that in 1921 60.6 per cent of all men over 20 years in England and Wales were either bachelors, or married men/widowers with no children under 16 years.

21.   Winifred Holtby, 'The Man Colleague' (1929) in Paul Berry and Alan Bishop (eds), *Testament of a Generation: The Journalism of Vera Brittain and Winifred Holtby* (1985), p. 62.

22.   Vera Brittain, *op. cit.*, pp. 24–7; J. Blainey, *The Woman Worker and Restrictive Legislation* (Prepared for the London and National Society for Women's Service, 1928), pp. 22–43; Jane Lewis, *op. cit.*, p. 188; Olive Banks, *Faces of Feminism* (1993 edn), p. 169.

23.   See *Ministry of Reconstruction: Report of the Women's Employment Committee* (Cd. 9239) (1919), pp. 6–7 in EMP 29/2 at the Imperial War Museum.

24.   Gillian Darcy, *Problems and Changes in Women's Work in England and Wales, 1918–1939* (London University PhD thesis, 1984), p. 144.

25.   *Ibid.*, pp. 148–9.

26.   Sheila Lewenhak, *op. cit.*, p. 189; Norbert C. Soldon, *Women in British Trade Unions 1874–1976* (1978), p. 104.

27.   Sheila Lewenhak, *op. cit.*, p. 168.

28.   Sheila T. Lewenhak, *Trade Union*

Membership among Women and Girls in the United Kingdom 1920–1965 (London University PhD thesis, 1971), pp. 276–7; Sheila Lewenhak, *Women and Trade Unions*, p. 177.

29.   J. Blainey, *op. cit.*, pp. 89–90.

30.   Sheila T. Lewenhak, *Trade Union Membership*, pp. 278–80.

31.   Quoted in Deirdre Beddoe, *Back to Home and Duty. Women between the Wars, 1918–1939* (1989), pp. 86–7.

32.   *Board of Trade. An Industrial Survey of the Lancashire Area (excluding Merseyside)* (Cd. 51–196) (1932), p. 111; Martin Pugh, *op. cit.*, p. 83.

33.   Alan Deacon, 'Concession and Coercion: The Politics of Unemployment Insurance in the Twenties' in Asa Briggs and John Saville (ed.), *Essays in Labour History 1918–1939* (1977), pp. 15–16; Martin Pugh, *op. cit.*, p. 82.

34.   Martin Pugh, *op. cit.*, p. 82.

35.   Stalybridge Oral History Transcripts, no. 037, at Stalybridge Local Studies Library.

36.   Joan Beauchamp, *Women Who Work* (1937), p. 56.

37.   Sir Hubert Llewellyn Smith (ed.), *The New Survey of London Life and Labour*, vol. 8 (1934), p. 276.

38.   *Ministry of Reconstruction: Report on Domestic Service*, 'Report of Domestic Service Sub-Committee IV' in Parliamentary Papers, 1919, vol. XXIX, p. 22.

39.   *Western Mail*, 1 January 1921.

40.   D. Caradog Jones (ed.), *The Social Survey of Merseyside*, vol. II (1934), p. 301; Sir Hubert Llewellyn Smith (ed.), *The New Survey of London Life and Labour*, vol. 2 (1931), pp. 444, 450.

41.   D. Caradog Jones (ed.), *op. cit.*, p. 317.

42.   *The Tatler*, 26 May 1926.

43.   Mrs Lilian Neal of Bath to the author, 23 August 1974.

44.   Mrs M. Fugill of Kent to the author, 30 August 1974.

45.   *Report of the Ministry of Labour for 1930*, Parliamentary Papers, 1930–31, vol. XV, pp. 39–41.

46.   *Ibid.*, p. 45.

47.   'Placing of Women and Girls from Non-residential Home Training Centres': Report of the Ministry of Labour in LAB.2.1219/20/ETJ/1178/1932 at the Public Record Office.

48.   Central Committee on Women's Training and Employment: Centre at Tonypandy (Ystrad), Rhondda for Women and Girls in LAB.2/1365/ED.730/19/1929 at the Public Record Office.

49.   See reports of students at the Centre at Tonypandy, e.g. Ethelwyn Harris, aged 16, who went as a parlourmaid to London in December 1928; she was 'promised 10/-, only received 8/-'.

50.   *Western Mail*, 25 June 1926.

51.   *1885–1935. A brief record of 50 Years' Work of the National Vigilance Association* (1935), p. 11. The records of the Association are at the Fawcett Library, Guildhall University, London.

52.   *Ibid.*, p. 12.

53.   *Ibid.*, pp. 9–10.

54.   Mrs L. Berry of Pontypridd to the National Vigilance Association, report dated 19 November 1930 in 4/NVA, Welsh Box no. 119 at the Fawcett Library.

55.   Stalybridge Oral History Transcripts, nos 037 and 083, at Stalybridge Local Studies Library.

56.   Girls' Department: Rules and Regulations (Bournville: Cadbury Brothers Ltd, 1922), p. 8. See also 1926 Rules.

57.   *Working Lives: vol. 1 1905–45: A People's Autobiography of Hackney* (Hackney WEA, n.d.), p. 54.

58.   Stalybridge Oral History Transcripts, no. 083, at Stalybridge Local Studies Library.

59.   Elizabeth Roberts, *op. cit.*, p. 61.

60.   Martin Pugh, *op. cit.*, pp. 98–9; Deirdre Beddoe, *op. cit.*, p. 85.

61.   Maggie Newbery, *Reminiscences of a Bradford Mill Girl* (Bradford Metropolitan Council, Occasional Local Publications, no. 3) (1980), p. 76.

62.   *Ibid.*, p. 77.

63.   *Ibid.*, p. 85.

64.   Elizabeth Roberts, *op. cit.*, p. 64.

65.   Maurice Corina, *Fine Silks and Oak Counters. Debenhams 1778–1978* (1978), pp. 80–2.

66.   *Ibid.*, p. 82.

67.   Richard Foster, *F. Cape & Co. of St Ebbes Street, Oxford* (Oxford City and County Museum, Publication no. 3, 1973), not paginated; section under 'Management and Staff'.

68.   Gillian Darcy, *op. cit.*, p. 226.

69.   P.C. Hoffman, *They also Serve. The Story of the Shop Worker* (1949), pp. 192–3.

70.   *The Tatler*, 2 June 1926; *Eve*, January 1920.

71.   *Special Report from the Select Committee on Shop Assistants*, Parliamentary Papers 1929–30, vol. VII, Evidence of Dr Ethel Bentham, Q. 2445–2447.

72.   Gillian Darcy, *op. cit.*, p. 238.

73.   *Special Report from the Select Committee on Shop Assistants*, Evidence of Dr Marion Phillips, MP and Mrs Bamber, Q. 1818.

74.   D. Caradog Jones, *op. cit.*, pp. 212–13.

75.   P.C. Hoffman, *op. cit.*, p. 182.

76.   Gillian Darcy, *op. cit.*, pp. 195–6.

77.   Mary Chamberlain, *Growing up in Lambeth* (1989), p. 119.

78.   Olive Howarth (ed.), *Textile Voices. Mill Life this Century* (Bradford Libraries and Information Service, 1989), p. 35.

79.   Pamela M. Graves, *Labour Women. Women in British Working-class Politics 1918–1939* (1994), p. 46.

80.   Gillian Darcy, *op. cit.*, p. 197.

81.   Kay Sanderson, 'Civil Servant Clerks in London, 1925–1939' in Leonore Davidoff and Belinda Westover (ed.), *op. cit.*, p. 151.

82.   Kay Sanderson, *op. cit.*, pp. 154–5; Winifred Holtby, 'The Wearer and the Shoe' (January 1930) in Paul Berry and Alan Bishop (ed.), *op. cit.*, p. 65.

83.   Kay Sanderson, *op. cit.*, p. 152.

84.   Teresa Davy, '*Female Shorthand-Typists and Typists 1900–1939; The Years of Transition and Consolidation*' (University of Essex MA thesis, 1980), pp. 100–2.

85.   Teresa Davy, 'Shorthand-Typists in London, 1900–1939' in Leonore Davidoff and Belinda Westover (eds), *op. cit.*, p. 133.

86.   Frances Donaldson, *Child of the Twenties* (1959), pp. 137–8.

87.   Teresa Davy, 'Shorthand-Typists in London, 1900–1939', p. 130.

88.   Charlotte Haldane, *Motherhood and Its Enemies* (1927), p. 109.

Chapter 5   Making Ends Meet: Working-class Family Life

1.   Elizabeth Roberts, *A Woman's Place. An Oral History of Working-class Women 1890–1940* (1984), p. 137.

2.   Stalybridge Oral History Transcripts, no. 037, at Stalybridge Local Studies Library, and Manchester Tapes, evidence of Mrs Bowker, from Hindley, Lancashire, who was born in 1899.

3.   Pat Ayers and Jan Lambertz, 'Marriage Relations, Money, and Domestic Violence in Working-class Liverpool, 1919–39' in Jane Lewis (ed.), *Labour and Love. Women's Experience of Home and Family 1850–1940* (1986), p. 197.

4.   Nigel Gray, *The Worst of Times. An Oral History of the Great Depression in Britain* (1985), p. 91; Pat Ayers and Jan Lambertz, *op. cit.*, p. 197.

5.   Carl Chinn, *They Worked All their Lives. Women of the Urban Poor in England, 1880–1939* (1988), p. 32.

6.   Mary Chamberlain, *Growing up in Lambeth* (1989), pp. 85–6.

7.   Eleanor F. Rathbone, *The Disinherited Family. A Plea for Direct Provision for the Costs of Child Maintenance through Family Allowances* (1927 edn), pp. 73–4. The book was first published in 1924.

8.   *Ibid.*, pp. 205, 319.

9.   Gail Braybon, *Women Workers in the First World War* (1981), p. 224.

10.   Mary Agnes Hamilton, *Margaret Bondfield* (1924), p. 183.

11.   Ann Hughes and Karen Hunt, 'A culture transformed? Women's lives in Wythenshawe in the 1930s' in Andrew Davies and Steven Fielding (ed.), *Workers' Worlds. Cultures and Communities in Manchester and Salford, 1880–1939* (1992), p. 89.

12.   Deirdre Beddoe, *Back to Home and Duty. Women between the Wars 1918–1939* (1989), p. 38.

13.   Log book of Bridgend/Penybont Girls' Homemaking Course 1918–24 at Glamorgan Archives, E/M.10/9.

14.   Log book for Hannah Street Girls' School, Barry, E/St.5/5 at Glamorgan Archives, Cardiff, entries for 9 February 1921; and Deirdre Beddoe, *op. cit.*, p. 39.

15.   Deirdre Beddoe, *op. cit.*, p. 39.

16.   Stalybridge Oral History Transcripts, no. 135, at Stalybridge Local Studies Library.

17.   Elizabeth Roberts, *op. cit.*, p. 33.

18.   Mary Craddock, *A North Country Maid* (1960), p. 17.

19.   Melanie Tebbutt, 'Women's talk: Gossip and "women's words" in working-class communities, 1880–1939' in Andrew Davies and Steven Fielding (ed.), *op. cit.*, pp. 54, 57.

20.   Charles Loch Mowat, *Britain between the Wars 1918–1940* (1983 edn), pp. 458, 507.

21.   Madeline McKenna, 'The suburbanization of the working-class population of Liverpool between the wars' in *Social History*, vol. 16, no. 2 (1991), p. 177.

22.   Madeline McKenna, *op. cit.*, p. 180.

23.   Mary Chamberlain, *op. cit.*, p. 15.

24.   *Ibid.*, pp. 14–15.

25.   Harry W. Richardson and Derek H.

Aldcroft, *Building in the British Economy between the Wars* (1968), p. 180.

26.   Louise Christie, *Gender, Design and Ideology in Council Housing: Urban Scotland 1917–1944*, paper presented at the Economic History Society Conference, 3 April 1993, p. 7.

27.   Louise Christie, *op. cit.*, p. 8.

28.   Madeline McKenna, *op. cit.*, pp. 183–4.

29.   Deirdre Beddoe, *op. cit.*, p. 94.

30.   Andrzej Olechnowicz, *The Economic and Social Development of Inter-war Out-County Municipal Housing Estates, with Special Reference to the London County Council's Becontree and Dagenham Estate* (Oxford D. Phil. thesis, 1991), pp. 149, 157, 167.

31.   *1931 Census of England and Wales: Preliminary Report – Housing* (HMSO 1931), calculated from tables on pp. 38–9.

32.   Margaret A. Pollock (ed.), *Working Days* (1926), pp. 256–8.

33.   Elizabeth Roberts, *op. cit*, pp. 134–5.

34.   Mrs Janet Davies, notes of tape no. 7088 by Mrs Minwel Tibbott, Assistant Keeper at the Welsh Folk Museum, National Museum of Wales. I am grateful to Mrs Tibbott for making this and other tape transcipts available to me; Eurwyn William, *Rhyd-y-car. A Welsh Mining Community* (1987), p. 17; S. Minwel Tibbott and Beth Thomas, *O'r Gwaith i'r Gwely. A Woman's Work. Housework 1890–1960* (1994), p. 37.

35.   Dorothy Flowers, *My Dukinfield Childhood* (1992), pp. 8–9.

36.   Stalybridge Oral History Transcripts, no. 093, at Stalybridge Local Studies Library.

37.   Dorothy Flowers, *op. cit.*, p. 9.

38.   *Ibid.*, pp. 15, 17.

39.   Steve Humphries and Pamela Gordon, *A Labour of Love. The Experience of Parenthood in Britain 1900–1950* (1993), p. 121.

40.   Stalybridge Oral History Transcripts, no. 004, at Stalybridge Local Studies Library.

41.   Mary Chamberlain, *op. cit.*, p. 114.

42.   Carl Chinn, *op. cit.*, pp. 34, 53.

43.   Marion Phillips, *Women and the Miners' Lock-out. The Story of the Women's Committee for the Relief of the Miners' Wives and Children* (1927), pp. 23, 70, 71, 76, 78, 79–80.

44.   *Ibid.*, pp. 82–5. When they arrived the children were so malnourished that they could at first eat nothing but bread and jam.

45.   Elspeth Lang, 'Women's Work at Maes-yr-haf Settlement, Rhondda Valley' in *The Common Room*, Spring 1933 (not paginated) at Glamorgan Archives, D/DMH.5/23c.

46.   Margaret Leonora Eyles, *The Woman in the Little House* (1922), p. 61.

47.   *Working Lives*, vol. I, *1905–45. A People's Autobiography of Hackney* (Hackney WEA, n.d.), p. 62.

48.   Pat Ayers and Jan Lambertz, *op. cit.*, pp. 201–3; Nigel Gray, *op. cit.*, p. 94.

49.   Walter Greenwood, *Love on the Dole* (1958 edn), pp. 22–3.

50.   Elizabeth Roberts, *op. cit.*, p. 151.

51.   S. Minwel Tibbott, 'Liberality and Hospitality. Food as Communication in Wales' in *Folk Life*, vol. 24 (1985–86), p. 45.

52.   Mary Chamberlain, *op. cit.*, p. 15.

53.   Elizabeth Roberts, *op. cit.*, p. 142.

54.   Pat Ayers and Jan Lambertz, *op. cit.*, p. 203.

55.   Stalybridge Oral History Transcripts, no. 085, at Stalybridge Local Studies Library.

56.   Steve Humphries and Pamela Gordon, *op. cit.*, pp. 63–4.

57.   Bill Jones and Beth Thomas, *Teyrnas y Glo. Coal's Domain* (1993), pp. 21–2.

58.   *Working Lives*, vol. I, p. 63.

59.   *Ibid.*

60.   Jane Lewis, *Women in England 1870–1950. Sexual Divisions and Social Change* (1984), p. 29.

61.   Madeline McKenna, *op. cit.*, p. 177.

62.   Carl Chinn, *op. cit.*, pp. 54, 172.

63.   *Ibid.*, p. 160.

64.   Freda Millett, *Childhood in Oldham 1890–1920* (1989), p. 23.

65.   Nicky Leap and Billie Hunter, *The Midwife's Tale. An oral history from handywoman to professional midwife* (1993), p. 12.

66.   *Ministry of Health. Report on Maternal Mortality in Wales*, Parliamentary Papers, 1936–37, vol. XI, pp. 14–17. The report noted that over the period 1924–33 the puerperal mortality rate for Wales was 35 per cent higher than the rate for England.

67.   Deirdre Beddoe, *op. cit.*, p. 112.

68.   Steve Humphries and Pamela Gordon, *op. cit.*, p. 8. By the mid-1930s the risk of a mother 'dying in childbirth was as high as it had been in the mid-nineteenth century'.

69.   *Report on Maternal Mortality in Wales*, pp. 15, 60, 61, 87–8. In Glamorgan puerperal mortality rates among single women were 8.68 per 1,000 live births in 1924–8 and 11.92 per 1,000 live births in 1929–33; in the latter period the death rate for single women was not far short of double that for those who were married.

70.   *Report on an Investigation into Maternal*

Mortality, Parliamentary Papers, 1936–7, vol. XI, p. 113 and Appendix 12.
71. Margaret A. Pollock, op. cit., p. 237.
72. John Stevenson, British Society 1914–45 (1984), p. 160.
73. Diana Gittins, Fair Sex. Family size and structure, 1900–39 (1982), p. 152.
74. Marie Stopes, 'Address on Ideals and Practice of Constructive Birth Control', lecture notes, 29 April 1930 in PP/MCS.D.19 at the Wellcome Contemporary Medical Archives Centre.
75. Steve Humphries and Pamela Gordon, op. cit., p. 9; C. Stella Davies, North Country Bred (1963), pp. 175–7.
76. Carl Chinn, op. cit., p. 172.
77. Nicky Leap and Billie Hunter, op. cit., p. 20.
78. Ibid., p. 23.
79. Ibid., pp. 35–7, 200.
80. Diana Gittins, op. cit., p. 152.
81. Elizabeth Roberts, op. cit., p. 93; Carl Chinn, op. cit., p. 166.
82. Margaret Leonora Eyles, op. cit., p. 142.
83. Ibid., p. 129.
84. Mary Chamberlain, Fenwomen. A Portrait of Women in an English Village (1983 edn), p. 77.
85. Ruth Hall, Marie Stopes (1977), p. 196.
86. Ibid., p. 246.
87. Marie C. Stopes, The First Five Thousand, being the First Report of the First Birth Control Clinic in the British Empire (1925), p. 17; Ruth Hall (ed.), Dear Dr Stopes. Sex in the 1920s (1978), p. 9.
88. Marie C. Stopes, (ed.), Mother England. A Contemporary History, Self-written by those who have no historian (1929), p. 133.
89. Nurse Bedford to Dr Marie Stopes, 11 October 1926, in PP/MCS/A22 at the Wellcome Contemporary Medical Archives Centre.
90. Deborah A. Cohen, 'Private Lives in Public Spaces: Marie Stopes, the Mothers' Clinics and the Practice of Contraception' in History Workshop, no. 35 (1993), pp. 98, 100.
91. Richard Allen Soloway, Birth Control and the Population Question in England, 1877–1930 (1982), pp. 192, 306.
92. See correspondence between Dr Marie Stopes and Mr E.W. Lambert and Nurse Naomi Jones in May and June 1927 in PP/MCS/C.21 at the Wellcome Contemporary Medical Archives Centre and also leaflet 'C.B.C. The Mothers' Clinic' (n.d.) in PP/MCS.C.45 at the Wellcome Contemporary Medical Archives

Centre; Ruth Hall (ed.), Dear Dr Stopes, p. 11.
93. Elizabeth Roberts, op. cit., p. 95.
94. John Rowley, 'Reminiscences of Alice Onions' in West Midlands Studies, vol. 16 (1983), p. 32.
95. Elizabeth Roberts, op. cit., p. 87.
96. Hansard, 5th Series, vol. 176 (20 July 1924), col. 2050.
97. Calculated from Appendix 14, p. 313, in Report on an Investigation into Maternal Mortality; Steve Humphries and Pamela Gordon, op. cit., p. 6.
98. Nicky Leap and Billie Hunter, op. cit., p. 93.
99. Ibid., pp. 95, 96.
100. Manchester Tapes, no. 949, at Stalybridge Local Studies Library.
101. Diana Gittins, op. cit., pp. 165, 167.
102. Ibid., p. 178.
103. Elizabeth Roberts, op. cit., pp. 85–6.
104. Steve Humphries and Pamela Gordon, op. cit., p. 6.
105. Inaugural meeting of the National Birthday Trust Fund, speech by Mrs Baldwin on 12 November 1928 in SA/NBT.C.1 at the Wellcome Contemporary Medical Archives Centre; Ken Arnold, Lesley Hall and Julia Sheppard, Birth and Breeding, the politics of reproduction in modern Britain (1993), p. 33.
106. Cicely B. Hale, A Good Long Time (1975), pp. 74, 78.
107. Lara V. Marks, Model Mothers. Jewish Mothers and Maternity Provision in East London, 1870–1939 (1994), p. 263. The Jewish community also made its own provisions for its mothers; four of the nine maternal and infant welfare centres in Stepney in 1929 were Jewish.
108. For details of tensions between Irish mothers and their English counterparts in Manchester and Salford see Steven Fielding, 'A separate culture? Irish Catholics in Working-class Manchester and Salford, c. 1890–1939' in Andrew Davies and Steven Fielding (eds), op. cit., p. 38.

Chapter 6 Professionalism, Politics and Power

1. Ruth Adam, A Woman's Place 1910–1975 (1975), p. 82.
2. Western Mail, 29 January 1919, p. 3.
3. Hilda Martindale, Women Servants of the State 1870–1938. A History of Women in the Civil Service (1938), p. 100; Harold L. Smith,

'British Feminism in the 1920s' in Harold L. Smith (ed.), *British Feminism in the Twentieth Century* (1990), p. 53.
4.   Hilda Martindale, *op. cit.*, p. 100.
5.   *Ibid.*, pp. 104–5.
6.   Andrew Saint (ed.), *Politics and the People of London. The London County Council 1889–1965* (1989), pp. 19–20.
7.   Dale Spender, *Time and Tide Wait for No Man* (1984), p. 131; Charlotte Haldane, *Motherhood and Its Enemies* (1927), p. 109.
8.   Charlotte Haldane, *op. cit.*, pp. 109–10.
9.   *Ibid.*, p. 110.
10.   Dale Spender, *op. cit.*, p. 253.
11.   Rebecca Abrams, *Woman in a Man's World. Pioneering Career Women of the Twentieth Century* (1993), pp. 37, 40, 42; Dale Spender *op. cit.*, pp. 246–53.
12.   E. Moberly Bell, *Storming the Citadel. The Rise of the Woman Doctor* (1953), pp. 182–3.
13.   Views of managers on the employment of women in the Westminster Bank in 1922 in the National Westminster Bank Group Archives, 7290.
14.   Westminster Bank staff numbers, 1921 to 1930 in the National Westminster Bank Group Archives, 7296.
15.   Report on staff conditions by the Chief General Manager of the Westminster Bank in National Westminster Bank Group Archives, 7296.
16.   John Carrier, *The Campaign for the Employment of Women as Police Officers* (1988), p. xx; Martin Pugh, *Women and the Women's Movement in Britain 1914–1959* (1992), p. 33.
17.   Clive Emsley, *The English Police. A Political and Social History* (1991), p. 148; Martin Pugh, *op. cit.*, pp. 117–18.
18.   Periodic Report to Constituents, February 1923 in Astor mss at Reading University Library, 1416/1/1/621.
19.   Martin Pugh, *op. cit.*, p. 118.
20.   Cicely B. Hale, *A Good Long Time* (1975), pp. 84–5.
21.   Cardiff and District Women Citizens' Association Archives in Glamorgan Archives, D/DX.158/2/34. See also a letter from the National Council of Women of Great Britain, 24 November 1930, discussing the need for 'propaganda work for the appointment of Women Police in Wales', D/DX.158/2/28. John Carrier, *op. cit.*, p. 179.
22.   Information provided by Mrs J.G. Clark, Archivist of the Loughborough University of Technology in correspondence with the author,
9 July and 20 August 1993.
23.   Information provided by Mrs J.G. Clark, 20 August 1993; *Woman Engineer*, March 1921, p. 55.
24.   See, for example, Fifth Annual Report of the Women's Engineering Society in *Woman Engineer*, June 1924, p. 338.
25.   Caroline Davidson, *A Woman's Work Is Never Done. A History of Housework in the British Isles 1650–1950* (1982), pp. 40–3; *The Women's Electrical Association* [n.d. c. 1925], *Origins and Objectives* in the British Library, WP 8500, *Woman Engineer*, December 1925, p. 112.
26.   Charlotte Haldane, *op. cit.*, p. 111.
27.   *Woman Engineer*, December 1926, p. 178, for details of the career of Victoria Drummond.
28.   Nellie Alden Franz, *English Women Enter the Professions* (1965), p. 282. Helena Normanton was a member of the Women's Freedom League. See Martin Pugh, *op. cit.*, p. 47.
29.   *Good Housekeeping*, March 1922, p. 97.
30.   Ruth Adam, *op. cit.*, pp. 78–9.
31.   Vera Brittain, *Women's Work in Modern England* (1928), p. 76.
32.   Gillian H. Darcy, *Problems and Changes in Women's Work in England and Wales, 1918–1939* (London University PhD thesis, 1984), pp. 312, 392–4, 408–13.
33.   Geoffrey Partington, *Women Teachers in the 20th Century in England and Wales* (1976), p. 25.
34.   Gillian H. Darcy, *op. cit.*, p. 338.
35.   Geoffrey Partington, *op. cit.*, p. 29.
36.   *Ibid.*, p. 31.
37.   Deirdre Beddoe, *Back to Home and Duty. Women between the Wars 1918–1939* (1989), p. 82.
38.   Geoffrey Partington, *op. cit.*, p. 31.
39.   *Good Housekeeping*, September 1923, pp. 136–7.
40.   Geoffrey Partington, *op. cit.*, p. 33.
41.   Leonore Davidoff and Belinda Westover (ed.), *Our Work, Our Lives, Our Words. Women's History and Women's Work* (1986), p. 112.
42.   *Ibid.*, pp. 111–12.
43.   Reminiscences of my sister-in-law, Mrs Margaret Horn, who was the daughter of the family.
44.   *Working Lives*, vol. 1 *1905–45: A People's Autobiography of Hackney* (Hackney WEA n.d.), p. 25.
45.   Asher Tropp, *The School Teachers. The Growth of the Teaching Profession in England and Wales from 1800 to the present day* (1959), pp. 273–4. See also P.H.J.H. Gosden, *The Evolution*

of a Profession (1972), pp. 46, 47, 52, 109–10;
Deirdre Beddoe, *op. cit.*, p. 81.

46. Ruth Adam, *op. cit.*, pp. 79–80.

47. Brian Abel-Smith, *A History of the Nursing Profession* (1960), p. 114.

48. Ruth Adam, *op. cit.*, p. 80; Brian Abel-Smith, *op. cit.*, p. 121.

49. *Ibid.*, p. 141.

50. *Ibid.*, p. 140.

51. Gillian H. Darcy, *op. cit.*, pp. 348–51, 376–8.

52. *Ibid.*, pp. 349–51.

53. Linsay Granshaw, *St Mark's Hospital, London. A Social History of a Specialist Hospital* (1985), pp. 390–1. St Mark's was a specialist colo-rectal hospital.

54. Susan Kingsley Kent, *Making Peace. The Reconstruction of Gender in Interwar Britain* (1993), p. 95.

55. Pamela M. Graves, *Labour Women. Women in British Working-class Politics 1918–1939* (1994), pp. 16–17.

56. Deirdre Beddoe, *op. cit.*, p. 134.

57. Harold L. Smith, *op. cit.*, p. 61.

58. Notes of Deputation from the Equal Political Rights Campaign Committee, which attended in the Prime Minister's Room, House of Commons, on 8 March 1927, in CAB.24/185/190 at the Public Record Office.

59. Memorandum by Lord Robert Cecil, Chancellor of the Duchy of Lancaster on the Franchise Question in CAB.24/185/85 at the Public Record Office.

60. For Churchill's views see, for example, Memorandum on the Franchise Question, dated 8 March 1927 in CAB.24/185/80 at the Public Record Office. Martin Pugh, *op. cit.* pp. 112–13.

61. Deirdre Beddoe, *op. cit.*, p. 134.

62. *Hansard*, 5th Series, vol. 215 (1928), cols 1361–1370.

63. *Ibid.*, col. 1367.

64. *Ibid.*, cols 1379–1380.

65. *Ibid.*, cols 1391, 1401.

66. Brian Harrison, 'Women in a Men's House: The Women MPs, 1919–1945' in *Historical Journal*, vol. 29, no. 3 (1986), p. 625; Martin Pugh, *op. cit.*, p. 150.

67. Martin Pugh, *op. cit.*, p. 159.

68. Pamela Brookes, *Women at Westminster. An Account of Women in the British Parliament 1918–1966* (1967), p. 67.

69. *Hansard*, 5th Series, vol. 215 (1928), col. 1393.

70. Martin Pugh, *op. cit.*, p. 168.

71. Leah Manning, *A Life for Education* (1970), pp. 78–86, 99.

72. Martin Pugh, *op. cit.*, p. 160.

73. Betty D. Vernon, *Ellen Wilkinson* (1982), p. 76.

74. Martin Pugh, *op. cit.*, p. 155.

75. Brian Harrison, *op. cit.*, p. 626.

76. Lesley Lewis, *The Private Life of a Country House (1912–1939)* (1980), p. 116; Pamela Brookes, *op. cit.*, pp. 43–4; Brian Harrison, *Prudent Revolutionaries. Portraits of British Feminists between the Wars* (1987), p. 132.

77. The Rt. Hon. Margaret Bondfield, *A Life's Work* (London, n.d. [1949]), p. 278; Martin Pugh, *op. cit.*, p. 179; Pamela Brookes, *op. cit.*, p. 45.

78. Annual Report to the Plymouth Conservative and Unionist Association for 1922 in Astor mss 1416/1/1/621 at Reading University Library.

79. Pat Thane, 'The Women of the British Labour Party and Feminism, 1906–1945' in Harold L. Smith (ed.), *op. cit.*, p. 135.

80. Brian Harrison, 'Women in a Men's House', p. 630.

81. Ellen Wilkinson to Lady Astor in Astor mss 1416/1/2/62; the letter was undated but was probably written in the early part of 1929.

82. Ellen Wilkinson to Lady Astor in Astor mss 1416/1/2/62; postmarked 28 January 1929.

83. Martin Pugh, *op. cit.*, pp. 63–4.

84. National Unionist Association: Women's Parliamentary Committee (Eastern Area) Minute Book in the Conservative Party Archives ARE.7/11/1 at the Bodleian Library, Oxford, meetings on 1 June 1921 and resolution at Third Annual Conference, 6 March 1923.

85. *Woman's Leader*, 30 January 1925, article by Evelyn Deakin, 'The Political Education of Women in the Conservative Party'.

86. Martin Pugh, *op. cit.*, pp. 68, 125, 152.

87. Pamela M. Graves, *op. cit.*, p. 1.

88. Pat Thane, *op. cit.*, p. 125.

89. C. Stella Davies, *North Country Bred. A Working-class Family Chronicle* (1963), p. 222.

90. Pamela M. Graves, *op. cit.*, p. 6.

91. *Ibid.*, pp. 1–2.

92. Labour Party: National Executive Committee Minutes on Microfiches 787 at the Bodleian Library, Oxford, meeting on 22 June 1927 and Report on Birth Control by Fred O. Roberts and Arthur Henderson.

93. David Doughan, *Lobbying for Liberation. British Feminism 1918–1968* (1980), pp. 8–9.

94. *Ibid.*, p. 9.

95. Martin Pugh, *op. cit.*, pp. 256–7.
96. *Woman's Leader*, 27 February 1925, article by Mrs S.B. Collett, 'What is being done for Liberal Women'. In 1920 the Women's National Liberal Federation claimed a membership of 95,217; this declined to 67,145 in 1922 and then climbed to 88,000 in 1926.
97. Martin Pugh, *op. cit.*, p. 114.
98. *Ibid.*, p. 115.
99. *Ibid.*, p. 107.
100. *Ibid.*, pp. 108–9.
101. Dale Spender, *op. cit.*, pp. 181–3, quoting from *Time and Tide*, 5 February 1926. See also Brian Harrison, *Prudent Revolutionaries*, p. 105.
102. Dale Spender, *op. cit.*, p. 274, quoting from *Time and Tide*, 15 October 1926.
103. *Woman's Leader*, 13 March 1925, p. 52. *Woman's Leader* was the journal of NUSEC.
104. Colin Cross, *The Fascists in Britain* (1961), pp. 57–9; Martin Pugh, *op. cit.*, p. 47.
105. Martin Pugh, *op. cit.*, p. 47.
106. *Ibid.*, p. 106; Brian Harrison, *Prudent Revolutionaries*, p. 7, for other examples of the 'peace movement'.
107. Vera Brittain, *Testament of Friendship. The Story of Winifred Holtby* (1980 edn), p. 132.
108. National Unionist Association: Women's Parliamentary Committee (Eastern Area) Minute Book, meeting 10 June 1926, *loc. cit.*
109. David Doughan, *op. cit.*, pp. 4, 6.
110. Martin Pugh, *op. cit.*, p. 57. In addition, 2,323 women were elected as poor law guardians in 1923. That office was abolished by the local government reforms of 1929, when elected boards of guardians were replaced by public assistance committees formed by local authorities.
111. Geoffrey Mitchell (ed.), *The Hard Way Up. The Autobiography of Hannah Mitchell, Suffragette and Rebel* (1968), pp. 28–9, 208.
112. Margaret Llewellyn Davies, *Life As We Have Known It* (1977 edn), pp. 103–4.
113. Geoffrey Mitchell (ed.), *op. cit.*, pp. 189, 203–4.
114. *Western Mail*, 31 May 1929, p. 8; *Oxford Mail*, 30 May 1929, p. 1.

Chapter 7 Life in the Countryside

1. John Saville, *Rural Depopulation in England and Wales 1851–1951* (1957), pp. 61, 63.
2. Adrian Bell, *Corduroy* (1982 edn), p. 64. The book was first published in 1930.
3. *A Pattern of Hundreds* (Buckinghamshire Federation of Women's Institutes, 1975), p. 102.
4. E.D. Mackerness (ed.), *The Journals of George Sturt, 1890–1927* (vol. 2) (1967), pp. 869–70. See also Adrian Bell, *op. cit.*, p. 243, with his reference to fields 'sprouting a pink and white fungus of bungalows and tea-houses'.
5. Alwyn D. Rees, *Life in a Welsh Countryside* (1950), p. 84.
6. H. St G. Cramp, *A Yeoman Farmer's Son. A Leicestershire Childhood* (1985), p. 24.
7. G.K. Nelson, *Countrywomen on the Land. Memories of Rural Life in the 1920s and '30s* (1992), p. vii.
8. *The Practical Education of Women for Rural Life: Report of a Sub-Committee of the Inter-Departmental Committee of the Ministry of Agriculture and the Board of Education* (HMSO, 1928), p. 10.
9. Alwyn D. Rees, *op. cit.*, pp. 62–3.
10. Transcript of Tape no. 5819 by Mrs Minwel Tibbott at the Welsh Folk Museum, National Museum of Wales.
11. Oral History Transcripts at Suffolk Record Office: Ipswich Branch, L.401/2/OHT/253.
12. W.M. Williams, *The Sociology of an English Village: Gosforth* (1956), p. 42.
13. *Ibid.*, p. 149; Alwyn D. Rees, *op. cit.*, p. 95.
14. Transcript of Tape no. 5819 at the Welsh Folk Museum.
15. *Within Living Memory. A Collection of Norfolk Reminiscences* (Norfolk Federation of Women's Institutes, 1971), p. 13.
16. Transcript of Tape no. 5819 at the Welsh Folk Museum. S. Minwel Tibbott, 'Liberality and Hospitality. Food as Communication in Wales' in *Folk Life*, vol. 24 (1985–6), p. 43.
17. Alun Howkins, *Poor Labouring Men. Rural Radicalism in Norfolk 1870–1923* (1985), p. 133; Alun Howkins, *Reshaping Rural England. A Social History 1850–1925* (1991), p. 286.
18. *Ministry of Agriculture and Fisheries. Report on Land Settlement in England and Wales: 1919–24* (HMSO, 1925), p. 56.
19. H. St G. Cramp, *op. cit.*, p. 42.
20. *Ibid.*, p. 15.
21. *Report of the Board of Agriculture and Fisheries on Wages and Conditions of Employment of Agricultural Labourers*, Parliamentary Papers, vol. IX, Report on Northumberland, p. 249; 1921 Census for Northumberland for details of the proportion of women in the labour force.
22. *Report of the Board of Agriculture and Fisheries on Wages, &c.*, Report on Cardiganshire, pp. 412, 414.

23. *Ibid.*, p. 414.

24. Oral History Transcripts at Suffolk Record Office: Ipswich Branch, L.401/2/OHT/255.

25. *Land Worker*, February 1925, p. iii; *Report of the Board of Agriculture and Fisheries on Wages, &c.*, Report on Lincolnshire (Holland Division), p. 158.

26. Hop-farmer's wife from Kent on *Farming Today*, Radio 4, 12 March 1994, *Report of the Board of Agriculture and Fisheries on Wages, &c.*, Report on Kent, pp. 124–5.

27. Charles Kightly, *Country Voices. Life and Lore in Farm and Village* (1984), pp. 37–8.

28. *Land Worker*, January 1921, p. 4.

29. *Land Worker*, May 1921, p. 6, letter from the chairman of the Sibsey branch of the National Union.

30. *Land Worker*, October 1921, p. 12, letter from Mrs R. Uzzell, a member of the Union's executive committee.

31. *Land Worker*, July 1921, p. 7, letter from Mrs C. Flory, a member of the Union's executive committee.

32. Charles Kightly, *op. cit.*, p. 38.

33. G.K. Nelson, *op. cit.*, p. 20.

34. Helen E. FitzRandolph and M. Doriel Hay, *The Rural Industries of England and Wales*, vol. II (1926), pp. 45–7.

35. Marie Hartley and Joan Ingilby, *Life and Tradition in the Yorkshire Dales* (1968), p. 55.

36. Marie Hartley and Joan Ingilby, *Life in the Moorlands of North-East Yorkshire* (1972), p. 45–6.

37. Reports of West Suffolk County Council, meeting of the Maternity and Child Welfare Committee on 15 April 1925. In February 1920 it was reported to the Committee that of forty-five midwives who had currently applied to practise under the terms of the 1902 Midwives legislation, eleven were untrained; the oldest was 83 and three others were in their seventies. See Reports at Suffolk Record Office: Bury St. Edmunds branch.

38. John S. Creasey and Sadie B. Ward, *The Countryside between the Wars, 1918–1940* (1984), p. 17.

39. David A. Pretty, *The Rural Revolt that Failed. Farm Workers' Trade Unions in Wales 1889–1950* (1989), pp. 182–3.

40. *Land Worker*, February 1921, p. 4.

41. David A. Pretty, *op. cit.*, p. 37.

42. Alan Armstrong, *Farmworkers. A Social and Economic History, 1770–1980* (1988), p. 190.

43. Howard Newby, *The Deferential Worker* (1977), p. 180.

44. S. Minwel Tibbott and Beth Thomas, *O'r Gwaith i'r Gwely. A Woman's Work. Housework 1890–1960* (1994), p. 21.

45. *National Farm Survey of England and Wales (1941–1943). A Summary Report* (HMSO, 1946), pp. 60–65, 104, 107.

46. G.K. Nelson, *op. cit.*, pp. 104–5.

47. John S. Creasey and Sadie B. Ward, *op. cit.*, p. 18.

48. *A Pattern of Hundreds*, p. 102.

49. Reminiscences of my husband, who was born in Ivinghoe.

50. Winifred Foley, *A Child in the Forest* (1985 edn), p. 15.

51. *Ibid.*, p. 35.

52. *Ibid.*, p. 17.

53. *Ibid.*

54. Mary Chamberlain, *Fenwomen. A Portrait of Women in an English Village* (1983 edn), p. 76.

55. Reminiscences of Mrs Pattie Lewis, transcription of Tape no. 5819 by Mrs Minwel Tibbott at Welsh Folk Museum, and of Tape no. 5822 for Mrs Winifred Jones, also at the Welsh Folk Museum.

56. Oral History Transcripts at Suffolk Record Office: Ipswich Branch, L.401/2/OHT/253.

57. Pamela Horn, *Rural Life in England in the First World War* (1984), pp. 120, 135.

58. *Ibid.*, p. 122.

59. *Ibid.*, pp. 124–33; Lord Ernle, *The Land and its People* (n.d. [*c.* 1925]), p. 188.

60. Mrs Rowland Wilkins, *The Training and Employment of Educated Women in Horticulture and Agriculture* (1927), p. 40.

61. *Report on Land Settlement in England and Wales: 1919–24*, pp. 8, 9.

62. See advertisements in Mrs Rowland Wilkins, *op. cit.*; and also Prospectuses of the Agricultural and Horticultural College for Women at Studley Castle in the University of Reading Library, WAR.5/14/5.

63. Obituary in *The Guardian*, 21 October 1993.

64. Information provided with photograph 94.312.60 at the Welsh Folk Museum.

65. West Suffolk County Council: Quarterly Reports at Bury St Edmunds Record Office, meeting of the Agricultural Committee on 19 October 1925.

66. *Farmers Express*, 18 June 1928, p. 601.

67. These advertisements appeared in the *Farmer and Stockbreeder*, 4 March 1929.

68. *Ministry of Agriculture and Fisheries. The Agricultural Output of England and Wales 1925* (Cmd. 2815) (HMSO, 1927), pp. 98, 102–3.

69.   Reg Groves, *Sharpen the Sickle! The History of the Farm Workers' Union* (1949), pp. 164, 170, Edith Whetham, *The Agrarian History of England and Wales*, vol. VIII (1978), p. 136.

70.   Reg Groves, *op. cit.*, p. 165. But see also Alan Armstrong, *op. cit.*, p. 185, suggesting a maximum membership of 93,000 in 1920 for the National Union; by 1923 that had fallen to 29,000 and in 1929 it stood at 23,000.

71.   Oral History Transcripts at Suffolk Record Office: Ipswich Branch, L.401/2/OHT/81.

72.   H. St G. Cramp, *op. cit.*, pp. 168, 170.

73.   *A Century of Agricultural Statistics. Great Britain 1866–1966* (HMSO, 1968), p. 82.

74.   Pamela Horn, *op. cit.*, p. 217.

75.   *Ministry of Agriculture and Fisheries. The Agricultural Output of England and Wales 1925*, p. 76.

76.   *The Practical Education of Women for Rural Life*, p. 13.

77.   Oral History Transcripts at Suffolk Record Office: Ipswich Branch, L.401/2/OHT/313.

78.   Reg Groves, *op. cit.*, p. 172.

79.   *Ibid.*, pp. 175–7.

80.   *Ibid.*, p. 178; Alan Armstrong, *op. cit.*, pp. 187–8.

81.   Mary Chamberlain, *op. cit.*, pp. 79–81; Alun Howkins, *Poor Labouring Men*, p. 163.

82.   Reg Groves, *op. cit.*, p. 198.

83.   Edith H. Whetham, *op. cit.*, p. 155.

84.   Reg Groves, *op. cit.*, p. 209; Alan Armstrong, *op. cit.*, p. 184.

85.   Reg Groves, *op. cit.*, p. 210–11.

86.   E. Mejer, *Agricultural Labour in England and Wales, Part II. Farm Workers' Earnings 1917–1951* (University of Nottingham School of Agriculture, 1951), p. 69.

87.   *Land Worker*, April 1925, Mrs Uzzell, 'A Woman at Work in the Villages', p. 1.

88.   Liz Bartlett, *Lace Villages* (1991), p. 55; Geoff Spenceley, 'The Lace Associations. Philanthropic Movements to Preserve the Production of Handmade Lace in Late Victorian and Edwardian England' in *Victorian Studies*, vol. XVI, no. 4 (June 1973), pp. 437, 439, 451, 452; *Within Living Memory*, p. 14.

89.   Geoff Spenceley, *op. cit.*, pp. 451–2.

90.   Reminiscences of my brother-in-law, Mr Ian Horn of Ivinghoe; Charles Freeman, *Luton and the Hat Industry* (1976 edn), p. 13.

91.   Interview with the late Mrs Wright of Leafield on 15 June 1988; Also interview with Mrs Mary Howse of Leafield on 12 May 1988;

K.S. Woods, *The Rural Industries Round Oxford* (1921), pp. 135, 138, 140, 141; N.L. Leyland and J.E. Troughton, *Glovemaking in West Oxfordshire, the Craft and its History* (Oxford City and County Museum Publication no. 4, 1974), pp. 17, 19, 25.

92.   Helen E. FitzRandolph and M. Doriel Hay, *op. cit.*, vol. I, pp. 204, 219–21.

93.   S. Minwel Tibbott, 'Liberality and Hospitality', pp. 47–8; Reminiscences of Mr Bill Morgan, Llangwm, Transcription of Tape no. 5821 at the Welsh Folk Museum and Reminiscences of Mrs Gettings, Llangwm, Transcription of Tape no. 5817 at the Welsh Folk Museum.

94.   Reminiscences of Mrs Annie Jenkins, Transcription of Tape no. 5812 at the Welsh Folk Museum.

95.   Caroline Baker, *Homedwellers and Foreigners. The Seasonal Labour Force in Kentish Agriculture, with Particular Reference to Hop Picking* (University of Kent M.Phil. thesis, 1979), pp. 308, 310, 313–15.

96.   Mary Lewis (ed.), *Old Days in the Kent Hop Gardens* (West Kent Federation of Women's Institutes, 1962), pp. 22, 32.

97.   Oral History Transcripts at Suffolk Record Office: Ipswich Branch, L.401/2/OHT/103; George Ewart Evans, *The Days That We Have Seen* (1975), pp. 201–3.

98.   George Ewart Evans, *op. cit.*, p. 203.

99.   *Ibid.*

Chapter 8   Leisure and Pleasure

1.   Rex L. Sawyer, *The Bowerchalke Parish Papers. Collett's Village Newspaper 1878–1924* (1989), p. 132.

2.   Bill Jones and Beth Thomas, *Teyrnas y Glo. Coal's Domain* (1993), p. 35; Paul Berry and Alan Bishop (ed.), *Testament of a Generation. The Journalism of Vera Brittain and Winifred Holtby* (1985), pp. 67–9.

3.   Bill Jones and Beth Thomas, *op. cit.*, p. 26.

4.   Andrew Davies, 'Leisure in the "classic slum" 1900–1939' in Andrew Davies and Steven Fielding (eds), *Workers' Worlds. Cultures and Communities in Manchester and Salford, 1880–1939* (1992), p. 115.

5.   Carl Chinn, *They Worked All Their Lives. Women of the Urban Poor in England, 1880–1939* (1988), pp. 66, 119–21.

6.   Mark Clapson, 'Playing the system. The world of organised street betting in Manchester, Salford and Bolton, *c.* 1880 to 1939' in Andrew Davies and Steven Fielding (eds), *op. cit.*, p. 169.

7. *Proceedings of the Select Committee on Betting Duty*, Parliamentary Papers, 1923, vol. V, Evidence of Canon Peter Green, Q. 6763–6764.

8. *Report of the Select Committee on Betting Duty*, pp. xiv–xv.

9. Pamela Horn, 'Women Workers in the 1920s – Cadbury's of Bournville' in *Genealogists' Magazine*, March 1994, p. 401.

10. See, for example, the *Bournville Works Magazine*, July 1922. The *Fry's Works Magazine* also mentioned a characbanc outing on 2 June 1923, to Savernake Forest. There are many other examples.

11. The Hon. Mrs Dighton Pollock, *Women of To-day* (1929), p. 45.

12. Melanie Tebbutt, 'Women's talk? Gossip and "women's words" in working-class communities, 1880–1939' in Andrew Davies and Steven Fielding (eds), *op. cit.*, pp. 63–4.

13. Melanie Tebbutt, *op. cit.*, p. 64.

14. Steven Fielding, 'A separate culture? Irish Catholics in working-class Manchester and Salford, *c.* 1890–1939' in Andrew Davies and Steven Fielding (eds), *op. cit.*, p. 38.

15. Steven Fielding, *op. cit.*, pp. 38–9.

16. Prunella Stack, *Zest for Life. Mary Bagot Stack and the League of Health and Beauty* (1988), pp. 110, 114–16.

17. *Evening Standard*, 30 October 1923.

18. Stephen G. Jones, *Workers at Play. A Social and Economic History of Leisure 1918–1939* (1986), p. 20.

19. Bournville Women's Works Council, 1918–1919 in Cadbury's Archives at Bournville, 002521, for details of holidays.

20. Rules and Regulations for Office Workers: Girls, October 1927, in Cadbury's Archives, 002227.

21. Rules and Regulations to be observed by all Lady Members of the Staff: National Provincial Bank, 28 June 1926 in National Westminster Bank Group Archives, no. 2948.

22. *Home and Country*, March 1926, p. 116.

23. The Hon. Mrs Dighton Pollock, *op. cit.*, p. 51.

24. See, for example, advertisements in the *Pall Mall Gazette*, 12 July 1923.

25. Ethel Mannin, *All Experience* (1932), p. 29.

26. *Evening Standard*, 9 November 1923.

27. *Pall Mall Gazette*, 2 August 1923.

28. Mark Pegg, *Broadcasting and Society 1918–1939* (1983), pp. 12–15.

29. *Ibid.*, pp. 44–5; *Evening Standard*, 9 November 1923.

30. Mark Pegg, *op. cit.*, p. 19.

31. *Ibid.*, p. 174.

32. *Evening Standard*, 18 and 25 October 1923.

33. *Evening Standard*, 30 October 1923.

34. *Evening Standard*, 20 October 1923.

35. Lesley Lewis, *The Private Life of a Country House 1912–1939* (1982 edn), p. 40; *Evening Standard*, 17 October 1923.

36. Carolyn Hall (ed.), *The Twenties in Vogue* (1983), p. 10; *Evening Standard*, 6 November 1923.

37. C. Stella Davies, *North Country Bred. A Working-class Family Chronicle* (1963), p. 228.

38. [Kate Meyrick], *Secrets of the 43. Reminiscences of Mrs Meyrick* (1933), pp. 212–14.

39. Carolyn Hall (ed.), *op. cit.*, p. 38.

40. Sir Hubert Llewellyn Smith (ed.), *The New Survey of London Life and Labour*, vol. IX (1935), pp. 297–8.

41. Deirdre Beddoe, *Back to Home and Duty. Women between the Wars, 1918–1939* (1989), p. 118.

42. Olive Howarth (ed.), *Textile Voices. Mill Life this Century* (1989), pp. 77–8.

43. Elizabeth Roberts, *A Woman's Place. An Oral History of Working-class Women 1890–1940* (1985 edn), p. 70.

44. *Ibid.*, p. 71.

45. Mary Chamberlain, *Growing up in Lambeth* (1989), p. 73.

46. Thomas M. Middleton, *An Enquiry into the Use of Leisure amongst the Working Classes of Liverpool* (University of Liverpool thesis, 1931), p. 149; David Fowler, 'Teenage consumers? Young wage-earners and leisure in Manchester, 1919–1939' in Andrew Davies and Steven Fielding (eds), *op. cit.*, p. 146.

47. Carolyn Hall (ed.), *op. cit.*, p. 86.

48. *Pall Mall Gazette*, 28 July 1923.

49. Carolyn Hall (ed.), *op. cit.*, p. 88.

50. *Ibid.*, p. 86; J.P. Mayer, *British Cinemas and their Audiences* (1948), p. 60.

51. J.P. Mayer, *op. cit.*, pp. 52, 61; David Fowler, *op. cit.*, p. 146.

52. Margaret Leonora Eyles, *The Woman in the Little House* (1922), pp. 117–19.

53. Georgina Howell, *In Vogue. Six decades of fashion* (1979 edn), pp. 63, 70.

54. Barbara Cartland, *We Danced All Night* (1970), p. 159.

55. See entry in *Dictionary of National Biography*. Miss Cooper died in 1971. Sheridan Morley, *Gladys Cooper* (1979 edn), pp. 100–2, 122–7, 131.

56. Georgina Howell, *op. cit.*, p. 71; Barbara

Cartland, *op. cit.*, p. 160.

57.   Barbara Cartland, *op. cit.*, p. 151; Carolyn Hall (ed.), *op. cit.*, p. 8; *Pall Mall Gazette*, 20 July 1923.

58.   [Josephine Ross], *Society in Vogue. The International Set between the Wars* (1992), p. 117.

59.   *Ibid.*

60.   Merlin Waterson (ed.), *The Country House Remembered. Recollections of Life Between the Wars* (1985), pp. 86, 94, 98.

61.   *Ibid.*, pp. 58–9.

62.   Lesley Lewis, *op. cit.*, pp. 113–14.

63.   Selina Hastings, *Nancy Mitford* (1985), p. 54.

64.   *Ibid.*, pp. 54–5.

65.   The Hon. Nancy Mitford, 'The Shooting Party' (1929) in Carolyn Hall (ed.), *op. cit.*, p. 130.

66.   Selina Hastings, *op. cit.*, pp. 57, 61.

67.   Steve Humphries and Pamela Gordon, *A Labour of Love. The Experience of Parenthood in Britain 1900–1950* (1993), pp. 92–3.

68.   Simon Goodenough, *Jam and Jerusalem* (1977), pp. 13, 32, 38.

69.   *Ibid.*, p. 19.

70.   Maggie Morgan, 'The Women's Institute Movement – The Acceptable Face of Feminism?' in Sybil Oldfield (ed.), *This Working-day World. Women's Lives and Culture(s) in Britain 1914–1945* (1994), p. 31.

71.   *Ibid.*, p. 34.

72.   Gervas Huxley, *Lady Denman, GBE 1884–1954* (1961), pp. 80, 83.

73.   Minutes of Stoke by Clare Women's Institute at West Suffolk Record Office, Bury St Edmunds, GH.503/20/1–2, meetings on 16 January 1924 and 17 February 1926. For Stoke by Nayland at West Suffolk Record Office, GH.503/21/1, meetings on 10 May and 11 October 1920.

74.   *Home and Country*, July 1923 266.

75.   Martin Pugh, *Women and the Women's Movement in Britain 1914–1959* (1992), p. 60; Maggie Morgan, *op. cit.*, p. 36. Lady Denman herself took an active part in the campaign for birth control, alongside her WI commitments.

76.   Maggie Morgan, *op. cit.*, p. 35.

77.   Simon Goodenough, *op. cit.*, p. 18.

78.   Mary Stott, *Organization Women* (1978), pp. 20–21, 26.

79.   Margaret Llewelyn Davies (ed.), *Life As We Have Known It* (1977 edn), p. xiii. The book was first published in 1931.

80.   W. Henry Brown, *A Century of Liverpool Cooperation* (n.d. [*c.* 1929]), pp. 132–4.

81.   Margaret Llewelyn Davies (ed.), *op. cit.*, pp. 67, 72.

82.   Stephen G. Jones, *op. cit.*, p. 68.

83.   Letter from Miss G.J. Goff of St Austell, Cornwall to the author, [n.d. *c.* 5 September 1974].

84.   Bill Jones and Beth Thomas, *op. cit.*, p. 27. See Thomas M. Middleton, *op. cit.*, Appendix II, 161 for details of religious observance in Liverpool. Nearly three-quarters of the women surveyed in 1930 had attended a religious service during the week in which they were approached.

85.   Oral History Transcript no. 005, at the Local Studies Library, Stalybridge.

86.   Oral History Transcript no. 158, at the Local Studies Library, Stalybridge.

87.   Carl Chinn, *op. cit.*, pp. 25–7.

88.   Reminiscences of my aunt, Mrs Phyllis Knight; Thomas M. Middleton, *op. cit.*, p. 156.

89.   Andrzej Olechnowicz, *The Economic and Social Development of Inter-war Out-County Municipal Housing Estates, with Special Reference to the London County Council's Becontree and Dagenham Estate* (Oxford D.Phil Thesis, 1991), p. 292.

90.   Nicola Beauman, *A Very Great Profession. The Woman's Novel 1914–39* (1983), pp. 174, 183, 192.

91.   *Times Literary Supplement*, 6 November 1919, p. 633.

92.   *Times Literary Supplement*, 2 June 1921, p. 355; Obituary of Mrs Hull in *Derbyshire Advertiser*, 14 February 1947.

93.   Deirdre Beddoe, *op. cit.*, p. 126; Nicola Beauman, *op. cit.*, pp. 10–11.

94.   Jean Metcalfe, *Sunnylea. A 1920s childhood remembered* (1980), p. 30; *First Annual Report of the BBC for 1927*, Parliamentary Papers, 1928, vol. II, p. 3, suggested music formed two-thirds of all programmes. During the course of that year a Wireless Military Band had been formed.

95.   Reminiscences of my aunt, Mrs Phyllis Knight.

96.   Reminiscences of Mrs K. Abney in Oral History Transcripts, Suffolk Record Office, Ipswich Branch, L.401/2/OHT/252.

97.   Carolyn Hall (ed.), *op. cit.*, pp. 20, 118–19; Georgina Howell, *op. cit.*, p. 86.

98.   [Josephine Ross], *op. cit.*, pp. 68, 70.

99.   Ethel Mannin, *All Experience*, p. 131; and Ethel Mannin, *Young in the Twenties, A Chapter of Autobiography* (1971), p. 38.

100.   *Pall Mall Gazette*, 1 and 3 August 1923.

According to the issue of the newspaper on 7 August 1923, over two thousand of the 'newer' type of buses had operated on country routes over the holiday period, with 3,800 buses of all kinds pressed into service in London. More than 80,000 passengers had been taken to Epping Forest alone.

101. Oral History Transcript no. 005, at the Local Studies Library, Stalybridge.

102. Oral History Transcript no. 063, at the Local Studies Library, Stalybridge.

103. Deirdre Beddoe, *op. cit.*, p. 125.

104. *Violet Magazine*, 27 July 1923, pp. 93–4; See also Robin Kent, *Agony. Problem Pages through the Ages* (1987), p. 86.

105. Ethel Mannin, *All Experience*, pp. 31–3.

106. Deirdre Beddoe, *op. cit.*, p. 124.

107. H.L. Beales and R.S. Lambert, *Memoirs of the Unemployed* (1973 edn), pp. 84–5, 87. The book was first published in 1934.

Index